DISTILLED

DISTILLED

*A Memoir of Family, Seagram,
Baseball, and Philanthropy*

CHARLES BRONFMAN

with Howard Green

 HarperCollins
PublishersLtd

HarperCollins Publishers Ltd
2 Bloor Street East, 20th Floor
Toronto, Ontario, Canada
M4W 1A8

www.harpercollins.ca

Library and Archives Canada Cataloguing in Publication
information is available upon request

ISBN 978-1-44344-847-5

Printed and bound in the United States of America
RRD 9 8 7 6 5 4

To my grandchildren—I love you all so very much.

In the days of my youth, Father William replied
I remember that youth would fly fast
So I thought of the future
Whatever I did
So I never might rue o'er the past
—Sam Bronfman's variation on Robert Southey's
"The Old Man's Comforts and How He Gained Them"

Contents

A Note from Charles Bronfman

⸻

I'm now eighty-five. Thankfully, I'm fit—both mentally and physically. My life, like most people's, has been a mixed bag—substantial achievements, serious disappointments; great loves, poor ones; various careers, some exciting, others mundane; critical illnesses, wonderful health. I wrote this memoir not to enhance my ego, but to indicate to others the possibilities that we all have, whether entrepreneur, inheritor, or whatever. It was time to reflect on all these and the other conditions and influences that have shaped, and will continue to shape, my life.

I've met and come to know many, many people. Most were bright; very few were wise. And wisdom, it seems to me, need not be reserved for those in their later years. However, it does take years to be honed. As George Bernard Shaw was wont to say, "Youth is wasted on the young." He also said, "A lifetime of happiness! No man alive could bear it; it would be hell on earth."

Despite being born with the proverbial silver spoon in my mouth, I have not suffered that "hell on earth." I have endured the horrid pain of suddenly, with no warning at all, losing a beloved wife, Andy, with whom I had spent twenty-five years. And the loss of Seagram was a huge blow for what it meant to my family and me, even more emotionally than financially.

Today, though, I'm one of the happiest of people. As you read this memoir, I hope you have discovered that I was often anything but. Yet I am now married to a wonderful woman. My children, as well as my stepchildren, have brought me great *naches*, and my grandchildren give me tremendous joy.

People probably know me best for what I call "entrepreneurial philanthropy." Certainly that has been the incredibly rewarding hallmark of my long career. These accomplishments, though, were based on business principles I learned from my father and my colleagues, both at Seagram and our family businesses—CEMP, and later Claridge. I really believe that, both for my loved ones and me, the best is yet to come.

Preface

O ver the years, I hadn't had much luck getting an interview with one of the Bronfmans. I recall a request I once made to speak with Charles, son of Mr. Sam, only to receive a tart letter from a lawyer saying no.

By virtue of their enormous wealth, the Bronfman family were equivalent to Canadian royalty—and later international royalty—because of what they controlled in the corporate sphere, their philanthropic heft, and their influence in certain circles, particularly in the Jewish community in Canada and globally. Sam Bronfman, who died in 1971, had turned Seagram into a global powerhouse and set the stage for a dynasty. This was the company that stocked the world's bars with Crown Royal, Chivas Regal, V.O., and many other well-known names like Martell cognac and Captain Morgan rum. Liquor sold, and sold well. The company gushed cash. Mr. Sam's sons, Edgar and Charles, took the family-controlled firm a step further, into the realm of chemicals and plastics, when Seagram became the largest shareholder of DuPont, one of the best-known companies worldwide. The Bronfmans were billionaires many times over and, in certain respects, on a pedestal because of their wealth.

My luck changed in the fall of 2012. One of my colleagues at Business News Network knew Charles Bronfman from a past interaction and convinced him to come on my program for an interview. The agreement was that the subject matter would be his philanthropy because he was joining the Giving Pledge, started by Bill and Melinda Gates and Warren Buffett—agreeing to leave more than half of his wealth to charity. I was pleased to hear we would have such a marquee guest. However, I was uncomfortable with only discussing philanthropy. For sure, Charles was, by any measure, a huge donor to many causes. But there was an elephant in the room. We had not heard other aspects of the Bronfman story—in particular, firsthand insights into the demise of Seagram after Charles's nephew Edgar Jr. pivoted the company toward entertainment and media, finally selling Seagram to France's Vivendi during the height of the 2000 technology boom for a huge stake in the French firm. Vivendi quickly withered, taking a chunk of the Bronfman fortune down with it. It was a shattering loss for the family—a humiliation and an embarrassment. To my knowledge, in all our years at the network, we had not had one of the key Bronfmans on the air to discuss what happened. The story had virtually gone away.

I thought it over. Most certainly we would honour our agreement to talk about philanthropy, but I felt that if we were sensitive and fair, we could reserve a segment to devote to other matters. On the appointed day, I went to the greenroom to meet Charles and we seemed to hit it off instantly. There was chemistry, as he would say. The section of the interview on philanthropy went well, so as we entered the final block of the show, I shifted to another topic, the separatist government in Quebec. That was my bridge to turn the interview away from philanthropy. Then I made the big turn. I told Charles we only had a few minutes left—a signal that he would not have to endure me for long—and with the greatest respect, I wondered all these years later what he thought about what happened to Seagram. The floodgates opened. He said he thought the same now as he did back then—it was a terrible tragedy and the family lost its identity. Did he speak with his nephew much? I asked.

"Not much," came the raw answer.

When I asked how it would have made his father feel, he began to tear up. He explained that to go against the sale of Seagram would have resulted in a family war. This was Charles Bronfman, finally speaking out. It was riveting.

After the interview aired, we corresponded warmly via email a few times, and the following year he came back, accompanied by his wife, Rita, for another interview. He told me that publicly expressing how he felt during our first interview had made him feel better. When Paul Desmarais Sr. died some time later, we called Charles again and he did a live phone tribute from New York. He was obviously greatly saddened by the death of his friend, a former Seagram director and another corporate titan in Quebec, whom he had visited just days before he passed away. By then, I felt that Charles Bronfman and I had developed a relationship of sorts. He felt comfortable speaking to me.

On Friday, July 29, 2014, I received a brief note from Anthony Wilson-Smith, the president of Historica, the organization that promotes the teaching of Canadian history and now produces Canada's Heritage Minutes, one of Charles's many philanthropic endeavours. Tony knew I was no longer at BNN and wanted my phone number because an "eminent" Canadian wanted to call me. Later that afternoon, my cellphone rang.

"Hi, Howard. This is Charles Bronfman," he said. "Do you want to write my biography?"

I was slightly thrown by this out-of-the-blue offer but managed to say I was flattered. I suggested we meet face to face to chat further, so I arranged to fly to Montreal the following Monday to meet him for lunch.

My spouse, Lynne, drove me to the airport. As I got out of the car, she advised me to get my shoes shined. I took her advice and got them spiffed up when I arrived at the Montreal airport, where I also picked up a Tide stick to wipe a stain off the lapel of my suit. I was arriving early, so Charles's assistant Angela Forster arranged an impromptu tour of the art collection at the sumptuous offices of Claridge, his family's private investment company. Everything surrounding Charles is elegant, so having freshly buffed shoes was a good call.

At noon, I met with him and after a minute or two of small talk we got down to what he wanted to discuss. He felt people didn't understand him, telling me that as a child, he was a "basket case," the youngest of four siblings with an overbearing brother and a domineering father. He said he wanted the manuscript published, not just written for his family. When I asked what the boundaries would be, he said there weren't any.

We soon walked up Peel Street to Ferreira for lunch. As we were guided to our table, we found ourselves walking toward former prime minister Brian Mulroney and L. Ian MacDonald, who were at the next table. Mulroney and Charles greeted each other like old friends, kibitzing about a glittering wedding they'd attended over the weekend, joking about how much it might have cost.

Charles ordered fish and I ordered chicken. When his meal was placed in front of him, it was a whole fish and he expertly lopped off the head and tail for the waiter to take away. As we tucked into our food, he talked about how, growing up, he never really noticed that he was unbelievably rich. If he went to the home of a friend, it didn't matter to him if the house was small. We also talked about anti-Semitism. He said he didn't experience it very much growing up in Quebec but did when he attended private school in Ontario. At one point, he asked me how much I'd charge to write the book. I laughed and said I knew he'd ask but that I wasn't sure of the answer, adding that I hoped he didn't think I was being coy.

"If I thought you were being coy, you wouldn't be here."

I went back to Toronto and thought about it. I knew by now that he'd tried to write his memoirs before, and for various reasons it hadn't worked out. The next time we spoke was on the phone and I said that while I knew *he* wanted it to be a good book, I *needed* it to be a good book, not just a vanity publication by someone who could afford such a thing. He said he understood, adding that he knew he wasn't perfect and had plenty of warts, like everyone else. I felt as though we now had an unwritten agreement between us. Our discussions proceeded over the next few weeks and I made another trip to Montreal on September 5, when we spent another six hours alone, talking about various chapters in his life. I could feel a book coming on. Then I was back in Montreal again on September 18 for another afternoon of conversation. It was no holds barred. He seemed willing to talk about anything—almost anything. One instance where he put a harness on me occurred when I asked about girlfriends when he was a young man.

"We're not going there," he said softly. Then he chuckled and told me to "mind your own effing business." I laughed and said we weren't finished the project yet, at which point he laughed harder. Another time he tried to put a leash on me was during a lunch in one of the world's most elegant restaurants, the Grill Room of the Four Seasons on Park Avenue in New York City, a quasi-club for the rich and famous since its opening in the late 1950s. Until it closed in the summer of 2016, it was, of course, in the Seagram Building, an icon of modernist architecture. I asked Angela, who had joined us for lunch, if we could get a copy of the menu.

"What do you want that for?" Charles asked, mildly irritated.

"Colour," I answered.

"Let me tell you something," he said. "Edgar, with his family, bought the restaurant without even asking me if I wanted to participate." Clearly hurt, he recounted how he'd phoned his brother and asked why he hadn't been told about the purchase before the deal was closed.

"We forgot," was the answer.

"Well," Charles said, "that kind of sums up our relationship, doesn't it? So we're not taking any effing menus."

"Fine," I said, "but I got the story, didn't I?"

He let out a very big laugh. Sometimes things come spilling out without a question being asked. The mere mention of a menu was a trigger.

A memoir has to give a sense, a feeling about someone's life. It's more than just a chronology. It's the sum telling of various stories, episodes, and phases that paint a life portrait. When we began this project, Charles was eighty-three years old, meaning he'd already experienced more than thirty thousand days of living. To extract the essential elements of that experience is a bit like building and residing in a house during the good times as well as when storms hit and dramas unfold within its walls.

The bricks to build this book came from Charles through extensive and intense interviews and conversations, the more than two hundred and fifty hours we spent together collaborating on how to tell his story. The result is his voice, from his heart. Our time together does not include close to one hundred hours spent with other people—in Montreal, Toronto, New York, Palm Beach, Los Angeles, Tel Aviv, and Jerusalem—to help fill in the blanks and recall details and stories that are impossible for one person to remember.

Most of the thousands of interviews I have done in my career have been timed to the second, conducted under bright lights, and viewed by people anonymous to me. These were very different. By way of example, one night in November 2014, after a delicious meal at an Italian restaurant in Palm Beach, Florida, we went back to Charles's beautiful home and sat in his spacious study. Generally, we did our talking for the project in the mornings and afternoons. But I was leaving early the next day and suggested it might be good to do another hour of work after dinner. The lights were low and there was no one else in the house. He started talking about his first wife, Barbara, his children, and then the love he lost—his second wife, Andy, who'd died after being hit by a car. It was quiet and I barely had to ask any questions; he just talked. Sometimes the essence of interviewing is not saying anything, but just being a receptor. When he was done, my eyes were moist—not because of a big, dramatic revelation or a great clip that we so frequently sought in television, but from the unadorned telling of loves lost, quietly related in the silence of a large, darkened home. Throughout this process, Charles opened himself up as few in my experience have done, and not all of it has been pleasant for him. He has led a remarkable life—filled with uncertainty, triumphs, and failures—and he has chosen to share it.

I've been lucky to have a lot of wonderful jobs and assignments during my career. My luck continued when Charles called me. It has been a privilege to work with him. Over the course of working with Charles, I think we have become friends (I hope he feels the same way) and I "get" what others say about him. The former president and prime minister of Israel, Shimon Peres, told me that Charles "led by trust, not by authority." Aliza Olmert, the wife of former prime minister Ehud Olmert, said of Charles, "He knew how to be a partner. He gave with what we call warm hands, with a deep understanding of the issues." His son Stephen told me he learned from his father that it's better to have people work *with* you than *for* you. In fact, Charles will tell you that his successes have always been the result of partnerships. Charles Bronfman has a lot of friends in this world. This book explains why.

—Howard Green, March 2016

DISTILLED

1

Basket Case Kid

───────────

I was the fourth of four, with all that goes with that. Each of us, the children of Sam and Saidye Bronfman, were two years apart in age. Minda was born in 1925, Phyllis in 1927, Edgar in 1929, and me in 1931. My parents wanted me to be born on June 20, the same day Edgar was born and the same day as their wedding anniversary. Phyllis says they went for a ride on a bumpy road to try to induce my arrival, but I was stubborn and didn't make an appearance until a week later. She chuckles that I was kind of a "squabby, long kid . . . like a chicken." Whether it was the poultry look or not, I was most certainly the overprotected youngest of the family, something of a toy for the others. Phyllis says I was an adorable little kid with blond hair, and cross-eyed, which meant I wore glasses with one lens frosted.

A skinny lad with big, protruding ears, I had several major illnesses, contracting double pneumonia at five, pneumonia again at nine, and streptococcus while in early adolescence. There were no antibacterial sulfa drugs when I got double pneumonia, and no penicillin when I subsequently got pneumonia. Both illnesses were very serious and potentially life-threatening. Phyllis

3

remembers our parents calling the situation a crisis. In the second instance, she says that Mother and Dad took the rare step in those days of flying back from wherever they were to be with me and that it was very quiet on the floor of the house where I was. When I got streptococcus, it was most certainly a threat to human life. I remember my mother crying as she stood in front of the window of my hospital room. A sick puppy, I found it too hard to open my eyes and I was too tired to close them. I was then one of the first civilians in the country to receive penicillin, via a huge needle jabbed in my skinny butt every three hours. Since then, the only time I've been in hospital has been as a visitor.

The world I was born into was the world of the Great Depression, but given who my father was, that would mean little to me. We were an extremely wealthy family thanks to our father, one of the leading industrialists of the era through Seagram, the spirits business he built and ran, the home of globally known brands such as Crown Royal and Chivas Regal. By the time I was two years old in 1933, the company had forty per cent of the Canadian whisky market. In 1948, when I was seventeen, *Fortune* estimated Sam Bronfman's wealth at $100 million, the equivalent of being a billionaire today. We lived in a world apart, described as Jewish royalty by historian Michael Marrus in his biography of my father.

Our home in Montreal at 15 Belvedere Road, known as "Oaklands," still sits on a steep hill in upper Westmount, a district that I now jokingly refer to as "the *shtetl*." With a high stone wall protecting it from the street and nosy passersby, it boasted twenty rooms. My father bought it while my mother, who was then pregnant with Edgar, and my sisters were holidaying on the coast of Maine. Robert Findlay, the architect who designed Westmount City Hall, designed the house. My parents gutted it and redid the interior, adding a sunroom, a breakfast room, bathrooms, and dressing rooms. All the furniture was custom-made, with oak in the dining room and mahogany for the living room. My mother emphasized what she referred to at the time as "Oriental" furniture, such as a Chinese inlaid table large enough for bridge games. My father once told me it's "the most beautiful house in North America."

"Dad? The most beautiful house in North America?" I queried.

"You heard me."

In addition to the main home, there was a multicar garage opposite the house. My brother and I were playing on the driveway when we heard that the Second World War had started. Our home was big, but it wasn't the biggest in the neighbourhood. The Timmins family—as in mining in Timmins, Ontario— had a huge mansion nearby to house nine children. My father's siblings lived close to us—Uncle Allan and his family practically next door, Uncle Harry a couple of blocks away, as well as Uncle Abe and Aunt Laura. I sat in front of Uncle Harry's house, dressed in short pants and a school blazer, to watch King George VI and Queen Elizabeth (later known as the Queen Mum) drive by when they were on their cross-country tour of Canada in the spring of 1939. In those days, there wasn't the same security as there is now to protect people like that. You could get close. By the way, that was the visit that inspired my father to dream up Crown Royal. He put five cases (sixty bottles) on the royal train in Quebec and another five cases on the train in Ontario. But he never drank Crown Royal. I asked him once why he only drank V.O.

"V.O. is for drinking. Crown Royal is for selling," he said.

In my dad's study, where he spent most of his time when he was home, he used to play solitaire at his desk. Mother played cards with her sister Freda in the sunroom. My son Stephen and daughter-in-law Claudine now own the property and have renovated it in a warm, yet stunning modern style. It is now heated geothermally and is LEED certified, an environmentally friendly home.

We also owned a second version of Belvedere about forty-five minutes outside of New York City, overlooking the Hudson River in a village called Tarrytown. My mother's description paints it as paradise.

The estate was magnificent, twenty-two acres planted with superb trees and lovely gardens. There was a small lake on the property and a large, heated swimming pool made of Italian tile. The house was modelled on a Spanish villa, a charming place with twenty-five enormous rooms and fire-places everywhere with mantels of marble or Dutch tile. The master bedroom was magnificent, its windows offering a sweeping view of the Hudson River. The place was beauti-fully furnished when we bought it. I didn't have to touch the dining room or the library. In Ogilvy's department store in Montreal an antique section had just opened, and I bought a lot of pieces there, mixing them with the furniture in the other rooms. I also bought some marvellous Chinese paint-ings in New York. The result was very pleasing. There was a two-storey recreation house by the pool, picturesque and rather romantic, and during the summer we spent most of our time there. On weekends, there was a lot of company. We lunched on the terrace, at umbrella-shaded tables. Often, my

Sam sat out there and chatted with friends for hours. Another of his favourite places was the pool table in the games room. He still loved to play the game. The house was well set up for entertaining. There was an arcade in the dining room, and we often had cocktails and dinner outside on the lawn. The children and their friends were often around.

My mother had her view of Tarrytown, but our views certainly don't synch. I look back on it as an enormous, nice jail because in order to visit anyone, you had to go by car. Prior to Tarrytown, though, when I was between the ages of ten and fourteen, we had a large stone country house north of Montreal that we rented from the Purvis family of Canadian Industries Ltd., more commonly known as C-I-L (the father, Arthur, had been killed in a plane crash during the Second World War). That home in Sainte-Marguerite was, according to Phyllis, "the one place where we were a family, eating together, and when indoors spending time in the same huge room that had a cathedral ceiling and a great imported stone fireplace . . . I see in my mind's eye Charles coming to Mother with a kitten upside down in his arms (asking), 'Is it a boy or a girl?' Charles asked Mother what sodomy meant; and my sister sang a song about Minnie the Mermaid where among the corals she lost her morals and Charles asked what 'morals' meant."

Our car was a Rolls-Royce with a chauffeur named Bordeau who wore the full regalia. At 15 Belvedere, we had a butler named Jensen who professionally played the part to the hilt. The girls had their nanny on their floor of the house, the second floor. Edgar and I had our nanny on the third floor of the house. Our bedrooms were next to each other. Edgar's was larger than mine and had a little nook thanks to the turret that went up that side of the house. We had our own small baseball diamond that was flooded in the winter so we could have a skating rink. It all made for comfortable living, to say the least.

My parents revered the style of the English aristocracy, particularly my father, who had a fascination, maybe an obsession, with royalty. The Jewish elite in Montreal wanted to emulate the Anglo-Protestant elite, and we were most certainly the Jewish elite. This royal fetish manifested itself in the names of Seagram's most successful brands like Crown Royal, 5 Crown, 7 Crown, and Chivas Regal.

Many people believe that those born to very successful, prominent people are instantly imbued with a supernatural self-confidence. That may be true of the Theodore and Franklin Roosevelts, but it was most certainly *not* true of me. I had none. I felt overwhelmed by my family and its high-achieving ways. I was, looking back, a childhood basket case, full of anxieties, fears, and an inner life that bore no resemblance to my outer, public life. Only in my thirties did this feeling start to reverse itself. And only in my later years have I begun to feel satisfied with who I am as a person, and who I have been.

When I grew up in Montreal, it was still Canada's number one city. Aside from not being affected by the depressed economy of the time, I also had no idea that I was living in a largely Francophone metropolis and province. There was a well-known book written by Hugh MacLennan called *Two Solitudes*, and I can tell you that's what it was like. The French lived east of St. Lawrence (St-Laurent) Boulevard and the English to the west. We lived in Westmount, the enclave where Montreal's richest English-speaking citizens lived. Our French counterparts lived in Outremont, where the Université de Montréal is located. McGill University is situated downtown in English-speaking Montreal. The only French people I knew were those who worked in our home, and they spoke English to us. I'm amazed that I was in my twenties before I knew French was spoken in the city—that's how cut off we were.

Such was the formality of our household that we rarely ate with our parents. My father, because of the pressing needs of his business empire, spent the week in New York City, running Seagram. He would take the overnight train on Thursday evening and be home in Montreal for the weekend. At *Shabbat* dinner on Friday night, we boys were dressed in our Little Lord Fauntleroy suits, while the girls wore flowery dresses. It was awful, but my parents meant well. Sunday lunch, featuring roast beef, was the other time we were likeliest to all be together.

My mother's guru was Emily Post, the maven of etiquette, and she grew to adopt a so-called European style of service—that is, formal. The food was English cuisine, if you can call English food "cuisine." Our cooks were cooks; they were not chefs. Still, there are foods from my childhood that still excite me when I think of them. Funnily enough, the famous Montreal bagel is not on the list, which includes sweetbreads and liver chopped in a little dish, flat crepes with maple syrup, tapioca and rice pudding, and bean *tzimmes* with marrow bones. My sisters loved the marrow, but I can't eat it to this day. As a result, I got extra beans in a sweet sauce.

Because we kept a kosher home (for the most part), we didn't have any sausages or bacon, although Edgar and I once ordered bacon and eggs in Boca Raton while having breakfast with our father. You could feel the roof blow off the place, such was Dad's volcanic reaction. Truth be told, a lot of families make up their own cultural/religious dietary rules to suit themselves. Shellfish isn't kosher, but we had it, although only when we were outside of the home. Somehow it seemed to be a lesser evil compared with meat from a pig. After all, the last part of the word *shellfish* is *fish*. Our father made the excuse that he grew up on the prairie so he didn't know about it. There was also something called *petcha* or *ptcha*, depending on which *shtetl* you're from. In today's delicate foodie world, jelly made from calves' feet doesn't exactly sound appetizing, but it was.

What I didn't want to eat was baked apple for dessert. One day it was placed before me and I had the temerity to say, "No, thank you." For that response, I was sent to my room for the afternoon. It took me fifty years to ever look at a baked apple again. It's actually not bad, I've discovered.

I remember the iceman coming to the house with big blocks of ice, manipulating them with a large set of forceps. There was also an equivalent to the Good Humor Man, who came around with ice cream for sale. In a neighbourhood store, we'd sit down and read comic books so we didn't have to pay for them. Typical kids. We'd get seven streetcar rides for a quarter and a chocolate bar for a nickel.

My hero was our chauffeur, Bordeau, because he could drink the entire contents of a six-ounce bottle of Coke in one gulp, without having to stop to belch. He wore the boots, the leggings, the cap, the whole uniform. When he'd drive my mother around, people would ask whose car it was and he'd always say it belonged to the governor general. During the war, however, we put the Rolls-Royce up on blocks. Because of rationing, you couldn't get gasoline for it. It was a glutton on gas. Besides the

Rolls, we had other cars. I recall two Packards, an American luxury competitor to Cadillac that went out of production in the late 1950s. We had a sedan and a convertible that was in my mother's name, but she never drove it. Some of my happiest times were spent upstairs over the garage, where Bordeau had an apartment. You could park three cars in the garage, but above one side of it is an apartment the size of a nice home, with two bedrooms, a kitchen, dining room, and sitting room. I used to hang out there with my black-and-white patched dog, Pat, the product of a mixed marriage and the best dog I ever had.

The car in which I learned to drive was the Packard convertible, complete with a rumble seat, a feature that disappeared from cars like tails disappeared from humans. I was taught on the back roads of the Laurentians, and by the age of twelve, I was a good driver. It was not unusual then for kids in rural Quebec to drive before they turned sixteen, given the need to operate farm vehicles.

My first job was delivering the *Montreal Star* for a couple of years after school, first on foot to the Gleneagles apartments on Côte-des-Neiges, then later on an easy route on bicycle. It was close to the store where we'd hang out. Apparently, according to my mother's memoirs, none of us children was extravagant. Each of us got an allowance, but we would make up lists about how we spent it. I grew up hearing business issues discussed around the table—not money, but business, and there is a difference. I think I learned more around the table than I ever did at school. Meantime, the classroom became an unhappy experience and place for me. I would get panic attacks on Sunday nights, knowing I had school the next day. That feeling got so ingrained it even carried on into my business life. My siblings, however, were good in school.

Edgar and I went to Selwyn House, a private school in Montreal. There were very few Jews there, only one other in my class. It was a prestigious school for the economic elite. You had to be from the top, top, top, probably what we'd call the one per cent now, or the point-one per cent. The Great Depression was not a topic of conversation. When we were younger, the chauffeur drove us but dropped us off at the corner nearby because it was embarrassing to be driven to school by a chauffeur.

Edgar, I think, established the record at Selwyn House for getting caned the most times on the bum, the bare bum. He was a good student, but he frequently got in trouble. Our mother would try to discipline him—although, in the 1980s, she wrote in one of her two privately published books that if any of us did anything that required discipline, she would take us into a room and sit us down to discuss the issue at hand. When it came to Edgar, I remember it a bit differently. He would test the limits and then my mother would take a belt and chase after him.

"Anywhere it lands, anywhere it lands!" she'd yell. To my memory, she never got him.

Although the kids we knew were pretty much all from well-to-do homes, most did not have anywhere near the wealth of our family. Yet I had no sense of that, not until my teenage years, when I felt that certain kids wanted to befriend me because of my father's riches. Funnily, I got used to the idea that maybe there was another reason below the surface for someone wanting to be my friend. But it never really bothered me. I never counted, nor did I care who had what. It's just the way it was, and I learned to be a little cautious.

For me, I was doing my best to manage at Selwyn House.

I was relatively comfortable in my situation in Montreal, with friends and sports. That changed drastically when I was sent to Trinity College School in Port Hope, Ontario, when I was ready for Grade 9. However, I skipped a grade and went right into tenth grade, and the problem with that was that I was behind in science, meaning trouble for me. I hated the place, hated the whole atmosphere. There was no kindness and no gentleness, a school fashioned on old British tradition. The teachers were an eccentric lot and it seemed the only way you could prosper there was if one of the nutty professors liked you. We knew them by their nicknames, like "Sharpie" Snelgrove and "Skook" Lewis. Sharpie had a sharp nose and taught chemistry. He liked me, so I did okay. Skook taught physics. He didn't like me so much, so I didn't do well. Later, Skook was teaching both chemistry and physics, so I failed both. I went to him to ask for help.

"Bronfman, you must study, study, study some more," he said. That's the help I got.

When it came time for us to get ready for our Spanish literature exam—an exam mandated by the province of Ontario—we were addressed by our teacher, Mr. Denny.

"Oh, chaps," he sighed.

"Yes, Mr. Denny."

"Oh, chaps. I have very bad news. It's about the book we've been studying. It's not the book the exam is based on." It was very bad news indeed, given that the exam was scheduled for the next day. Six of us went and signed our names at the top of the exam paper and then left. We felt it was hopeless to take the test because we could not possibly read the proper book in just one night in order to prepare.

I feel as though TCS ruined my education, it was such a screwed-up place—at least for me. Edgar went two years before me and therefore he was present for only part of my time there. In those days, whichever school one kid in a family went to, the other kid followed. They sent Edgar there to toughen him up, after rejecting the idea of sending him to Royal Military College. I was the only Jewish kid at TCS after he left. We had been the first two to ever attend the repository for the children of the WASP elite. It's also where I experienced my first, vile taste of anti-Semitism. In one situation, a boy warned me to "keep my big Jewish nose out of it." I belted him in the chin. During my first year, twelve of us lived in a big area that was divided into cubicles, and before sleeping, the other eleven would say in unison, "King Item, King Edgar." They were speaking in thinly veiled code. When you took the first letter of each word, they were really saying "K.I.K.E.," a slur word for Jew that dates to immigrants arriving at Ellis Island. I already didn't want to be there, but then I had to put up with that. Only recently I heard that we were referred to as the "horrible Hebes."

Edgar had a better experience there. He wasn't nearly as sensitive as I was. Although as kids we fought and he'd beat me up, at TCS he was my protector in many respects. Thus the pattern of our relationship was established.

Years later, though, a successor headmaster of TCS came to see me at the Seagram office. He wanted money. I prefer to describe it as *schnorring,* a wonderful Yiddish word that means scrounging or begging in a wheedling, cagey sort of way. Let's put it this way: it's not a favourable description. After he asked, I told him my story of the time I'd spent at the school he was now running. Then I asked him, "If you were me, what would you give TCS?"

"If I were you, I wouldn't give them one plugged nickel."

The word apparently got out, because at a later date, when I was speaking in Toronto, another headmaster approached me from TCS.

"I understand you had a terrible experience there." I thought the guy was trying to be nice, but after lunch, didn't he *schnorr* me. I said, "You've got to be out of your mind."

The man I knew and liked the best at TCS, ironically, was the chaplain, the Reverend E.R. Bagley, who was a heck of a decent fellow. In addition to being my housemaster, he was also my history and English teacher as well as soccer coach. We had to go to chapel every night. I'd always say "amen" before he got through saying "Jesus Christ." He gave a sermon that was one of the best I've ever heard. It was so simple. Most things that are good are simple, I've found. The sermon was entitled "*If* is the biggest word in the English language." It's true. *If* can be the biggest word in the English language.

Luckily for us, we were too young to fight in the war. But that period is very clear in my mind. I remember hearing some of Churchill's speeches on the radio—"We will fight them on the beaches, we will never surrender." Those were the darkest, gloomiest days. I didn't know of *Mein Kampf* or what had happened at the 1936 Olympics. I also knew nothing of the Holocaust, nothing at all. There was, to my knowledge, no reporting of it until the end of the war. Then I recall seeing the pictures in the newspaper of the Allied troops coming across these starving, sick, and ghostly-looking people when they liberated the camps. Although we didn't know the horrors until the war ended, we most certainly knew who the enemy was. We had a song we'd sing, to the tune of "The Caisson Song":

Hitler has only got one ball.
Goering has two, but they are small.
Himmler is somewhat similar.
But poor old Goebbels has no balls at all.

Although the song was classic schoolyard ridicule, it reflected the fact that we knew something very serious was happening, the most serious things you ever heard. The world was in danger. Certainly Europe was in danger. We were lucky in our family because we had no relatives who were lost in the Holocaust. I have strong memories from that time, though—the sinking of the famed British battleship HMS *Prince of Wales* by the Japanese just a few days after Pearl Harbor in December 1941 and the Battle of Dieppe in 1942, which took the lives of so many Canadians. From 1943, I remember the Tehran Conference with Churchill, Roosevelt, and Stalin and the Quebec Conference with Roosevelt and Churchill. I remember Roosevelt in his cape. And I remember most vividly when FDR died. I was in the kitchen of our house. The news came on the radio. That was a big shock and I felt very, very sad. But I also remember the elation and great celebration of V-E Day.

If you haven't lived in Montreal, you don't know what a cold winter is. Perhaps it's comparable to Moscow's, or winters experienced by those hardy northern types who huddle in Winnipeg or the Northwest Territories, but Montreal has its own special cold. The snow starts early and stays late, and looking at the mighty St. Lawrence only makes you feel colder. What it does, though, is provide the perfect backdrop for a sport I loved playing as a kid, hockey. I didn't have much of a shot, and for some reason I would reduce my odds of scoring even further by aiming right for the goaltender's pads rather than where he was vulnerable. Although I had speed on my side and enjoyed participating, I never saw myself as a particularly good player.

Montreal was and is a hockey town with *Les Canadiens*, known as the Habs, having won twenty-four Stanley Cups, more than any other NHL team. To put that in perspective, the New York Yankees have won twenty-seven World Series, so the Habs have one of the best records in professional sport. My parents had season tickets, and my brother and I had season tickets as well. First we were in the blues, which were mid-priced seats, then the reds, which were just a few rows behind the players bench. Before we'd go on our own, we used to go with our parents to Sunday afternoon games. Phyllis says Mother was a very enthusiastic fan who cheered loudly. I was even more enthusiastic. I'd get so emotionally involved in the game that I would move around constantly. By the time it was over, I was more tired than the players. My favourite players were the goalie Bill Durnan, the defenceman Doug Harvey, and, of course, Maurice "Rocket" Richard. Harvey was the most intelligent hockey player on the Montreal squad. He initiated the idea of the rushing defenceman, years before Bobby Orr came along. He was a great setup man and the first offensive defenceman I had seen. As for Richard, it's true what they've said about his eyes. He'd come down the ice with those flaming eyes. The beauty of the NHL then was there were only six teams, so you knew all the players and, more specifically, all the lines. Detroit had the "Production Line" of Gordie Howe, Sid Abel, and Ted Lindsay. Boston had the "Kraut Line" of Milt Schmidt, Bobby Bauer, and Woody Dumart. Montreal, of course, had the "Punch Line" of Richard, Elmer Lach, and Toe Blake.

We used to play hockey with our cousins, Peter and Edward (Uncle Allan's sons), who lived almost next door. After a rift between my father and my uncle, Peter and Edward would go on to form their own business empire known as Edper, a conglomerate that controlled Brascan (now Brookfield), Noranda, John Labatt Ltd., and many other companies. But when we were kids, we were buddies. Dad and Allan ripped down the house between ours and made a playground on which there was a backstop and a plate where we played baseball and a game called "running bases" in the summer. What used to make us angry, though, was that the World Series would often fall on the high holidays, either Rosh Hashanah or Yom Kippur—how the hell could we get out of dinner and listen to the game? In the winter, it was hockey on what was called the Bronfman Brothers Hockey Team. God forbid we should have had to go to one of the parks! In many ways, we were pretty well confined to the property. Our parents were always worried about the outside world, specifically kidnapping. This was not long after the Lindbergh baby was kidnapped and found dead, which clearly made our parents nervous.

Their fears were not misplaced. In the summer of 1975, my brother Edgar's eldest son, Sam, was abducted and held for ransom of more than two million dollars, all in twenties. I spent the entire week with Edgar at his New York apartment. The FBI set up a "hermetically sealed" household, meaning no one was allowed to leave. When it was time for Edgar to "make the drop," I rode with him downtown in an "FBI taxi." It was a Yellow Cab owned by the Bureau and it even included a meter—a perfect decoy car. I tried to pay the fare, but the agent said, "Don't worry, it's one of ours." The FBI then purchased a shirt for Edgar because the one he was wearing was made of thin material, which meant the wire they were fitting him with would be visible. When it was time for him to leave to make the drop, I wanted to go with him. The FBI had to physically restrain me. I suddenly understood how people in war do things they would normally be terrified to do. I simply wanted to be there for my brother. He had protected me at TCS, and now it was my turn. Fortunately, Sam was released after Edgar did the deed. In the end, the perpetrators got no money, were captured, and were convicted of extortion. That incident brought Edgar and me closer than ever. Eleven years prior to that, in August 1964, my parents would have their own brush with terror at our home in Tarrytown, New York, when two thieves broke into the house, tied them to a sink using stockings, pointed a revolver at my father, and made off with my mother's jewels.

Baseball was also part of my youth. My mother maintains I was crazy about it as a kid. However, if she was implying that I played it, that's not the case. I just followed it. The nice part about the game is that it's a pastoral sport, played in summer. It also meant hot dogs, Cokes, Cracker Jack, and ice cream. Later, it provided a pivotal phase in my life when I brought the Montreal Expos and Major League Baseball to Canada. In the U.S., knowing baseball was also a way to be accepted. For the children of immigrants, it was your way into society at large. In Canada, hockey played that role. Let's face it: you wanted to be like everyone else, rather than separate and apart. As a kid, I went to see the top farm team of the Brooklyn Dodgers, the Montreal Royals of the International League. It was Triple-A ball and it was darn good. Little did I know that I was also witnessing history. In 1946, the Royals had a player named Jackie

Robinson, the first African American to ever play in organized baseball (read: white baseball). He played for Montreal before being promoted the next year to the Brooklyn Dodgers. Thanks to the Royals, I knew of the up-and-comers in the Brooklyn Dodgers organization before they were Dodgers. And if you loved the Dodgers, you hated the Yankees. It was the underdogs versus the overdogs.

Robinson was sensational. He played second base for us. In his first game, he got four hits in five at-bats. For that season, he hit .349 and stole forty bases. Although he was a great base stealer, he was not the fastest runner. What he could do, though, was read the pitcher and the catcher. He knew when to bluff and how to drive a pitcher crazy. That use of psychology would give him the upper hand. Robinson on third base—oh my god. He'd start to run toward home and then he'd stop. If you were a right-handed pitcher and you'd see that out of the corner of your eye, you'd start going nuts. He also had amazing acceleration. He might not have been the fastest, but he was the quickest and the smartest.

Later, it occurred to me that the United States is an amazing country. Americans love their myths about freedom. However, until the late 1940s, in what's billed as the world's paragon of democracy, a professional life in America's pastime was off-limits to men of colour. Black men could not play in Major League Baseball or its minor leagues, but rather were confined to the negro leagues. It's shocking, absolutely shocking. A memorable incident in the Jackie Robinson story is what Pee Wee Reese did at a game in Cincinnati during Robinson's first year with the Dodgers. Reese was the shortstop while Robinson played second base. Reese was from Louisville, Kentucky, a southern town about a hundred miles southwest of Cincinnati. Before the game, when the players were doing their warm-ups, the crowd was picking on Robinson. Reese walked over and put his arm around his black teammate, essentially saying to America and the world, "He's my friend, he's my teammate." But one gesture from Reese, while huge, was still just a gesture. John McHale, who had been a player for Detroit and later president of the Expos organization, told me that there was a worry among players in the majors that the black guys would take their jobs. McHale said to those players, "Then we just have to play better."

Edgar and I used to take the streetcar on Sundays to go to Royals doubleheaders, and we would also go to hockey games together. He would bet with me, but against the Montreal Canadiens. I'd say, "How the hell could you bet against the Canadiens? It's our team." Pointing to his heart, and then to his wallet, he said, "This (money) has nothing to do with this (the heart), and that's the difference between you and me."

As for playing sports, I played soccer and hockey and did some sprinting in school but never learned to swim properly because I couldn't master the breathing. I also skied, in spite of the prehistoric equipment we used back then—leather ski boots that we had to lace up when it was freezing outside, bamboo ski poles. Steel edges on the skis had just been introduced, allowing you to turn more easily and stop. There weren't chairlifts back then; there were rope tows and something called a J-bar, shaped like the letter J, and you'd plunk your butt on the curved part and it took you back up the hill—as long as it was a small hill.

In order to get a bit of attention, I knew how to get my siblings in trouble. Although Edgar was two years older and stronger, I'd get him into hot water. Impishly, I also occasionally got Phyllis into tight situations. Once, when I was in my twenties, we were skiing in Aspen. After some time on the slopes, Phyllis had her rear end aimed at the fireplace to warm up. There was a gentleman sitting there—Howard Head, who was the inventor of metal skis. He and I had been chatting in front of the fire. I asked Phyllis, "What do you think of the new metal skis?" She started criticizing Head's product. I interjected and said, pointing to the gentleman who was there, "Oh, Phyllis, I'd like you to meet Howard Head."

In spite of my anxieties and lack of self-confidence, my mother says that I was a natural orator, giving my first public speech when I was about fifteen years of age. It was in New York City and it came on as something of a surprise. There was a distributors' meeting at the Waldorf-Astoria and the head of one of the Seagram subsidiaries was being honoured. His name was Bill Wachtel. He was very friendly with my father, and I loved the guy, calling him "Uncle Bill." Dad was supposed to give the address that night, but he and Uncle Allan were in Scotland or Ireland and neither could make it back. So the word came down from Dad: "You'll give the speech."

I had a couple of days' notice but couldn't escape the fact that I'd be in front of six or seven hundred people at the Waldorf. I was standing there, shaking, the focal point of all those expectant faces, the son of the great Sam Bronfman. If I didn't do it, it would have been an insult to my "Uncle Bill" and public speaking would have been more difficult to surmount later in life. So I did it and found out I was still alive at the end. I spoke personally about "Uncle Bill" and managed to get through the ordeal. The speech was probably terrible, but decades later my mother wrote about it as though I was a veteran orator who absorbed the skill by being present at family dinner parties where there were frequent lively exchanges. Jewish mothers!

Eight or nine years later, when I was running the Adams Company, one of the firms in the Seagram stable, we had a meeting in the Windsor Hotel in Montreal (where my Canadian office is today), and I gave a speech to my salesmen. My father heard it. Afterward, when I saw him, he didn't say a word, not a word.

I said, "That bad, eh?"

"Yes, it was," came the answer. Although he demolished my performance with that terse line and offered no tips on how to improve, his reaction sure motivated me to do better.

On the surface, as a kid, I was a "hail fellow well met," as they say. But it was a veneer. I was terrified of girls. I didn't know how to talk to people, really. It wasn't until the Expos, when I was in my late thirties, that I was self-assured enough to talk to people because I could talk baseball. Even today, at a dinner party, I'm quite quiet unless I feel like I have something to contribute. I'm not good at local gossip.

At one point during my time at TCS, they conducted psychological tests on us, trying to determine what we wanted to do in life. We were asked if we were part of an orchestra, would we rather play a string instrument, a wind instrument, or be the conductor or manager. I wanted to be the conductor. I'd also dream of myself in slalom races on skis. And I would have loved to be a pitcher, because that's the most important guy on the team. I loved to watch a pitcher take his stride and watch that beautiful motion. I also loved to sit behind the netting and watch the pitch come in. I used to try to throw curves and sliders myself, using different grips. But reality was one thing, while fantasy was another.

There weren't just dreams, there were also nightmares. I had a recurring one as a child. We had a staircase leading to a wall that protected the house from the street. I'd be on my toboggan at the top of the steps, but in my dream I'd go over the wall and there'd be a car coming.

In spite of the good times I had as a child, with baseball, hockey, and comics, there always seemed to be a sense of foreboding. Even my bar mitzvah, which is supposed to be a joyous family and community occasion, was freighted with heaviness. It was a somewhat subdued affair compared with Edgar's because my Uncle Harry's son Allan had died a few weeks before at only thirty-eight years of age. But the thoughtful tone came in the form of a letter from my father—a beautiful letter, actually.

"The key to every man's future is himself," my father wrote to me, quoting his own grandfather. Without a doubt, there is a strong grain of truth in the line. As a man, you have to rely on yourself and apply yourself in a determined fashion to whatever you choose to do. But in my view, it's also true that the key to a person's future, however defined, depends on other things as well—luck, the society one is surrounded by, and factors beyond one's control.

Dad's letter continued, imploring, "To you who have been born to many comforts, your lot entails corresponding responsibilities . . . Well it is to walk with Kings, but never lose the common touch. I cannot impress upon you too emphatically the ideal of services to the less fortunate than yourself." The fact that we had many comforts meant we were, to some regard, on display in Montreal. Others had their noses, metaphorically speaking, pressed up against the glass, trying to peer into our lives, which must have seemed idyllic.

Of course, as a kid, you have other thoughts, selfish thoughts, like being upset about presents. When my cousin Edward had his bar mitzvah, he got two hundred presents. Edgar got three hundred. Peter got four hundred, and I was in line to get five hundred presents, and then, unfortunately, Cousin Allan died. I don't remember how many presents I got, but it was back in the two hundreds. I was close to Peter, who was almost two years older than me, and after my bar mitzvah we were invited on a fishing trip to Gananoque, Ontario. My parents wouldn't let me go unless I'd thanked everyone for my gifts with a written note. Confession: Peter helped me write the notes, signing my name on cards to people neither of us knew.

My father finished on an up note: "Your sociable temperament and your tenacity of purpose, your strength of mind and anything in which you feel yourself . . . in other words, a good head and stalwart spirit." It was, in the main, a loving letter and laced with a sense of duty.

I remember my brother, Edgar, saying to me, also on the back steps of the house, "Whatever we do, we can't win. If we fail, we're idiots. If we succeed, it's 'cause Dad built it." Wealth has its privileges. It also has its burdens.

2

Overwhelming Family

―――――

Despite coming from the family I did, I had no great pretensions to glory. In fact, when I was eighteen I began seeing a psychiatrist three times a week. My parents knew this, of course, but going for treatment was my decision. I think it's fair to say that I did not love myself as a younger person, although it would be wrong to say that I didn't have fun. Psychologically speaking, I've learned there are essentially three types of people: the pleaser, the loner, and the one who won't be pushed around. Minda, the oldest of my siblings, was the pleaser. Phyllis, who came second in our foursome, has always been the loner. Edgar, the third child and first son, was the one who wouldn't be pushed around, and then I came along as the fourth, settling back into the first persona of the group, the pleasing role. In each case, it was clearly just us kids looking for attention in the family pecking order.

The doctor I saw regularly told me that if I had been destined to be a shoe salesman, I wouldn't have to come to see him. He meant that if I were not the son of Sam Bronfman, pre-programmed to be more than a shoe salesman, I probably wouldn't have had the issues I had. Not to denigrate those who sell shoes, but he had a point. Although we all led a rather protected life, with staff to look after our every need, much would be expected of us, from our days at the highfalutin private schools we were required to attend, to what we were going to do in life and whom it would be appropriate for us to marry. Dad, for instance, would tell us it was just as easy to fall in love with a rich girl as a poor girl. As Edgar recounted, we were driving back with Dad from Lake Placid, where we'd spent the weekend. "What happens if I fall in love with a poor girl?" Edgar asked. "Don't go out with any," was Dad's answer. For my sisters, the expectation was even clearer—shut out the fortune hunters by marrying wealthy guys. It's hard enough to find a spouse in life, let alone one from the right social strata. I didn't get married (for the first time) until I was thirty, late for my generation.

At home in Montreal, there was always someone between our parents and us—namely the help, of which there was a lot. Phyllis, in the 1996 documentary *Whisky Man*, described how governesses and nurses would present us to our parents at the appointed hours when we were scheduled to see them, generally at a mealtime. Edgar also recalled our home being "rather a cold place," adding that we were not encouraged to bring friends there. He told the filmmakers "it was not much fun to bring people into a house that Queen Victoria would have felt ill at ease at, it was so stiff." Edgar also said, "If you did something terrific, 'Of course you did, you're my son.' It was never 'well done.' I don't think I ever heard the words 'I love you.'"

I think it's clear that of the four of us, I'm the only one who was left with fondness, even love, for our father, although as I said in that film, "I fell in love with my father after he died . . . he was no longer a threat to me." As for our mother, I never felt we had a warm mother–son relationship. Let's put it this way: she wasn't the type to bake cookies for us. In fact, she was a mother who couldn't cook to save her life. Once, when she was trying to make up with Edgar about something, she offered to fry some eggs for him. It turns out she didn't have a clue how to do it, so finally Edgar took over and did it himself.

Our parents were busy people, not only with the business, Jewish community issues, and philanthropy, but also climbing the social ladder, something both of them wanted to do from the get-go and something that became the shared glue of what was a happy union. It's not unusual for the children of powerful people to be wimps or middling achievers. But I think it's fair to say that in spite of each of our issues—and there were many— my siblings and I turned out to have done well.

The die for me among my siblings was most surely cast in large part by the behaviour, patterns, and traits of those in the previous generation. Between Dad and his siblings—there were four boys and four girls—our father was the dominant figure, even though he was not the oldest. He was the go-getter and the business builder, ultimately claiming the family business for himself and his children. Later, there would be trouble between Dad and his brother Allan. For many years, though, they were very close. Allan had studied law and was arguably a more pol- ished person publicly than my father, adding a more classic sheen to the operation. Dad was the soul of the company and the businessman, and he wanted Allan to be the voice, the PR man. Dad, however, could sniff out weaknesses in Allan and exploit them for all they were worth, to the point many years later of shutting Allan's sons, Edward and Peter, my first cous- ins, out of any possible jobs at Seagram, even a summer job. By outcontrolling Allan by a ratio of two to one through ownership vehicles that had been set up, Dad ensured that Seagram would pass without obstacle to his children via CEMP, a trust named for Charles, Edgar, Minda, and Phyllis.

Later in life, I would start to think of myself as Uncle Allan—not a very helpful way to view my place in the family. My older brother, Edgar, took on the role of my father when he became Dad's successor as the CEO of Seagram—even though Edgar and I were equal partners when it came to share owner-ship. He was chairman and I was co-chairman, whatever that meant. I was the kindly one, the one my father thought would burnish the family name, while Edgar was the tough guy, the one who could take the rudder of Seagram after Dad was ready to relinquish it. The question of whether sons of founders or family of founders should steer the mother ship is one we'll come back to in detail later.

I got a sense of the contrast and enmity between Dad and Allan while on a fishing trip with my uncle and cousins in Gananoque, Ontario. Something happened, I don't remember precisely what, but I joshed my uncle and said, "You'd better be careful or I'll tell the boss," meaning my father. Allan lost it and reamed me out in front of his sons, assuring them he was an equal partner in the business with Dad. That was a lie. I always liked Allan and I think he liked me—I would defend him when Dad ranted and raved about him. But Allan certainly made a fateful decision for himself when he hitched his wagon to my father, rather than blazing his own trail as a lawyer. Eventually, all of Dad's brothers found themselves diminished in the busi-ness—he outgrew all of them. I just happened to be privy to the angst and battle between Dad and Allan.

Edgar described how he'd got wind of Uncle Allan trying to "sneak Peter into the business." He called Dad in New York, who asked how he felt about it. Edgar said, "If he comes in, I go out." Asked why, Edgar said, "'Cause there will be too many Bronfmans in the company."

It wasn't that Edgar disliked cousin Peter or thought ill of him; he just didn't think it was good for the company, and our father agreed, then hung up the phone and blasted Uncle Allan. I have said publicly that Dad made Allan a "not unreasonable offer." Cousin Edward disagreed and told documentary maker David Paperny, "The price was lousy, but we had to accept it. And I think my father was quite humiliated and sometimes took his frustrations out on us and our family." He said that Allan must have hated Dad for how he was treated and that Dad had taken advantage of his father.

For sure, Dad was one tough hombre. In a sense, he had to be. He came from parents who had escaped eastern Europe in the latter part of the nineteenth century. They hailed from the *shtetl* Ataki in Bessarabia, now known as Moldova. Dad's parents made it to Saskatchewan in the late 1880s with four children, a rabbi, and a nanny. My grandfather brought tobacco seeds and tried to cultivate the plant on the prairie. That didn't last long. He must have had some capital at his disposal, though, because he ended up buying a hotel in Brandon, Manitoba. A hotel in those days in a place like Brandon wasn't the Four Seasons, or even a Motel 6, for that matter. It consisted of a bar, a pool hall, and maybe three rooms upstairs. Perhaps the rooms upstairs were rented for short-term transactions, possibly a number of times each night.

On my mother's side, the family had also settled in western

Canada, in Plum Coulee, Manitoba, where her father was the co-owner of a general store. As a result of Jews being forbidden to own land in eastern Europe, the Canadian arm of the Jewish Colonization Association had bought land in the area. Eventually, my mother's father bought farmland and had a man cultivate it for him, making him a gentleman farmer, as it were. When I was sixteen, I asked him why he married my grandmother. In a tellingly practical story, he told me that she was eighteen and she was pretty. He said that he was twenty-one and that he needed somebody who could keep house and cook, while she needed someone who could earn a living. It doesn't sound like hot romance, but it was certainly a partnership that made sense in the cold reality of western Canada in that era.

He also once told me an amusing story about why he poured himself a large glass of V.O. (Seagram's signature whisky) each day. "Because my doctor told me I should have only one drink a day. But he didn't say what size."

My father's date and place of birth are somewhat controversial. He personally claimed he was born in Brandon in 1891, but I believe it was in Wapella, Saskatchewan, where they settled initially. After Dad's death, Edgar discovered documents that clearly indicate he was born in Bessarabia, part of Russia, two years prior. Other reports are that he was born on the sea voyage to North America. The discrepancy would likely have its root in a strong desire on his part to not be viewed as an immigrant. There are stories of him having to endure the humiliation of wearing torn clothes to school. Dad was not big on being poor, and perhaps such experiences spawned the drive and determination that contributed to his remarkable success in business.

Sam Bronfman was a man of common sense who made

common-sense observations. To his father, who went into the hotel business, he remarked that it seemed like the real money was made behind the bar, so why not concentrate on liquor instead of renting rooms and a few pool tables? In many cases, he turned his common-sense notions into homilies or lessons in life, which he liked to share around the dinner table. My siblings tended to roll their eyes when he'd launch into them, but many have stuck with me throughout my life. For instance, when I met someone as a young person, I'd often look down when I shook hands. Dad told me to look that person straight in the eye when I shook hands, otherwise he or she would think I'd done something wrong. It's a simple rule for conducting oneself and it makes total sense. As for the business, he'd say, "Distilling is a science, blending is an art." The latter spoke to his perfectionism and his tendency to micromanage, but also to the granular understanding he had of his industry. He knew his numbers, he knew his product, he knew his labels, and he knew how to market his merchandise. But he had founder's syndrome, and although Edgar later criticized him for trying to manage what had grown into a huge business, he most surely operated on a level with few peers. Although the word *genius* can be overused, I wholeheartedly believe it applies in his case.

By the age of twenty-four, Dad was already so successful he had his own chauffeur. That was a good thing. He was a terrible driver because he was always thinking about business rather than driving. But someone told him he could be even more successful if his bartenders didn't steal from him. That person then told him about a newfangled measuring device that could be attached to a bottle so he could compare what was poured, the number of drinks sold, and what ended up in the till. Dad replied that he knew the bartenders were stealing but that the bartenders knew that he knew—and he added that they had an unspoken pact.

"As long as they know that I know, then they know if they steal too much, it will mean trouble. But if they use that new measuring device, they'll just water down the whisky and the customers will complain, and the last thing I want is a complaining customer."

Common sense. He also wanted to run a business that could be boiled down to a simple concept. He wanted a business where people could walk into a shop and say, "Give me that," and he was the one who had made what they wanted—an elementary business on a grand scale.

Genius aside, the downside of my father was that he could be terrifying. He was frightening to many, and I lived in fear— as did my siblings—that we could be the next target of one of his explosive rages, which often included a string of profanities that shocked even hardened, grown men. Phyllis described being scared of Dad, probably because of his angry outbursts, to the point of being "terrified to be alone with my father." My late cousin Edward also described Sam Bronfman as "a hard-nosed, shrewd dictator who always got his way and had everybody trembling." There are infamous stories of him in a fury, pulling phones out of their wall sockets or throwing a glass full of ice.

The taint of bootlegging accusations deeply troubled him, perhaps contributing to his temper. Leo Kolber, a lifelong friend who managed CEMP's investments, described being on the receiving end of one of Dad's blasts in which our father, in a blizzard of anger, called him something quite offensive. His legendary fury could even be targeted at people like Leo, of whom he was fond. Leo suggests in his own memoirs that some of Dad's frustrations were connected to not being invited onto bank boards or into exclusive clubs. Leo and I helped rectify that by going to see a senior officer of the Bank of Montreal, the bank we dealt with at Seagram. Dad was soon on the board. But by then he was getting old and his time had nearly passed. So, at the tender age of thirty-five, I was named to the bank's board. The things my father dearly wanted were now open to me, but he *needed* them, whereas they didn't matter to me. He also put tremendous pressure on himself, not only in trying to constantly grow the business, but also by always engaging in some form of personal self-improvement, frequently in the pursuit of social acceptance. He loved poetry, for instance, which he would quote. Among his favourites were John Masefield's "Sea Fever" and Lewis Carroll's "You Are Old, Father William." He had his own complexes that would have kept a shrink busy.

Prohibition is a whole other story. I don't remember saying it, but Michael Marrus quotes an exchange between my father and me in his book.

"Daddy, what's a bootlegger?" I supposedly asked from my innocent, boyhood perch.

"Don't you ever use that word again," came the response from my father.

Was he or wasn't he? That's the question that people will always ask and about which they'll come to their own conclusions, no matter how much evidence they have or don't have. I, for one, don't know and I don't give a damn. He would have succeeded, in my view, in any business. But my father certainly devised ways to sell liquor through ingenious channels when more traditional channels became unavailable. Liquor was once shipped via mail order from province to province—all legal. When that was shut down, liquor was shipped for medicinal purposes—all legal. However, when Prohibition was in full force in the U.S., were there other means? Edgar wrote that Dad was not a bootlegger, but the company certainly sold to bootleggers. Does that make Dad a bootlegger by extension? Maybe. However, when the Bronfman brothers began exporting liquor from Canada to the United States during Prohibition, the Canadian government did not block the exports. Ottawa wanted the tax revenue, so if the family was selling to mobsters, the federal government was complicit.

Still, our family name was continually blemished with the brush of bootlegging, and there were several low points. On October 4, 1922, Dad's brother-in-law Paul Matoff was murdered at two in the morning in Bienfait, Saskatchewan, as he counted the take from that night's sale of booze. The crime had all the hallmarks of a mob hit, and the killer—or killers—made off with six thousand dollars plus diamond jewellery Matoff was wearing. Then, in 1929, Dad's brother Harry was arrested and charged with bribing a customs official and tampering with witnesses. He did time in the slammer for a number of weeks, but two trials both resulted in verdicts of not guilty. In 1935, the RCMP charged all four Bronfman brothers with smuggling booze back into Canada, but the charges were thrown out, although under suspicious circumstances. Even as late as the 1950s the Bronfman name was mentioned in unflattering ways at a U.S. Senate inquiry into organized crime in Washington, D.C., headed by Tennessee senator Estes Kefauver. As I told the producers of *Whisky Man,* Dad "walked a fine line, but whatever he did was legal and the Canadian government was his partner."

I told the interviewer that we never discussed it at home "in any shape or form," and I didn't ask (other than that one time) "because I knew my father in my way—and you could say to me I didn't want to ever have an image of my father that was sacred to me destroyed or changed, and I would say you might be right."

The impact of Prohibition and the bootlegging chatter is the lingering taint. That's clearly why Dad snapped at me that morning at the table when I asked the direct question. He was never able to wipe clean the smear of bootlegging accusations. The stench stuck and he had to live with it all of his life.

Our father—what he did, how he behaved, and what he provided for us—set the tone and context for our upbringing. As Edgar said, "Business was one of his children, his first child." That speaks volumes, at least from Edgar's perspective. Unlike the others, I also saw a sweet side to our father, perhaps because I was the youngest and had been sickly. Our mother was a different story. While I said earlier she was not an archetypal mother, she was a born leader and organizer. She studied at the University of Manitoba, noteworthy for a young woman of her era. She had a great sense of humour, was a baseball player in her day, and later her leadership skills came to the fore when she orchestrated the merger of the YMHA and YWHA in Montreal. She was, of course, legendary for hosting community and charitable events. That included organizing a tea at our home for none other than Eleanor Roosevelt. When she was not entertaining one of the most famous women in the world, she was responsible for the house and for raising us, even though the help did much of the raising. To be fair, though, Mother had to play the role of both parents because

Dad was away most of the week in New York. But they would talk strategy about how to bring us up, while she was in charge of the tactics and rules—with whom we played, what we were allowed to do and not do, what we ate, and our relationship with the help. I assume it was Mother who made the decision to send us to the school I loathed, Trinity College School, since she was in charge of our education.

While she was a headstrong person, she could sometimes be lost outside of the Bronfman bubble. Back when I was a kid, it was against the law in Quebec for children to go to the movies. When I was fifteen, a year short, Mother and I were driven to a movie house by the chauffeur. They wouldn't let us in, and then we had another problem: the chauffeur had left, leaving her with the perplexing question of how to get home. I think I said, perhaps with a bit of a smart-alecky tone, "Well, Mother, we'll take a taxi."

I don't think my parents had any inkling that the overwhelming nature of our family had anything to do with the anxieties of my youth. My mother wanted me to join the junior committee of the Montreal Symphony when I liked symphony as much as I liked garlic, which was not at all. She wanted me to do it as a stepping stone to becoming a society person, something in which I had absolutely no interest. For a while, I bent to her will and, funnily enough, worked with future prime minister John Turner, who was in charge of ticket sales while I handled the publicity for an Andre Kostelanetz concert at the Montreal Forum. John and I became good friends during that stint, but that was more because it played to a strength I didn't realize I had: I like people and have for the most part enjoyed working with them and sharing in the camaraderie. At the time, however, it felt as though I was being force-fed the required meal in order to achieve a certain station in life. Eat some symphony. It's good for you.

When I was young, I had a history of worrying. I was very naive and didn't like school. As a result, I found myself getting overloaded, and then I'd want to bolt. When time management became more important, I discovered I was not good at organizing my time. When I was little, my mother used to say, "Give Charles your worries. If you have any, give them to Charles because he's the best worrier," an indication of how unsure I was of myself. Mother's line, of course, was a tease. However, when she called me a "shnookie," that hurt. It felt like she was calling me an elf, implying I was little, sweet, and not very brilliant. I felt it was derogatory, and she said it in front of my siblings more than once. For sure, though, I was a worrywart as a kid. As for who I am today, I'm most certainly not related to that fellow.

Down one level from my parents were my siblings, all older and all smarter—at least, I thought so back then. My big sister Minda, the oldest of the four siblings, also went to a psychiatrist for many years for family-related problems. She would often fight with Dad about money. She wanted more; he wanted to provide less. Minda said about Dad, "He would use the voice." There's some truth in that because he had a somewhat derisive voice. At one point during her school days, Minda was sporting a newfound interest in socialism and she pranced into his study, where he was playing solitaire. I happened to be there at the time. She had just come back from the doctor, where she'd taken allergy tests, and she told him with great joy that she was never meant to be a rich man's daughter because she was allergic to mink.

"Yeah? What about sable?" he replied.

In later years, long after she'd tossed aside her flirtation with socialism, Minda thought she should have been anointed to run Seagram rather than Edgar. It was her view that Edgar drank too much, was a playboy who womanized too much and often operated based on flawed reasoning. Although Edgar was a good businessman in many ways, I always felt he wasn't as intellectual as my sisters, but he had the sharp elbows and the rebelliousness that made it hard to get around him. At one point in later years, Minda wanted me to fire Edgar as CEO of Seagram. I could have called a shareholders' meeting on the matter, but it would have been difficult to win the vote. And anyway, I didn't want to do it. However, once, when he really screwed something up—like running up a bank debt of $300 million in the mid-1970s—I called him on it and he said, "Do what you want, but don't take away my title."

While I have a very warm memory of Minda as a kind, lovely person—the sibling with whom I felt closest—Edgar felt totally different. He was quite blunt about how they did not get along, how she wanted to be CEO and resented him for getting the job. Minda and Phyllis also resented how Dad divided up the family fortune among us, with Edgar and I each getting thirty per cent while the girls got twenty per cent each, but that's another story.

Minda was six years older than me, so when she went off to Smith College in New England, I was just twelve, a huge difference. She married in her late twenties, but not before she worked for *Time* in New York City. Due to the magazine's production schedule, her "weekends" were Monday and Tuesday. My parents were very keen to know how she intended to meet

anybody, given that she was unavailable for courting on weekends. In those days, if you were twenty-two and not yet married, people wanted to know why. Ultimately, Minda married
not only a "title," but a European so she could get out from
under her overwhelming family. Her husband was Baron Alain
de Gunzburg of Paris. His grandfather had been made a baron
in Russia. Minda took on the title that came with the marriage:
Madame la Baronne. Ironically, Alain's own brother and their
two children don't recognize their title. But Minda embraced
it, to the point where her butler used to throw open the doors
to the dining room and say with a straight face, "*Madame la
Baronne est servi.*" We used to give her the business about this
pretentious indulgence and she laughed with us. It certainly
didn't take away from her sweet nature. Alain was also a nice
guy and had gone to Harvard Business School. He had a small
private bank and, among other things, an interest in a sausage
factory. He always said if you want to stop eating sausages, go
to a sausage factory. I said I wouldn't because I loved eating
them. In any event, Alain was complex. He did all the things
Jewish people don't typically do. He liked going on shoots,
hunting. He loved non-Jewish society and denied there was
any anti-Semitism in France.

Phyllis, we all felt, was Mother's favourite, and she does not
disagree. Mother paid more attention to her and was sweeter
to her, perhaps seeing in Phyllis the free-spirited woman she
may have inwardly wished to be. Phyllis was artistic, independent, and knew her own mind. She was also talented, sculpting
beautiful pieces from a young age, including one of our mother.
Phyllis attended Vassar, where she wrote her thesis on Henry
James and later studied at Yale, followed by the Illinois Institute

of Technology in Chicago—Mies van der Rohe's school—where she earned her master's in architecture. Her position as mother's pet was clear to the rest of us, and we used to throw that back at her, not that it did much good. Phyllis was a beautiful young woman who got whatever the hell she wanted because she was a rebel.

In addition to being naturally talented when it came to art, she also had a bit of the tomboy in her, joining in our hockey and touch-football games. The tomboy side was perhaps her tough, fierce personality coming to the fore. In retrospect, it's no surprise she and Edgar got along (although not until they were adults). Phyllis's temper is also akin to Dad's short fuse. It's no doubt connected to the other trait she shares with him, perfectionism, which is her curse as well as her blessing.

However, she's taken a keen interest in family in her later years. As for her opinion of me, I think she always viewed me as a compromiser—she would say "populist" or "middle of the road"—while she's a draw-a-line-in-the-sand type. It's true, I am prone to compromise, except on things about which I feel strongly. I pick my battles. Although Minda has been gone for many years after dying of cancer in 1985, it seems like Phyllis had no time for Minda. She could be harsh about her. Was it simply a rivalry between first born and second born, both of whom were female, that went back years to when they were schoolchildren? Phyllis says it goes back to how Minda treated her—not well, I gather.

All told, Phyllis is a complicated broth, like all of us. In spite of her short temper, hard-edged behaviour, and the fact that she and I didn't have a close relationship, she is a decidedly accomplished woman for whom I have the highest respect. She is very, very highly

regarded. She was married for a relatively short and unhappy period in the 1950s. Her child is metaphorical: the Canadian Centre
for Architecture is her baby, and it's most certainly something that
should make her proud, as it does me. She founded it in 1979 as
an international research centre and museum dedicated to "the
conviction that architecture is a public concern" and to promote
understanding and debate about its role in society.

Before that, though, there was the Seagram Building,
which undoubtedly made her a force to be reckoned with when
it comes to architecture. It is clearly a great building because
she was not a compromiser. She had the moxie to stand up to
Dad, who was ready to erect a dull building. Her eight-page,
single-spaced, typed letter to him is now legendary, in large part
because of how it begins. On June 28, 1954, she wrote from
Paris: "Well now I will set about writing the letter about which
I have been thinking for a few days and this letter starts with
one word repeated very emphatically NO NO NO NO NO,"
essentially saying, "You mustn't put up that building, Daddy,
you must build something great." To do the job, she plucked
the modernist maestro, Mies van der Rohe, whose clean lines,
bronze structure, and wide-open plazas are on display not
only at the Seagram Building, which opened in 1957 and still
looks like it came out of the wrapper, but also the Toronto-
Dominion Centre, headquarters of TD Bank (built ten years
later by Cadillac Fairview, a Bronfman-owned real estate firm),
among others in Montreal, Chicago, and elsewhere.

The nadir of my relationship with Phyllis was probably in
1976. René Lévesque was on the cusp of being elected as the
first separatist premier of Quebec, and Phyllis became quite
sympathetic to the cause.

"I mean (I) understood the French situation here because they had been so maligned by the British always. And in my house and the school I went to. It was always the same thing. The French were always the fall guys . . . it was very much the white Negro. And they were treated that way. The French were the servant class," she says.

Although French-speaking Quebeckers, who were in the majority in the province, had undoubtedly suffered as second-class citizens, I didn't feel that separation was the answer. At the time, I gave an ill-advised speech the day before the vote in which I accused the separatists of being anti-Semitic and threatened to pull out of the province (I was the majority owner of the Montreal Expos then). I had been told by a well-placed source that victory for the Liberals was secure, so I let loose, not knowing there was a reporter in the room. My comments made it into the news media and I was excoriated. To make matters worse, I had the feeling Phyllis wanted to drum me out of the family because of it.

"I think I thought what he said was grotesque," Phyllis still says today.

I don't think she had a lot of regard for my brainpower, at least back then. Funnily enough, these days, as octogenarians and the only two siblings left, we get along very well. I was very proud of her winning the Lion d'Or for lifetime achievement at the Venice Architecture Biennale in 2014 and of Rem Koolhaas's comment, "Architects make buildings, Phyllis makes architects."

I have left the most perplexing member of my immediate family, my brother Edgar, to the last portion of this chapter. It is with him that my feelings are the most tangled and conflicted. At the root of these feelings lies the most basic of issues: who I am as a person. But who was Edgar, who passed away in December of 2013? How did his character and behaviour affect my character and my life? In a lot of ways, as life goes on, we learn that it becomes as much about a series of questions as about answers. Edgar has written, "I was really close only with my younger brother, Charles." He goes on to say that as the baby of the family, I looked like the perfect model for the undernourished kid in "Milk for Britain" ads. He wrote that I was "treated as a love object" by my father, who was always squeezing my hand, and that I was "regarded as an insurance policy, in case something should happen to me," which brings up the notion of royal succession—"first the heir, then the spare," as they say in England.

Edgar wrote, "If I resented the love he received, I'm certain Charles must have struggled with growing up in the shadow of both Father and me. Still there was always great affection between us. Thankfully, we never engaged in competition over our eventual position with Seagram. Somehow, it was just understood that I would be in charge."

Edgar was handsome, built like a bull, and he moved through life in such a fashion, in a domineering way, writing that he "started with Seagram the day I was born." The domineering side was the Sam Bronfman apple that had fallen close to the tree. Like Phyllis, Edgar was rebellious and not one to be pushed around, except perhaps by our father. In Edgar's opinion, Dad was always saying no to him, particularly when Edgar was running Seagram. In his later years, our father called himself the president of presidents, meaning they were going to have to carry him out of the business he built. This was no picnic for Edgar, for sure, but it also highlights what was, at its core, a competition between the two of them. I think Edgar wanted to compete with Dad, because he was always striving to be better than him and different than him.

Edgar wrote that Sam Bronfman didn't want an heir, he wanted a clone. He'd wanted to be somebody, had become somebody, and wanted a repeat performance from his first-born son. Edgar's youthful escapades at Williams College in the Berkshires region of Massachusetts, involving drinking, a hair-raising motorcycle accident, and an impetuous engagement before he was out of his teens, were all so blatantly obvious. While Dad wanted a clone, Edgar wanted love. Our parents didn't demonstrate that emotion very readily, and it was in many respects what Edgar craved the most, above all from his father. Without the comfort of love, he was going to show the great Sam Bronfman. By bettering him, he'd finally get his attention, if not in the form of affection, then in the form of respect. It wasn't enough that Edgar was the anointed one, the child of Sam who was chosen to run the mighty empire. There had to be something more. Edgar literally set himself up at a desk in Dad's office to learn how the business ran so he could one day run it, and run it better than his old man.

To illustrate how Edgar was always trying to break out and show Dad, at one point my brother wanted to buy a bourbon business. That was like taunting a hungry tiger. Dad had spent his entire adult life taking on the bourbon people. He didn't think he could turn himself away from his beloved blends that had made him his fortune. The two of them also battled over vodka, a business Edgar wanted to break into, again trying to forge his own path in opposition to his famous father. Dad, meanwhile, had the not-unreasonable view that the vodka business wasn't as good as selling whisky. Distilling whisky is a business for patient people, he argued. Once you distill it, you have to lay it down for years to let it age. Vodka can be distilled and sold the next day. To any business student, Dad's reasoning was clear: the whisky business, because it was more difficult, had a barrier to entry or a protective moat that gave it a competitive advantage. That barrier to entry was capital—the capital required to build warehouses and buy barrels for aging whisky, the capital to see a business through the long period while its product ages and generates zero revenue.

As well, Dad had built a business on selling flavour, a taste. In his view, the vodka industry was selling no taste. He argued that if any Joe could make vodka one day and sell it the next, the product couldn't be very valuable. While Dad and business students were right in theory, the vodka market turned out to be huge. Edgar's nose detected a trend, and we got into the business of selling vodka after Dad died. It was a way for my brother to differentiate himself from our father, whose presence always loomed large.

Eventually, the one area where Edgar would outdo Dad would be in the realm of world Jewry. He became president of the World Jewish Congress, while Dad had only been vice-president of the organization and president of the Canadian Jewish Congress. In his role at the WJC, Edgar helped unmask a Nazi guard who turned out to be none other than Kurt Waldheim, the president of Austria and former secretary general of the United Nations. He also led a successful appeal to Swiss banks to return billions of dollars of purloined property to Holocaust survivors. These powerful acts may be among my brother's most enduring legacies.

Before all of that, though, in the business Dad would put obstacles in front of Edgar, dismissing his ideas. None of us would suspect that such behaviour would ultimately sow the seeds for what would befall the empire our father had so carefully built. The line that is emblematic about family fortunes being frittered away haunted him.

"Shirtsleeves to shirtsleeves in three generations," was the saying.

One of Dad's other favourite expressions was "blood counts." He used to say we pay more attention to the breeding of horses than to the breeding of humans. As Edgar said, it was Dad's belief that we as Bronfman boys would do well and not screw up *because we were his sons,* implying that he had passed on the magic molecules—and that, in a sense, the company he built was our birthright because we were his blood. This would play out in spades decades later in our family, and not in a way that ended well. But clearly, it would be Edgar who would take up the mantle after Dad.

In spite of my brother's considerable skills, there is, however, a strong argument to be made that we should have hired a professional, outside CEO rather than having family management after our father. Dad, however, could not have done that because of his mantra "blood counts" and because he had groomed Edgar for the job. But after Edgar, I firmly believe that had we had the wisdom and closeness our father had desired, the family should have recommended that the board hire non-family management and Seagram would today still be prospering and we would still control it—and for years have been the largest and most influential shareholder in DuPont as well.

As for who should have followed Edgar, his son (Edgar Jr.)

says that Dad indicated to him that he would be "the one." We all have selective hearing. I don't dispute that Edgar Jr. heard that. However, knowing my father, I doubt that he would have said that to any of his grandchildren. That's simply not who the man was.

We were visiting neighbours in Sainte-Adèle when the housekeeper came to tell us the news that Dad had died. Barbara and I drove to Montreal and I didn't say a word, nor did I cry on the drive—I cried later, but I don't remember huge tears. The last time I spoke to Dad was probably the day before he died. I don't think he knew he was dying. *I* certainly didn't know he was. He went to the office until pretty near the end, still playing the role that he called "president of presidents." The doctor didn't want Dad to know he had prostate cancer because he worried Dad would get so depressed that death would come sooner. The doctor also didn't want any druggists to know, so he'd get ingredients for medications and mix them up himself. Dad, who had no idea the lengths to which his physician, Abe Mayman, would go to protect him, would cuss him out. Abe would take it, though, because I think he genuinely loved Pop.

I don't remember much about Dad's funeral, other than the fact that it was huge. The news footage from 1971 shows an endless line of limousines. Although I have no recollection of this, it was reported that regularly scheduled flights to Montreal were interrupted to allow for the slew of private planes carrying executives and dignitaries to the city for the funeral. Dad was an original to the end. Someone making the arrangements thought that because Dad was a Companion of the Order of Canada, his casket was to be draped with the Canadian flag. That was a breach of Jewish custom, but the rabbi relented and the Maple

Leaf was there. It rained that day and all those big names got wet, but on the way to the cemetery, the sun came out.

Bizarrely, after Dad died, Mother worried about running out of money and even went so far as to ration meat to once a week for the staff. Two of my colleagues at Claridge had gone to see her and informed her that she had reached the limit of her philanthropy budget for that year, which she interpreted as meaning she was broke. This was quickly clarified by telling her she was far from insolvent and the staff could have meat for breakfast, lunch, and supper, seven days a week.

The day after Dad's funeral, Edgar and I quietly made a trip to the cemetery to stand over his freshly filled-in burial plot. We made a vow over our father's grave that we'd always stick together. It was much like Dad and his brothers had done when his mother was on her deathbed. Although it was made in the heat of emotion, our vow was made with the best of intentions. It's a cliché, but the road to hell is paved with good intentions. We did stick together—although I held my nose. We would pay the price.

3

Young Man in Business

———

W hen I went to McGill University, I did well, except when it came to exams. I froze. Although Dad couldn't manage to secure a seat on the board of governors—a prestigious appointment he was denied—he had no problem getting me face time with the principal of McGill so I could discuss my anxieties. Cyril James ran McGill from 1939 until 1962, and when I went to see him in 1951, he told me why I should stay in school. There were two reasons James cited to advise me against dropping out, and I'll never forget what he said: I wouldn't be able to join the University Club, and even though I'd be on the boards of directors of a number of companies, I'd have to hang my head in shame when my fellow directors talked about their respective alma maters. Such a convincing argument by such a learned man! In retrospect, it reminds me a bit of my mother's desire to involve me in the symphony so I could have a seat at the table of polite society.

James's persuasive encouragement resulted in me going home and asking my father if I could come work for him at the company the following Monday. I always knew I would end up at Seagram. I *was* Seagram. Ever since I was old enough to check, I'd look to see which brands were for sale on the back of the bar. I was nineteen years old and I had just morphed into a university dropout who was fortunate enough to have a father who'd built a company for his sons to eventually take over. On Monday, March 12, 1951, I went to work at Seagram's distillery in LaSalle, Quebec, the facility my father had decided to construct after he moved to Montreal in 1924. It was a decision that would cement his position above his brothers as the true leader and key shareholder of Seagram.

At LaSalle, I started visiting every part of the operation to learn how it all worked, writing notes and bringing them back to my supervisor so he could review what I had absorbed. My approach was different than Edgar's. I wanted to know how things functioned in the trenches. Edgar wanted to know how to run the place, whereas I yearned to learn from the ground up. I wanted to know what a salesman did, what an accountant did, how you made whisky, and to get a feel for the business and the people. What kind of a guy worked in a blending lab? What does a secretary do? Edgar was more interested in how to manage the company and he was, for the most part, damn good at it. But I still prefer my approach because you get to know the people. You get to like them, get to feel part of the team, although I will allow that it may be easier to be tougher if you don't know the people.

That likely explains why Edgar embraced the opposite approach. "I have avoided such relationships and in fact have never developed an intimate friendship with anybody who works with me," he wrote. Not quite. At Seagram, Edgar unfortunately surrounded himself with poor advisors whom he befriended.

But his statement about working relationships reflects the same modus operandi as his bet against the Montreal Canadiens when we were kids—the heart versus the wallet. For me, it was the heart, for him the billfold. There's a strong case to be made, however, that over the long haul, the heartfelt approach wins.

Had it not been for the Bronfman empire I could have easily ended up in a retail job—the shoe salesman my psychiatrist had described. But my first real break in the business, aside from getting a job there in the first place, was going to run the Adams label that we established in 1954. It was a small company-within-the-company that had forty salesmen whom I had never met, a few offices, and some so-so whisky to sell. We owned it because, in the early 1950s, we bought a company in Vancouver called United Distillers. It had several brands, none of which was very good. One of them was Adams Old Rye. So Dad sent one employee up to Ottawa to check the registry to see if there was ever someone named Adams who happened to have a distillery in the 1800s. It turns out there was a Thomas Adams who owned a gristmill in Ontario. After making the grist for bread, the mash that was left over was used to make the liquor.

Adams had his mill in 1802, and so Dad created a company called "Thomas Adams, Distiller Since 1802." In keeping with widespread industry practice, my father came up with the pretentious-sounding line, aping some sort of fusty English shopkeeper's sign that conjured up something respectable. The fact that the industry did this all the time is why so many whiskies are christened as "old." Everyone wanted to label his products that way. The younger the whisky, the more the industry called it "old." It was all about creating an aura of tradition and craft that would make people pay money for a shot of rye that claimed its distinguished roots reached back to the early 1800s, a claim that somehow was designed to make them think it was better.

When I first started in the business, I was making thirty-five dollars a week in the blending lab. Much later, someone there told me I was awfully young to be doing the job I was doing.

"Well," I said, deadpanning, "I've had an absolutely startling career at the company."

"How did that happen?"

"You have to be smart enough to choose the right parents," I wisecracked, trying to keep my lineage coated in lightheartedness.

Everyone knew who I was and that I'd got the job because I was Sam Bronfman's son. There was no point trying to hide it. It seemed smarter to turn the issue on its head by making a joke about it, thereby making myself some allies. Subconsciously, I guess I wanted to reframe the issue of being the boss's son. I wanted the questions to be about how I handled the job, how I performed it, and how I dealt with people.

Adams already had an Ontario sales manager, a tough but lovable old codger named Sam Newman. I said I would take the job of running Adams but only if I could have Jack Baker, a Seagram salesman I knew well, as the new Ontario sales manager—rather than Newman. My boss protested my preference for Baker by saying, "He's never run anything." I countered by saying, "And neither have I," and off we went to run Adams.

We lost money the first year, and never again. I think my honesty about my qualifications—or lack of them—kept me from overreaching. I knew I was a guy who had dropped out of college. I knew I got the job because I was the boss's son.

But I was never a victim of the Peter principle, never promoted beyond my level of competence to a level of incompetence.

One way I made my mark at Adams was to follow a tried-and-true method, keeping a hawk's eye on expenses. I vowed that of our three sales companies—Seagram, Calvert, and Adams—we at Adams would have the lowest expenses per capita. Previous to arriving at Adams, I had been, along with another fellow, responsible for creating what our boss viewed to be a foolproof expense account. The one that had been in use took three-quarters of an hour to complete, but the one I instituted at Adams was basic as hell: you'd put your name on it, plus whatever the expenses were—such as car and hotel—and that was that. If you wanted to, you could cheat it in five minutes, whereas the expense system being used in our other sales companies was so complex it would take you close to an hour to cheat it. This approach spoke to my deeply held belief that the simplest things are the best. Not only did my system reduce the amount of cheating, there was an added bonus: I also got more work out of my sales staff because they weren't spending all that time trying to cook the books.

I would also go through all the expense accounts myself. If I saw them rising, I'd pick on one guy and dock him twenty or thirty dollars and the word would go through the organization, "They're watching us." It wasn't rocket science; it was just the kind of common-sense route my father would appreciate. I always think of my time at Adams as getting the equivalent of my MBA, or better. Not to denigrate those who earn that degree, but I was *living* the case studies rather than reading them. It was my first real responsibility in the business and my first real success.

Of our three sales companies, Seagram was the captain of the industry, Calvert was the middle guy, and Adams was the fighter—and I can proudly say I made it the fighter. Here I was, Sam Bronfman's son, and I had this sales company and everyone figured I couldn't or wouldn't do anything rough and tumble because I was the son. I'm not talking about anything illegal, but rather, edgy, aggressive measures, if you like. So I said to my guys, "We're going to be the down-and-dirtiest of the whole bunch." If one company's salesman was giving a bottle a case to sell his goods, we would give two. My point was that we needed to get noticed so we could be better positioned in liquor stores, bars, and restaurants.

To get people's attention, all sorts of things were worth trying, and we did. Packaging was a big part of it, because packaging by its very nature is marketing. It creates a sense of the brand, and when something becomes a brand, it means it's recognizable, and once it's recognizable, the odds are better that it will sell. It's painfully obvious. In the liquor business, the bottle is almost sacred. Everyone knows Crown Royal because of the shape of the bottle and the purple silk sack that comes with it. As a kid, you were probably even aware of Crown Royal without connecting it to alcohol because your parents gave you the purple sack to schlep your marbles around, but I'm dating myself. If people think they're getting something fit for royalty because of a bottle and a regal colour, fabulous! That's how you sell something.

For my father, who fussed over names, labels, and other marketing marginalia, you didn't mess with bottles. One day, Jack Baker came into my office and cracked a hard, plastic bottle—a prototype—on my desk. *Wham!*

"I want this goddam bottle," he said. I looked him in the eye and I saw the way he was looking at me. There was no mistaking he was a man on a mission.

"Well, I guess you'll have that goddam bottle," I replied. Unfortunately, this was totally against the ethos of the company. With its rectangular shape, Baker was wielding what my father referred to as "fancy bottles"—he firmly believed bottles should be round (with one exception: Crown Royal). In spite of this, having worked up a head of steam, Baker and I paraded into my father's office.

"Dad, Jack wants this bottle and I think he's right."

"Okay," he said, which completely floored us. There was no argument, no chewing off my head for bringing him a cocka-mamie idea. I think he swiftly thought to himself, *They need a fighting chance,* and our unorthodox approach was a way for us to get it. It also wasn't a Seagram brand—it was Adams, so he wasn't putting the Cadillac in harm's way. Perhaps most crucial, he liked Jack Baker, which probably figured into the equation. Whatever his overriding reason, he was right to let us go our own way with our own bottle because that brand's sales climbed exponentially.

Although in later years the size of the company would become such that he couldn't have, and shouldn't have, been involved in every aspect of the business, at that time in Seagram's evo-lution, the stratospheric plane on which he operated was truly remarkable. Among his considerable strengths was strategically setting the tone when it came to quality. He decided early on that Seagram should be a "quality house," and in order to be a quality house, you and your employees had to live and breathe excellence. As a result, he spent a great deal of time sniffing and tasting whisky to show everyone at the company that the big boss was involved. It sent a message.

My father also had an uncanny command of detail when it came to the business. Having such granular knowledge undoubtedly gives a CEO a competitive edge as long as he or she doesn't get lost in the particles of the business, but understands them in the context of a larger framework for making sound decisions. When it comes down to it, the strength afforded by that level of knowledge gives the boss a huge leg up. The bottom line is you couldn't bullshit a man like Sam Bronfman. To illustrate, our Newfoundland agent, Henry Collingwood, came to Dad's Montreal office and my father asked him about the business. After about five or ten minutes of questioning, Hank was stumped, the limit of his knowledge reached. At that time, Canada comprised only about nine per cent of Seagram's business and Newfoundland might have accounted for just about five per cent of the Canadian business. It was virtually a rounding error in the overall scheme of things. But with Collingwood tapped out, Dad started spouting figures about our operations in Newfoundland. He knew them all and hadn't just looked them up right before Collingwood came in to see him. All the great ones are like that. They have micro-level knowledge of their industry, even stretching to the remote crevices of the business.

Not only did Dad preach quality, he practised it by spending more money on it than anyone else in the industry. The way he aged his goods, the way he blended them, it all contributed to first-class merchandise. Although this was a more expensive way to go, the investment always came back to him in profits. If you sold quality, you could charge more, and more expensive products meant higher profit margins.

Ultimately, I became head of sales for the three companies, and I did my job well. I was still in my twenties and frankly, at the risk of sounding boastful, I didn't find the work too tough or challenging. In retrospect, I was much smarter than I gave myself credit for. In 1958, at the grand old age of twenty-seven, I was made president of the House of Seagram (which oversaw Canada, the Caribbean, and Israel) and put on the board of the parent company. Today, it's hard to imagine someone of that age on the board of a major publicly traded company, unless it's someone like Mark Zuckerberg at Facebook or Sergey Brin and Larry Page at Google, companies they founded themselves, a bit like the Sam Bronfmans of their era. When I ascended to this relatively lofty level, I couldn't read a balance sheet properly and am not much better at it today, to be honest.

The part of the financial statements I've always been most interested in has been the income statement, where you see if the company is actually making a profit. That might stem from the fact that when I ran Seagram Canada, the biggest part of our business was the manufacturing component. We had six plants, four of which were bottling plants, and the key thing to control was the cost of manufacturing. Obviously, if the costs were too high, a profit would quickly become a loss. So when it came to that part of the business, I channelled my father and his *Rain Man* persona with figures. Once, I couldn't resist showing off a bit. There was a man who worked with us as head of the Seagram sales company. He was carting around a big pile of books.

"What are those books?" I asked.

"They're the numbers."

"I know what the numbers are. Don't you know what the numbers are?" The poor guy didn't know what hit him, but his father wasn't Sam Bronfman. Blood counts—in some ways, at least.

My mentor in those days was a wonderful man, Jack Duffy. To this day, his face looks back at me from a black-and-white portrait that sits on the windowsill of my New York office, a testament to how much certain people meant to turning my life around and putting me on the pathway to success. Duffy worked for us as a blender in Louisville, Kentucky, and Edgar brought him to New York, where we also did blending and where Dad and Edgar personally reviewed the blends. Edgar soon recommended to Dad that Jack move to Canada to run our distilleries, and that's how we met. He had a terrific intelligence about the people working at our various distilleries, and maybe that's why we connected—he was a people person. Above all, he trusted them and instructed them to do what they thought was best. In the parlance of modern business gurus, he was empowering the troops, respecting their own abilities to think through the issues themselves and figure out ways to do better. The theory was, if you have the responsibility, you have the authority. It was a great lesson.

Even though Jack was my mentor, I still outranked him. One time, when we were both in Vancouver, he came to me and said, "Boss, I really screwed up. I did something terrible." What did you do, I asked? He told me, and he had read the situation correctly—he had indeed screwed something up, although all these years later, I have no recollection of what had been so terrible. So I asked him, "Jack, what time were you up?" He answered that he'd been up at six so he could phone the Montreal office, where it was three hours later. I then asked him why he had fessed up to me about this particular incident and he said, "'Cause if I tell you, you're not going to fire me. You'll give me hell and we'll work it through. But if someone else tells you and they don't like me, they can put a twist on it. If I make a mistake, I'd much rather be up front about it."

That tells you all you need to know about Jack Duffy and why he was my kind of fellow. Sadly, he died of cancer at just forty-seven years of age in 1967. His illness led to one of the only times I had a fight with my father. I knew Jack was sick and so did Dad, but Sam Bronfman's temper didn't cool down for any man, even one who was dying. After Dad yelled at him about something, I went into my father's office and pointed my finger at him.

"Dad, you know Jack's a sick man. You will never raise your voice to him again." And he never did. I have my own lines in the sand.

This was also the time in my career when I learned how to do certain unpleasant things, like firing people, the toughest thing a manager has to do. There was the case of Bill, who was running our Calvert sales company. Our Ontario business was declining and I was after him to fire his sales manager for the region. After all, Ontario accounted for fifty per cent of our business in Canada. But Bill didn't want to be told what to do, and in a fit of bravado, he told me he didn't need the job—so if he and I were to have a policy disagreement, he vowed he would leave. But with Ontario underperforming, the situation soon became intolerable for me, so on a Friday afternoon I went to Bill's office and said, "Will you please fire the Ontario sales manager?"

"I won't."

I said, "Bill, we just had a policy disagreement." He went totally ashen.

"Did you just fire me?"

"Yes, I did." I then called up the Ontario sales manager and fired him as well.

But it wasn't easy. The first time I had to terminate someone, I got physically ill. I ended up lying on the couch in the apartment of Dave Liss, the Adams sales manager for Manitoba.

"Charles, I'll fire the son of a gun if you can't do it," Dave said. At that point, I realized I'd have to fire many people in my career, and if I didn't do it right then, the next time would be even tougher.

For all his bluster and explosive bursts of rage, Dad wasn't very good at firing people. He'd get others to do it for him. He would get all riled up and call the poor victim all kinds of names and then say, "Now you go fire him."

There was the case of an executive, which made the deed all the more challenging. I didn't have the foggiest idea why my father was angry with him, which also made terminating the person dicey. In any event, I did it, and right away he went to Dad, pleading with him not to fire him because he was going through a difficult family situation. So my father, showing his softer side, rehired him. A few months later, Dad insisted I fire him again. I did it the second time on the condition that Dad would not rehire him anymore.

So much of it was common sense. Whenever I'd go out to a restaurant for dinner, I'd check the establishment's bar and order a V.O. If the taste was off-putting, I'd question the waiter. If he could, he'd bring me the bottle to prove it was V.O. Then there was the case of Elm Ridge, the golf club where we played.

We had just come out with Seagram's Golden Gin. It had a light yellow colour because it had been put in barrels with wood chips that softened it and gave it that hue. This was a selling point, and you could get a nickel more per drink for it. At the golf club, the purchasing manager was a fellow named Louis Crevier, who was not what you'd call the ace in the deck. I gave him a whole promotional speech about Seagram's Ancient Bottle Golden Gin, how it was better and how he could sell it for more. Meantime, Harold Fischel, our sales manager for the southern United States, came to Montreal for a wedding. Harold was the biggest seller of that gin in the company and I wanted him to test out how good I was at promoting the new product.

So there we were with Louis Crevier, and I asked Harold to quiz Louis about Seagram's Golden. Louis then proceeded to tell him that the gin had the light yellow colour because we didn't distill it as much, meaning there was more fusel oil in it, which is not a good thing. Harold looked at me, laughed, and said, "You sure got your message across." So I said to Louis, "Let me make this very clear to you."

"Yes, Mr. Charles."

"If you serve any other brands but ours in our golf club, I'm going to kick you in the balls."

"Yes, Mr. Charles." Clearly, I wasn't going to kick the man where it hurts, but he got the point. I also got the point that you had to use different approaches with different people.

Louis taught me another lesson. We had a brand of scotch called Usher's OVG. Louis would pour the Usher's OVG into a Dewar's Scotch bottle. All proud, he'd tell me, "Mr. Charles, I passed five bottles of Usher's last night."

"Did you pour them into Dewar's?" I'd ask.

"Yeah."

"Louis, please don't do that." The lesson I learned is that people are so anxious to please, they can go too far. And to me, pouring an off-brand into a bottle for a known brand is certainly going too far.

Many of my business instincts I absorbed from being around my father. Although his was often a simple, straightforward approach, it was far from simplistic. For instance, when I was at Seagram Canada, I was totally against organizational charts. My view was that if someone saw a chart that put him a quarter of an inch higher than someone else, it indicated seniority and higher pay and created morale issues. On this point, Jack and I paid a visit to Gil Mead, our VP of human resources. Jack Duffy took me to see him. Lo and behold, in Mead's office there was an org chart for Seagram Canada.

"Let me ask you a question," I said. "Does everyone in Seagram Canada know who they report to?"

"Yes."

"If New York calls the bottling manager in LaSalle or New Westminster, do they know who to call?

"Yes."

"Then can you please explain to me why we need the chart?"

"'Cause New York wants it."

"Well, that's too damn bad."

Maybe because the Canadian division was smaller, there wasn't the fear factor that existed in New York. Giving myself a bit of credit, it might also have been due to the way I dealt with people. When I was first put in charge, I realized that the accounting people weren't talking to the production people, the production people weren't talking to the ad people, and the ad people weren't talking to the sales people. I addressed this by eliminating the "silos" that existed in the organization and made it more collegial. In fact, I used to have bridge games at home with my top guys—the opposite approach to Edgar's. But my approach never prevented me from doing what I had to do.

Take the case of short-shipping. Jack Baker, who'd started with me at Adams and later ran the Seagram sales company in Canada, discovered that we had been short-shipping to Ontario stores. That meant if the order was for a hundred cases, we could only ship seventy or eighty because we didn't have the bottled inventory. We didn't have the stock to keep up with the orders, which gave our competitors an opening. This set up a war between Baker and my mentor, Jack Duffy, who was our head of production. So I went to Duffy and asked him how bonuses and penalties were determined for the bottling house manager. It turns out the manager was not financially penalized for short-shipping stores. The bonus formula was changed immediately and the problem was resolved. The lesson was to look at the disease behind the symptoms.

By then, Edgar was working in the U.S., having moved to New York in 1955. His view was that because the company was doing ninety per cent of its business there and he was the heir apparent, New York was where he should be. I did not disagree. As Edgar wrote, "We had both witnessed the terrible fights between Father and Uncle Allan, and he (Charles) was determined to avoid that kind of confrontation. From his viewpoint, my relocation to New York solved the problem." He's right. I was happy where I was and I really didn't want to pursue the path that led to being a titan of industry. To be honest, I was also kind of scared of New York, while Canada felt comfortable.

Again, once he was in Manhattan, Edgar settled into a

desk in Dad's office. It created a lot of static with people who had worked with Dad for a long time and were loyal to him, yet there was Edgar, operating as quasi-boss. The fights that occurred were momentous. In some respects, I had the same problem in Canada. Take the situation involving one Merle M. Schneckenburger, known around the company as "Shneck." He was in charge of advertising when I became the boss of House of Seagram. However, he simply overlooked the fact that I was in charge, ignored me, and would go directly to Dad to get his way. So when he went on holiday, I decided to visit the ad manager—Shneck's number two, a fellow named Bob—and told him we were going to do such and such an ad and we were going to put it in *Time* magazine in Canada. Clearly, based on Bob's reaction, I was proposing a boneheaded idea.

"It's going to cost me my job," Bob said.

"Don't worry, I'll protect you." I had set the bait. That Friday, I told Shneck's secretary that I wanted to see him in my office at 11 a.m. on Monday, leaving him wondering and worrying about the meeting all weekend. When he came in, I had *Time* opened and said, "What do you think?"

"It's not very good," he said.

"No, it's not. It was placed in *Time* and you weren't around to stop it. Does that tell you anything? It should tell you that I hold all the aces. Either you'll have to accept that or you'll have to leave." Two months later, I told Dad I couldn't work with him anymore, so he moved Shneck to international advertising in New York, where he only lasted a few months. It was very tough for both Edgar and me to suddenly become bosses of people who were used to reporting to our father. The generation gap was an emotional gap, a lot to overcome. In fact, I vowed that, if my son wanted to succeed me upon my retirement, I would take my senior colleagues with me.

Although these situations show that I wasn't always the compromiser Phyllis suggested I was, I was also a good diplomat when required. In those days, one of our fierce competitors was Hiram Walker–Gooderham & Worts, which made Canadian Club. The original boss there was Harry Hatch, who was one of my dad's two sworn enemies in the business, the other being Lewis Rosenstiel of Schenley. Sometimes, though, in spite of them being your enemies, you had to sit down with these people. For instance, we faced a problem with the Ontario Liquor Board, which wanted to cut one category of whisky. This was a big deal, because the province of Ontario accounted for about half the volume of the distilled spirits industry in Canada. A change in the number of brands we'd be allowed to place on the shelves in the province could have been complex. The authorities that ran the liquor board wanted the industry to solve the issue for them. As a result, I thought I should sit down with Harry's son, Cliff, who was now CEO. As head of Seagram in Canada, I was all of twenty-nine years old. Cliff was seventeen years older than me. After quite a bit of negotiating as to whether we should meet at all, we did so in a suite at the Royal York Hotel in Toronto. He entered quite hesitantly, and I remember smiling at him and saying that our fathers may have hated each other, but it was a very profitable hatred. Furthermore, I said I wanted to go to jail as much as he did, so there would be no collusion. By the time an hour went by, we had resolved our differences and had arrived at a solution that the liquor board implemented. I admired and liked Cliff and said to him, "You can't put me out of business and I can't put you out of business, but I must admit, I enjoy switching people from Canadian Club to V.O." He admitted that he felt the same way. I had successfully defused a problem. That's when being a peacekeeper is useful. Looking back, there were other times in the business when I should have made war, but I don't want to get ahead of the story.

All of this time, I was still living in my parents' house in Montreal. Often, they weren't there so I had the run of the place and was waited on hand and foot. In spite of staying at Mom and Dad's for longer than my friends, I lived my own life. In 1961, that changed. I met Barbara Baerwald on a blind date, set up by her grandmother and one of my mother's best friends. It was a Sunday evening in New York. She had hurt her finger and it had been bandaged, so she greeted me by flipping me the bird, so to speak. I took her to a restaurant that turned out to be much too fancy for the occasion. We were both uptight but got along well, and we kept getting along well. Love bloomed and the courtship lasted a year. I proposed to her in a car, a two-seater Thunderbird convertible, like the kind in *American Graffiti*. I was driving and said to her in a matter-of-fact way, "I'm in love with you, you're in love with me. Let's get married."

"Would you please stop the car?" she said.

Barbara was living in New York and I was living in Montreal, and she wanted to move. Aside from that, she liked me and said yes. She also had a boyfriend in San Francisco, who was a nice guy, but she chose me instead. We got married at the Plaza Hotel in New York City in 1962 by a rabbi from Temple Emanu-El and then honeymooned in Bermuda.

Barbara was from a well-known family, but not a wealthy one. Her grandfather was one of the founders of the Joint

Distribution Committee, perhaps the best-run Jewish organization in existence, and my father knew him. He was also a founder of the investment bank Lazard, and when the crash came, he retired and devoted himself to the JDC. It turned out he lived longer than he figured he would, which was good. The bad part was that he ran out of money. Her father was Herman Baerwald, a sweet, fine man of whom I was very fond. Unfortunately, he died of breast cancer, generally not known to afflict men as well as women, although rarely so. Barbara was the oldest of three and a very, very nice, bright young woman.

I was so damn immature, though. Barbara and I didn't really understand each other when Stephen, our first child, was born in 1964 in Montreal, where we made our home. But the first few years of our marriage were very good. We built a home in Montreal that I thought was much too expensive—very forbidding on the outside, although warm on the inside. We also had a nice home in the Laurentians, the hills north of Montreal. Stephen resembled Dennis the Menace, thus our first dog we named Ruff, after Dennis's dog. Ellen, our precious daughter, came along in 1969. It would only be a matter of years, though, before Barbara and I began drifting apart and had difficult times, eventually leading to a divorce and me remarrying.

During my coming of age as a businessman in the 1950s, there was another theme running concurrently—family investments. In preparation for passing on the family fortune, Dad had set up the trust I referred to earlier, CEMP, a name derived from the first letter of each of his children's names. The trust divided up shares in the business. It was not particularly fair, but by bequeathing sixty per cent to the boys, it was Dad's way of making Edgar and me allies as well as unassailable through a large block of stock, assuming we were the ones who would take over running the business. If it had been twenty-five per cent for each of us, it could have been three against one or deadlocked.

Once CEMP was set up, someone had to manage it and invest the money it generated, which was considerable. That person was my best friend from my time at McGill, Leo Kolber, who would later become Senator Leo Kolber. Leo was the son of a dentist and an ambitious mother who sold hats. His father died of a heart attack when Leo was just sixteen, so he had to learn how to fend for himself and his mother. A lawyer by training, he caught the real estate bug at a young age and became one of the savviest property investors Canada—or North America, for that matter—has ever seen. Put it this way: there would be no Cadillac Fairview—meaning no TD Centre and no Eaton Centre—without Leo. He wrote in his memoirs that, after his father died, there was a $40,000 estate, allowing his mother to purchase a small apartment building for $25,000. Leo was the one who would go and collect the rent for her. As he did so, it struck him that real estate could be a pretty good business—borrow money to buy a building and get cash flow from the rent. Dad also saw something else in Leo that sounds—and is—very crass, but it accounted for why he hired him. He's a Jewish boy on the make, Dad told Mother, just the kind of person we should have looking after our money. He also liked that Leo hadn't lived a sheltered, protected life like Edgar and me, giving him a hard-edged, unvarnished view of the world. That's certainly the truth. Leo tells a funny story about being at our home when our butler announced there would be tomato soup at lunch.

"Is it Campbell's?" he asked.

The butler looked down his nose and apparently said, "At 15 Belvedere Road, we do not serve canned soup." So there.

Leo's streetwise upbringing also included nasty brushes with anti-Semitism while growing up in Montreal. All in all, he was a tough nut and Dad was right to hire him.

Edgar and I had a chance to work with Leo on our first real estate deal in 1953, but we passed, much to my embarrassment, when we couldn't agree on terms. The plan was to finance the construction of a handful of homes on lots in the town of Mount Royal. Leo made money on that, and not long after, he had a second deal ready to go on land at the top of Westmount, which I knew to be valuable. In his book, he described how Edgar and I put up the money to buy sixty thousand square feet of property for sixty cents a square foot. Six months later, a developer bought us out for $1.20 a square foot. We'd doubled our money in half a year and we were off to the races with Leo, paying him a retainer to bring us deals.

Leo's mother, meanwhile, was not crazy about her son working for the Bronfmans, believing that he could do as well on his own without us getting a cut of the action. According to Leo, perhaps in a heightened pique, she dramatically announced that she would sit Shiva if he worked for the Bronfmans. For non-Jewish readers, Shiva is the traditional week of mourning after the death of an immediate family member, so this was somewhat theatrical talk from Mrs. Kolber, to say the least. As Leo wrote, she got over it and there was no Shiva. He stuck with us and we stuck with him, and all concerned did pretty well by it.

By 1958, we'd moved to bigger deals through a company we called Fairview. I actually came up with the name, and now, when you see buildings owned by Cadillac Fairview (which is currently owned by Ontario Teachers' Pension Plan), that's the same Fairview. At that time, Leo had his sights set on building a shopping centre in Toronto called Parkway Plaza, which involved purchasing and putting together several properties. From then on, things moved rapidly. In 1962, Fairview told the public it was planning to build the Toronto-Dominion Bank's new office tower, the TD Centre, which at the time was the biggest office-tower development in Canadian history and the city's first skyscraper. It would be a fifty-fifty venture with the bank. As my co-author and collaborator, Howard Green, wrote in *Banking on America*, his book about TD Bank's expansion into the United States, the tower put Toronto-Dominion, the smallest of the big five Canadian banks, on the map in the country's financial district, bolstering the bank's confidence and helping set the stage for it to grow into what it is today.

Although Leo ran Fairview and oversaw the TD project, Edgar and I were kept in the loop and participated when necessary. For instance, when the TD Centre project was getting going, Leo wrote that he, at a mere thirty-two years of age, had to fly to Toronto to meet with the bank's chairman, Allen Lambert. I went with him so that a Bronfman would be in the room. Again, Mies van der Rohe would get the call as architect, given Phyllis's relationship with him from the Seagram Building, which had opened in New York in 1958. As Leo has reminded us, we put up $6 million to build the TD Centre and ultimately sold our half for $500 million. Not bad.

The TD Centre led to the construction of another Toronto landmark, the Eaton Centre, again a blockbuster investment. With no money down, in the end we made $360 million. In 1974, Fairview merged with Cadillac to become Cadillac Fairview. The projects are almost too many to mention, but Canadians will know Erin Mills Town Centre and Cedarbrae Mall, both in the Greater Toronto Area; Galeries d'Anjou in Montreal; Portage Place in Winnipeg; and the Pacific Centre in Vancouver. In the U.S., we built in Dallas, Los Angeles, Atlanta, and Fairfax County, Virginia.

In 1986, we decided that Cadillac Fairview should be sold, and we did just that in 1987. Leo doesn't hold back his anger about this, miffed that the reasons were never clear to him, that he hadn't been consulted, and that neither Edgar nor I had bothered to call him. He couldn't understand why we wanted to sell such "gold-plated assets." The reason we sold is that we didn't want to be cash-strapped and felt that we needed more flexibility. Between the Seagram holding and the Cadillac Fairview holding, it was clear which one would be sold to achieve that flexibility. It also turns out that a couple of years after, there was a crash in the real estate market whose effects lingered until the mid-1990s, so from my point of view, it was the right decision at the right time for the right reasons.

As for how we handled Leo, it was unusual. It's true he was not consulted. I told him it was going to happen rather than discussing it. It was a *fait accompli*. Frankly, I could have handled it better, but while Leo was very close to the family, he was not a family member. He would have tried to convince us not to sell, and I think at that time, we just didn't want to hear it. As for the deal itself, he handled it brilliantly. He worked with Goldman Sachs to get top dollar for us—and for him, given that he had a stake in it as well. It appears that after his anger subsided, he subsequently reflected on the sale and reassessed the fact that we got a terrific price for the company, just as stocks were melting down in the October 1987 market crash. The family's share of the Cadillac Fairview sale was an eye-popping $1.2 billion. Leo's share was worth $100 million. Again, not bad.

While all of this was happening, I thought that business, when practised at the highest levels, was tough and I wasn't. As I said earlier, I was also scared of New York. It was too big in my eyes. When Edgar went there and said, "That means I'll probably end up running the company," I said that was fine with me. My brother wrote there was never any question about my ambitions. "True, he and I were equal partners, and he wanted to be treated as such. But he also wanted me, not him, to succeed father in running the company," Edgar said.

Some people run things while I ran away from things, or at least I thought I did. But as I look back on it all, the evidence is clear that I succeeded in Canada. I ran the Canadian operation—as much as ten per cent of the business—and I ran it well, through the people I knew, liked, and respected. I also brought Leo into our family affairs, and that had enormous impact. To avoid any conflict, it was my father and Edgar who actually hired him, but they wouldn't have known Leo if he hadn't been my friend. In a sense, it was perhaps my good instinct for people manifesting itself—an ability to spot talent. It was all a huge lift for me, and it set me up for my next major uplift, Major League Baseball and the Montreal Expos.

4

Bringing Major League Baseball to Canada

I f you had to pick an activity that's the polar opposite of being involved with the symphony, you might consider becoming an owner of a Major League Baseball team. America's pastime was not quite what my mother had in mind for her youngest, but in 1968, I was in Puerto Rico for a meeting of the Young Presidents' Organization when the phone rang. On the other end of the line was Gerry Snyder, vice-chairman of the executive committee at Montreal City Hall. He was calling on behalf of none other than Jean Drapeau, Montreal's larger-than-life mayor.

If there was ever a big-picture man and someone who didn't sweat the details, it was Jean Drapeau. His shortcomings didn't seem to matter to Montrealers. They kept electing him. His first stretch in office was from 1954 to 1957, then again from 1960 to 1986, a staggering twenty-nine years in total as chief magistrate of what was, for a lot of that time, Canada's largest and predominant city. Drapeau was, at his core, a salesman extraordinaire, eventually securing for Montreal the World's Fair (Expo 67), the performance hall Place des Arts, and, eventually, the Olympics.

In the late 1960s, however, he was putting a major sales job on Major League Baseball, trying to land the first team outside the United States. If Montreal were approved, it would be not only the first team outside the U.S. of A., but the first team in a city whose predominant language was not English. It was a brazen attempt, but brazen was Drapeau's stock in trade. In Mexico City in December of 1967, the barons of baseball listened to the man with the horn-rimmed glasses and moustache promote his town, and on May 27, 1968, they too succumbed to the mayor's charms by granting Montreal a team at the same time as they gave the nod to a franchise in San Diego.

The plan was to start playing just a year later, in 1969, a tall order given that there were no investors lined up and the city did not have a stadium that was close to being suitable. But if you were Jean Drapeau, obstacles didn't exist. Hurdles were for other people to worry about, not the concern of the man with the master plan. He had an expression, "There are no problems, only solutions." It wouldn't be long before Drapeau was referring to me as his best friend, even though I had never been to his house nor he to mine. Details, details!

Back in Montreal, the call went out to the business establishment, and that included me. Major League Baseball's entry fee for a new franchise was $10 million, so the mayor wanted ten investors, each ponying up a million dollars. When the solicitation came to me, I said if there's a roof on the stadium, we're in. You want a roof? No problem. Drapeau & Co. promised the moon. They just didn't say *when* the roof would make an appearance, but again, stop with the details. Meantime, I told my wife, Barbara, that they wanted a million dollars from us and that I'd agreed. She replied, "A million dollars and you just say yes?"

"Well, it's never going to happen anyway."

Things then went silent for a while, and the next time I heard anything, Barbara and I were in bed and we heard a radio announcer say that professional baseball was coming to town.

"Oh shit. Now we're in the glue," I said to her. Fortunately, Barbara was in favour of the investment, but only mildly.

Montreal may be known far and wide as a hockey town, the home of the Montreal Canadiens of the National Hockey League, but the city has baseball in its blood, too. Not only did Jackie Robinson play there for the Montreal Royals—a team that dated back to 1897 and was the farm team of the Brooklyn Dodgers—but the Royals also showcased the wares of future major-league stars and Hall of Famers like Cy Young Award winner Don Drysdale, three-time Most Valuable Player Roy Campanella, and eight-time All-Star Duke Snider.

The built-in handicap to playing professional baseball in Montreal, however, was always the weather. The cold temperatures start early and the snow stays late. The contrast between throwing a pitch in April in Houston or Anaheim versus doing so in Montreal is stark, to say the least. Thus, my condition that there be a stadium with a roof. But again, Jean Drapeau was hell-bent on putting Montreal on the board as a globally known city, and the Expos would be one more chess move that would also include vying for the 1976 summer Olympics. He had a stadium on the brain for reasons beyond the Expos.

Aside from my love of sports, as opposed to symphony, a sense of Canadian identity was flourishing within me. In the 1960s in Quebec, the province had been experiencing the so-called Quiet Revolution. Weary of discrimination at the hands of the English minority, Francophones were standing up for themselves, and separatists were beginning to become a force politically. There had also been violence, and the country was noticing that all was not as calm as Canadians liked to advertise. Aside from being a sports fan, I thought baseball would be good for the city, the province, and the country. It would be something else for everyone to root for, a potential unifying force. I also liked the idea that it would thicken our ties to the United States.

As things evolved, of the ten investors Drapeau wanted, only six actually came to the table. In my view, only two of us had leadership abilities—Jean-Louis Lévesque, a leader in the Montreal business community whose name adorned the securities firm Lévesque Beaubien, and me. Lévesque was rich, well known, and also active in the sports world as the owner of a racetrack in the area. Most important, from a political point of view, I thought it was crucial that we have a Francophone as the chairman, and I told him so. He agreed, but to my dismay took himself out of the investing group in the summer of 1968, just when we needed the money.

Suddenly, yours truly was chairman and majority owner, eventually winding up with a seventy-five per cent stake in the enterprise. When I hesitated, a good friend whose opinion mattered told me I had to go ahead with it. "You can't lose," he said. "You'll either make it happen, or if you don't, you'll have at least given it a good shot." That reinforced my decision to proceed.

Then there was my father. When he'd ask me what I was doing, I'd say I was working on "this baseball thing."

"I thought you were supposed to be selling whisky for me," he'd counter.

When it finally looked like we were going to get the team, I decided to see him directly about it. I had no idea what his reaction would be, so when I went, I kept thinking to myself,

"Keep your cool, no matter what he does." Dad loved reading the New York *Daily News*, which included Walter Winchell, *Dick Tracy*, and *Little Orphan Annie*. When I walked into his office that morning, he had the paper in front of his face. I said I had to speak to him.

"Yes, my son, about what?"

"About baseball." The paper went back over his face. "It's about who's going to pay for it," I said. Then the paper went down again. I said I didn't think the team would make money, so it would be wrong for me to invite my siblings to join me in the purchase.

"So I'll pay for it myself." His expression changed.

"Have you got that kind of money?"

I said, "Barely, but I do." Immediately after our conversation, he checked that with Leo.

From then on, Sam Bronfman was the biggest Expos fan in the world. The only thing he wanted to know was whether his kid had balls, and not baseballs.

Meantime, ironing out the details with Drapeau was like a French farce. The mayor's point man on the Expos file was his alter ego, Lucien Saulnier, the chairman of the city's executive committee. While Drapeau was a salesman deluxe, Saulnier was a finance man deluxe. If you were to give him a nickname, it might have been "Dr. No." It seemed to me that his favourite expression was "definitely not." One day, I was talking with Saulnier and I asked him about the covered stadium. He looked at me like I was from Mars.

"What covered stadium?"

I recounted to him that Drapeau had written a letter to the league, promising a covered stadium in two years.

"Well, that's nice," Saulnier said. "Show me where he's authorized by the city council or the executive committee to write that letter."

"What? He would write a letter without any authorization?"

"Look. You can write a letter. I can write a letter. The guy who cleans the floor can write a letter. He wrote the letter. He was not authorized."

Hearing that, I was stunned. Had I too been conned by that smoothie Drapeau? Would Sam Bronfman's son look like the city's biggest sucker after investing in a baseball team that didn't have an adequate place to play? I decided I had to resign, wrote a letter saying so, and delivered it in person to Drapeau. Undeterred, he then continued his seduction, asking me to hold off for twenty-four hours. He had, he said, been advised by his father not to make emotional decisions, and if you give people twenty-four hours, things can change. So I waited.

The next morning, there were four of us in my office in mourning for the team that would never be. Aside from Leo Kolber and me, there was Lorne Webster of the prominent Montreal family who would be one of my partners and John McHale, who had been deputy commissioner of Major League Baseball when the franchise was granted and who was destined to be the first president of the Montreal Expos. While we were there, Drapeau called and asked me to please come to his office—alone, nobody else. So I went down to see him after lunch, and when I arrived at his office, he had a lovely coloured drawing of Jarry Park, a field I had never visited.

It turns out that Warren Giles, the president of the National League, had come to Montreal, and two newspapermen took him to a hokey baseball field, where they looked down the sight lines. The reporters asked Giles if Major League Baseball could be played there. Yes, it could be, he said, so Drapeau had engineers and architects stay up all night, drawing a stadium that would hold 28,000 people—rather than the 3,000 Jarry Park could seat at the time—so it could become the first home of the Montreal Expos. Once again, the big-picture man had let others pull an all-nighter to look after the details.

Leo, who had discouraged me from investing in the team, then negotiated our deal with Saulnier and the city for use of the ballpark. They would build the stadium, we would have the concessions and the parking, and we'd give them a percentage of the revenue, which was not very much, but they'd own the stadium.

In honour of getting the franchise, there was a celebration for the presentation of the cheque to Warren Giles of the National League. It was held at the Windsor Hotel, and Lester Pearson, who had just left office as prime minister, was there in the capacity of honorary president of the Expos. Pearson had played semi-pro baseball and was a huge and knowledgeable fan, one reason he and John F. Kennedy hit it off. The story was that, while Pearson was in office, if the World Series was on and there was an afternoon game, he wouldn't have any appointments so that he could watch the game. Apparently, one day the U.S. ambassador called to see about getting an appointment, and Pearson's secretary said no. "Well, then," the ambassador said, "would you please tell him I'd like to watch the game with him?"

At one point later, we flew Pearson down to Florida for training camp—on the Seagram plane, no less. Today, using the jet of a publicly traded company for baseball business would be a big no-no—and should have been back then—but it happened.

Pearson and his wife, Maryon, travelled with us to Palm Beach for our first spring training ever. When I asked John McHale where we should stay, he intimated there was only one really fine hotel, the Breakers. It's an imposing, iconic, and very fine beachfront hotel in the Italian Renaissance style. But I was disturbed about two things. No tennis clothes were allowed in the lobby, thus it was a "walk around the block" to play. Significantly more disturbing, there were no black or Hispanic people at the place at all—not a staff member, let alone a guest. Thankfully, times have changed and the resort reflects cultural diversity. But this was intolerable to me. So the next morning, I handed in our key and moved to the motel where players, team management, and directors were housed. Pearson told me I had deserted him. However, he relented when I said that I didn't think his wife would be comfortable at the motel. But he added that, the following year, he would come alone and stay at the motel with "the boys." He was true to his word. The next year, he came alone and stayed with the rest of us. He had a ball.

As for Warren Giles, the president of the National League, I never went to any of his league meetings to try to sell Montreal. Gerry Snyder went on behalf of Drapeau. At one point during the process, though, Giles phoned me. He said he'd noticed that I had not gone to any of the National League's meetings and he wanted to know why. I told him that Montreal was the type of town where my name would be splashed all over the papers. If someone else had won the franchise, I would not have wanted to look bad in the eyes of my fellow citizens. Giles then asked about the money, trying to make sure it would be there when the payment for the franchise was due.

"Mr. Giles, if we get the franchise, the money will be there."

He said, "Thank you," and hung up. Some time later I asked him about the call.

"How'd you know I wasn't some sort of playboy just fooling around with Dad's money?"

"I liked the sound of your voice. That's why."

Once we had the franchise, the backbreaking work began. Not only did the stadium have to be upsized by a factor of almost ten, but in less than a year we had to assemble appropriate staff, which included coaches, scouts and yes, players.

"I don't think we realized at the time how frantic it really was. We didn't have a ballpark, we didn't have a player, we didn't have anything. We just had a franchise," recalled the late Jim Fanning, our first general manager, who ended up staying with the organization for twenty-five years.

Heading the operation was John McHale, who was named president and CEO in August of 1968. As it turns out, he and I had each come up with the name "Expos" independently, on the same day, at the same time. McHale had played for the Detroit Tigers and had retired to become the team's general manager. Later, as GM in Milwaukee, which became Atlanta, he worked with Jim Fanning. He knew the game from a field perspective. He eventually became deputy commissioner of Major League Baseball, meaning he knew the issues from the front-office side of the ledger. And he also had a human perspective. As a minor-league player for the Buffalo Bisons, he said, his salary was so tiny he always aimed for the "Knit to Fit" sign over the right field fence that would win him a free suit if he hit it.

A logo and uniforms needed to be designed as well. And to clarify any misconceptions about the team insignia—some people thought it was my initials—the logo has an *M* for Montreal, an *e* for Expos and a *b* for baseball. On January 14, 1969, the day he was announced as our first manager, I remember showing Gene Mauch the red, white, and blue colour scheme, particularly for the hat. Mauch, who had previously been with the Phillies before they sacked him, was a traditionalist and was horrified when he saw the cap. He thought it looked like a beanie.

"Gene," I said to him, "we're going to sell a million of those hats." And we did. We also had the largest attendance of any expansion team in the history of baseball. I had announced before the season started that we'd draw 1.2 million fans, and we got 1.212 million. I also told the tax department, Revenue Canada, that we were a young team, not very good, and who knew what would happen if we lost twenty games in a row. And we did. But I'm proud to say that, all these years later, even after the dissolution of the team in 2004, hipsters are still wearing Expos hats.

Amazingly, there were only two months to get ready for the draft. As Jonah Keri wrote in his history of the Expos, there were two schools of thought about how to approach the selection of players. From a fan perspective, there was clearly a yen for a certain number of recognizable names. In other words, you wanted a few veterans who'd bond with the fans, or already had. The risk with that strategy was that you'd probably get players who were a bit past their "best before" date, but maybe they had another year or two in them and could provide leadership and then be traded in short order. The second strategy was to go with young, untested talent, which was a high-risk, high-reward route.

Jim Fanning said the philosophy was actually to draft as many players as possible "who had value" so that they could eventually be used to make trades.

I decided from the outset to stand back and let the baseball people run the baseball business. I also let everyone know it was the John McHale Show. There was only one instance later on, when I recommended the Gary Carter trade, but for the most part, I resisted the temptation to run the team. The professionals had to lead the enterprise. What was I going to say? Draft this guy over that guy? What did I know when it came to the nuances of baseball?

Anyone of a certain age who followed the game will remember whom the Expos got in the first draft: Manny Mota, Mack Jones, Jack Billingham, Jesús Alou, Bill Stoneman, Maury Wills, Jim Fairey, and Coco Laboy. Maury Wills turned out to be an object lesson, and one that I imparted to management, much like one of the life lessons or homilies Dad used to share at the table. Walter O'Malley, the owner of the Los Angeles Dodgers, had become annoyed with Wills for allegedly having an affair with Doris Day. (Wills wrote in his book that he and Day were lovers and that they'd agreed to always deny it. In her autobiography, Day did deny that she and Wills had an affair.) Wills was shipped off from Los Angeles to Pittsburgh—one demotion—and then to the Expos, a second demotion. Frankly, when he joined the team, he did not perform.

What I learned from the Wills experience was this: if you were bringing a player to Montreal, the frontier of baseball, he had to think the move was a promotion, not a demotion. Wills played as though it was the latter. You might say I was already sticking my nose into running a baseball team when I vowed I wouldn't. But the Wills case was a business lesson, not a baseball lesson. It was psychology that could have applied in any business, not just baseball.

Which brings us to the Expos' first true star. The flip side of the Maury Wills situation was trying to find the diamond in the rough, the great player who was underappreciated somewhere else, or maybe a substitute who rarely even got on the field or into the starting lineup. Someone like that could blossom on a new team like the Expos, where the expectations were not those of an established team. Heck, it would be a miracle if we just got up and running in eight months and were ready for our first game.

If there was ever an underappreciated player, it was right fielder Rusty Staub toiling under unfriendly management with the Houston Astros. Staub wanted out, and for him, the arrival of the Expos for the 1969 season was like drawing the "Free Parking" card in Monopoly. Jackpot!

Jonah Keri quotes Staub: "I knew nothing about Montreal. What got me was how much respect I had for Mauch, and how much he wanted me on his ball club. I knew I had to get out of Houston because of how they were operating."

Mauch, McHale, and Jim Fanning, our general manager, decided we had to have Staub. So we traded first baseman Donn Clendenon along with Jesús Alou (uncle of outfielder Moisés Alou and brother of manager Felipe Alou) to Houston for Rusty. Staub was a hell of a hitter with a good throwing arm. He was also intelligent, and not just about the game. Then suddenly, Clendenon, who was simultaneously working for a pen company out of Atlanta, said he was going to retire rather than go through with the trade. In fact, he would not report to Houston because the late Harry Walker was the manager, and Clendenon, who was black, believed Walker was a racist. As a result, Houston protested and declared that the trade was voided. We countered by arguing that our agreement was "buyer beware." If the man decided to retire or not report, that was Houston's problem, not ours.

Enter the commissioner of Major League Baseball, Bowie Kuhn, who would later earn my enmity—and did he ever—because of what happened after the Toronto Blue Jays came into existence. Kuhn ruled the trade was valid. But because Clendenon wouldn't report, we settled by sending Houston two more players, Jack Billingham and Skip Guinn, plus $100,000. Eventually, we traded Clendenon, who was a so-so hitter for us, to the New York Mets, where he was the MVP of the 1969 World Series.

Staub, it turns out, had been at our camp the whole time, but as long as the Clendenon dispute was pending, he couldn't practise with any of our players. However, our people knew Kuhn was going to visit our training camp at a certain time on a certain day. Rusty, who desperately wanted to play with us, was told to be ready to meet the commissioner. So Kuhn arrived and a group of us got to the field—Bronfman, McHale, Mauch, Fanning, Staub, and Kuhn. I was standing next to Kuhn when I felt a hand pull me out of the line and I was plunked somewhere else. A picture was then taken that went out on the wires all over North America of Staub in an Expos uniform—replete with his requested number 10—standing next to Commissioner Bowie Kuhn. That sealed the deal. Rusty was now an Expo.

The photographer that day was Denis Brodeur, the father of NHL goaltending great Martin Brodeur. He became our photographer, and Rusty became known as *Le Grand Orange*. He was very important to the team, becoming an instant hero and our first star. Staub looked like the model for the poem "Casey at the Bat," only with orange hair. I used to play catch with him, and he would make the same throw to me as he would from the outfield. He said, "It's the only way I'll throw the baseball," telling me that the last thing you should think about is how to throw.

"I can only throw one way," he said.

I thought to myself, *Now there is a student of the game.* Staub also endeared himself to the Francophone community by learning a bit of French, to the point of doing some broadcast interviews in Canada's other official language. He also hit twenty-nine home runs in our first season and, in terms of on-base slugging percentage, was the fourth-best hitter in the National League, behind some of the most famous names in baseball: Hall of Famers Willie McCovey, Hank Aaron, and Roberto Clemente.

But the weather, oh, the weather. The winter of 1968–69 was brutal and long, with fifteen centimetres of snow falling on April 2. Fortunately, the team's first game would not be played in Montreal. It was against the New York Mets, on April 8, 1969. As the team took the field, Jim Fanning said some of the Mets were ribbing the Expos about the uniform and cap design. Mauch responded by giving them a dose of seasoned baseball psychology to scare the hell out of them. He announced to the New York dugout and the wisecracking Mets that he had a bunch of young, wild pitchers who didn't know where their pitches were going. Their minds filled with images of getting bopped in the head by wayward balls, there were no more disparaging comments from the Mets.

For their first game ever, though, the Expos had their own

fears to surmount. They would have to stare down one of the greatest pitchers of all time, Tom Seaver of the Mets. Seaver would, over the course of his illustrious career, be rookie of the year, win more than three hundred games, garner three Cy Young Awards as best pitcher in the National League, and lead the Mets to a World Series win that season. On the mound for the Expos: Mudcat Grant, already thirty-three years old, with arguably his best years behind him. Throwing out the first pitch at Shea Stadium, however, was the man who'd dreamed the dream, Montreal mayor Jean Drapeau, while John McHale and I stood next to him. Canadian contralto Maureen Forrester, who hailed from Montreal, sang "O Canada" in both English and French.

Attendance at Shea Stadium was 44,451, and all the Americans in the crowd were standing up for my national anthem. Tears were running down my cheeks. That's what it was all about, right there. And then, in the furthest thing from a pitching duel, we won our first game, beating the Mets 11–10! Mudcat only lasted an inning and a third, giving up six hits, while Seaver lasted five innings, also giving up six hits. Rusty Staub, Coco Laboy, and Dan McGinn (a relief pitcher) all hit home runs for the Expos. McGinn's was the first homer in Expos history—off Tom Seaver, no less. What an oddity. Here you had the first major-league team from outside the United States, wearing funny hats, and a *left-handed relief pitcher* hit the team's first home run off the great Seaver. It was a wonderful, weird start to the Expos.

We would not play our first home game until April 14, 1969, after six games on the road. A crowd of 29,184 showed up at Jarry Park, which three days before didn't look anywhere close to ready. A last-minute blizzard didn't help. On the morning of the first game in Montreal, they were still putting seats in the stands down the right-field line. We played the St. Louis Cardinals. Their centre fielder, Curt Flood, let everyone know how he felt about the playing conditions on what must have seemed like the tundra. Of the new grass in the outfield, Flood said you could kill yourself out there because it was so bumpy, the ground having heaved, post-winter.

Expos pitcher Bill Stoneman was also quoted about the playing conditions. "The field was really soft. I mean really soft. It was a bit rough ... the ground was so soft that behind home plate, the catcher was John Bateman—I forget who the umpire was that day—but both of them ended up standing about two or three inches lower at the end of the game than they were at the start of the game, just sinking into the ground as the game went on."

Those calling the game, broadcasters Dave Van Horne and Russ Taylor, spoke about all the high rollers coming out to the ballpark, with Taylor saying it was all of my friends, that the community would not dare turn its back on something I started, given my involvement in Montreal with business, hospitals, museums, and charities.

Whatever, it was a great day and again we won, this time 8–7. The game would instantly make Mack Jones part of Expos lore after he knocked in five runs, including a three-run homer. The left-field bleachers were nicknamed "Jonesville" because of all the home runs he hit there. During spring training, Jones would rib me, calling me "Money."

"How you doin', Money?"

The great slugger Willie Stargell of the Pittsburgh Pirates was also legendary in Montreal from the Expos' beginnings and was a particular favourite of my son, Stephen. Early on, Stargell smacked a ball so far outside Jarry Park that it landed in a public swimming pool behind the right-field fence. The pool even got a nickname out of the deal—"*La Piscine de Willie*"—and whenever Stargell came to bat, someone would always yell, "Everyone out of the pool!"

Thus began the life story of the Montreal Expos. Although we won our first game and our first home opener, our first ten years were not winning seasons. The 1978 campaign was our tenth season below .500. And then the fun began. Although we'd had our share of stars, it was at times difficult to recruit players to play for the Expos. There was a great right-handed pitcher from Los Angeles whom I once tried to woo at a meeting at a private airport in Montreal.

"Is there any chance of signing you?" I asked.

"No," said Don Sutton. "It's a foreign country, they speak French, and the taxes are much higher."

Fortunately, not everybody felt that way. Many of the Expos' wives absolutely loved Montreal, the greatest city most of those people had ever visited or lived in. But still, it was at that point that I made up my mind. If we couldn't sign big stars, we'd have to make our own by developing talent. As a result, you have to build up a farm system to spawn and grow talent. We really hadn't done much of that until baseball changed in 1975 and players could become free agents. That meant the big-time bidding wars were on for superstar players, as well as for many who were nowhere near to being superstars. Since we couldn't sign them, we would create them.

To kick off this new strategic goal, I invited Expos staff, coaches, scouts, and supervisors to our apartment in Palm Beach, Florida, where I made the announcement. In addition to that, to motivate the troops to rally around the flag, everyone would get a twenty-five per cent raise immediately. In spite of this generous gesture, there was a certain amount of skepticism among the group. "Bloody owners, they don't mean it" was the grumbling below the surface. That lasted until the fattened-up cheques arrived the next month and they quickly realized I meant it. I'm proud to say we went on from there to build the best farm system in the majors. Tim Raines, Andre Dawson, Gary Carter, Larry Parrish, Warren Cromartie, and many more had already been developed and signed by us, resulting in a stretch of winning seasons between 1979 and 1983. It was truly the golden age of the Expos.

The stadium, however, would not be a golden experience. It was not until 1977, the year after the Montreal Olympics, that the Expos moved into the "Big O," as it was nicknamed. As for the roof, that didn't come for another five years. As for retracting, it worked on and off from 1988 until 1992, when it was closed permanently. The Big O was also known as the "Big Owe," given the huge cost of building it. Keri wrote that it was initially estimated to cost $124 million. That rose to $310 million and was finally projected to cost $600 million. CBC News reported that the Olympic Stadium ended up costing more than $1.5 billion, and the debt wasn't finally paid off until late 2006.

In addition, the stadium was in the east end of the city, somewhat awkward to reach for many. The Big O also had zero appeal as a place to play a pastoral, summer sport like baseball. It was oversized and concrete was everywhere. The angle of the seating wasn't right, so you were never close to the field. The rows of seats needed to be set on a steeper incline so people in the thirtieth row could see the players. The artificial turf wasn't very good, and it was bad for the players. Andre Dawson's knees may have paid the price, although they were bad before he came to us.

As for the roof, it was a convoluted design. It worked, it didn't work, it half-worked. Drapeau never consulted with us about the design or location. It was all about the Olympics, with nary a thought about the baseball team the mayor had gone to the barricades for during the previous decade. I remember saying to the Quebec premier's right-hand man that he should stop Drapeau. "You'll have the Expos for decades," I said, "while the Olympics will just last ten days." To no avail.

In spite of it all, we fielded a hell of a team for four or five years. The 1979 season was the first in which we witnessed flashes of greatness and what would come. The Expos had a six-and-a-half game lead by July, with a record of 46–29. It was also the first season the team drew two million fans, which happened again in three of the next four years, interrupted only by the 1981 strike. By 1982 and 1983, the Expos were getting better crowds than the New York Yankees. But in September 1979, we came the closest in our short history to winning our first playoff berth. After a doubleheader on September 24, the Expos were leading the Pittsburgh Pirates by half a game, only to lose four of their last five, giving Pittsburgh the division crown. The Pirates then went on to win the World Series, propelled by their theme song, "We Are Family," by the R&B/disco group Sister Sledge. Although we lost to the Pirates, the Expos had the third-best record in baseball that year, better than the Western Division champions in either league.

By 1980, the team had Gary Carter, Steve Rogers, and perhaps the best outfield in baseball with Ellis Valentine, Andre Dawson, and Warren Cromartie. We had developed our own ensemble cast, even though in 1976, with the advent of free agency, we had been tempted by the availability of Reggie Jackson. Fanning described how he and McHale flew to the Carolinas to meet with Jackson and his agent, were impressed, and made him an offer. After that, we flew him up to Montreal, and I organized a party and dinner for him at my house. The leading lights of Montreal were there. Leo and John McHale interviewed Jackson at Leo's house, only after the famed slugger had been delayed. The Associated Press reported that authorities said that a small amount of pot was found in his suitcase at the airport—"not even an ounce," according to a federal Crown prosecutor. Canadian officials did not prosecute Jackson. All we really knew was that he was late, although Jim Fanning recalled Reggie being "agitated." In any event, Montreal turned out not to be of interest to Jackson, while New York City was. Can you blame him? George Steinbrenner signed him to the Yankees, where Jackson's star continued to shine brightly. The Yankees' owner, gloating over the signing, said, "Bronfman may have Seagram, (Ray) Kroc (who owned the San Diego Padres) may have McDonald's. But I've got the Big Apple." He was right. He did. And that would become more and more significant as time went on and the business case worsened for the Expos.

But the early '80s were a blast for us. By then, Dick Williams had been our manager since 1977, one of the reasons Reggie Jackson flirted with us, having played for Williams during two World Series–winning seasons with the Oakland Athletics in the early '70s. Williams was a gentleman of the old school. Although he got results, he had a peculiar modus operandi. He had the reputation of being something of a drill sergeant. Let's just say he didn't mollycoddle the players.

Williams led the team to a terrific season in 1980, but it turned out to be another heartbreaker when all was said and done. The Expos spent more than nine weeks of the season in first place and in mid-September led the Philadelphia Phillies by a couple of games. That lead dribbled away, and by the time the last series of the season rolled around, the two teams were tied. Just like the year before, the Expos were eliminated via a loss to the Phillies, this time on a Mike Schmidt home run in extra innings. Like the Pirates, the Phillies went on to win the World Series. We kept getting close but couldn't clinch it.

It took the bizarre season of 1981 for the team to get into the playoffs for the first time. That season, the players of Major League Baseball went on strike, and it was a stroke of good luck for us. We were third in our division when the strike happened, and then, on August 6, after a settlement was reached, the owners agreed to split the season. Playoff spots were guaranteed to the four teams that were leading their divisions prior to the strike. Then, whichever teams had the best records in the second "half" of the season also got playoff berths. Once part two of the season was on, the Expos had a hot hand and finished half a game ahead of the St. Louis Cardinals. We faced the dreaded Phillies in the first round of the playoffs, and the series went to five games, but thanks to a Steve Rogers shutout, the Expos advanced to play the Los Angeles Dodgers in the National League Championship Series. If they won that, they'd be headed to their first World Series.

After losing the first game, the Expos took the next two. Again, even though Montreal could have sewn it up in game four, the series went the distance of five games. In the fifth game, in very cold weather in Montreal, our ace starter and one of the best in the league, Steve Rogers, got the call to come in and pitch in relief of Ray Burris. He faced Rick Monday, who had been a solid centre fielder and reasonably good batter but was by no means a marquee player. With two outs in the ninth inning, Monday hit a two-run homer off Rogers to win the game, 2–1, securing the National League pennant for the Dodgers, who went on to win the World Series. The game has been forever enshrined as "Blue Monday." It was perhaps the darkest hour for those of us with the Expos, as a sense of disbelief fell over the team. In 1979, it was the Pirates. In 1980, it was the Phillies. Then, in 1981, it was Rick Monday. While Steve Rogers did not suffer the personal humiliation that Bill Buckner of the Boston Red Sox would five years later, letting an easy ground ball bobble through his legs when the Sox were just one out away from winning their first World Series since 1918, the loss was a massive downer. It was the closest the team ever got to winning a league championship. And although we were contenders again in 1982 and 1983, it was never the same, and certainly after that, the team began a long demise.

By then, the economics were beginning to rear their ugly head. Revenues were in weak Canadian dollars, while expenses, such as the ever-increasing player salaries, had to be paid in stronger American dollars. And no player's salary demands during my time as owner of the Expos were more off-putting than those of our star catcher, Gary Carter.

Let me first say that Gary died at far too young an age from cancer in 2012, a terrible shame for his family and all who admired him. However, back in the early 1980s, as the Expos were cresting, Carter's career was cresting as well. We were contenders again in 1983, but once again we faltered in September.

In 1984, the trend line changed and the Expos' win-loss percentage was under the .500 mark for the first time in six years. Our best years were behind us, even though that year we'd brought in Pete Rose—a.k.a. Charlie Hustle—to play for us in Montreal. But Carter was our biggest star. He knew it, and he was, in the view of many, the best catcher in baseball. In September of 1983, when we faced the Phillies in a division-deciding double-header, Carter went 0-for-8 at bat.

Some thought the Carter situation changed my view of the team—that until then I had thought of the players as family but had become disillusioned. That wasn't true. I never thought of the players as family, or "my guys," even though I would write each one of them a personal letter when they joined or left the team—highly unusual behaviour for team owners, I'm told. The economics of owning a baseball team and what happened with the Toronto Blue Jays and our loss of broadcasting rights were a much bigger issue than Gary Carter. But I can't deny that the Carter situation was part and parcel of the overall.

Even though there are certain people who loved him from the beginning, Carter was, in my view, too much of a rah-rah guy playing a professional game, and other players didn't like him much. We never won with Gary Carter, and when he was asking for two million dollars a season—which sounds quaint, compared to what's being paid today—McHale and I were furious. Still, we held our noses and did the deal with Carter because we felt we had no choice. We had no other catcher of that calibre. To illustrate how pissed off we were, though, we didn't even have a signing ceremony.

Eventually, I put it to Carter *mano a mano* in my apartment in Palm Beach, because I had said some unflattering things. I told him, "Here's my problem with you. We're down a run, with men on first and second. You come up to bat, and if you slap a single into right field, we tie the game. But you don't want to hit the other way! You want to hit the game-winning home run and see the headline in the paper. So when you get up to bat in that situation, I go to the bathroom because I know you're going to hit into a double play."

It wasn't long after that conversation that I said we should trade Carter. He did not add chemistry to the club, and you don't win without chemistry. Rusty Staub had charisma when it came to the fans, but he was also good with the other players. Carter had charisma with the fans, but his star status made him, from my viewpoint, selfish. We traded him to the Mets on December 10, 1984, where he was just one of several "stars." As for Carter's take on it, he was quoted as saying he was disappointed and had wanted to stay with the Expos for his entire career, adding that Bronfman's approach was "If the Expos can finish in fifth place with Gary Carter, they can do the same without him." He was right about that. It turned out to be a great trade for Carter. He was one of the Mets' heroes when they won the World Series two years after the trade.

Some thought emotion drove my decision to trade Carter, and yes, it makes me recall Edgar's line about me thinking about the heart while he thought about the wallet. But the Expos, I can assure you, became a wallet issue, even though they may have started out as a heart issue. The economics continued to get worse. Aside from the salaries and the currency disadvantage, it was also becoming clear that our worst-case scenario regarding our fan base put us in a position of weakness. What I mean by that is that, in the worst conditions, the Phillies would have twenty thousand people in the stadium. On our worst days, we'd have ten thousand or fewer. In 1984, when we started to lose more games than we won, our attendance fell more than thirty per cent.

There was also competition for Canada's baseball fans. The Toronto Blue Jays had arrived, and we had happily supported and assisted the birth of that team, figuring we could create more excitement for baseball through a Montreal–Toronto rivalry, akin to the long-running history between the Habs and Maple Leafs in hockey. Unfortunately, it was the American League that was expanding, not the National League, so the Jays ended up in the AL, meaning a rivalry was not in the cards. However, it clearly resulted in split loyalties. Prior to the Jays coming on the scene, baseball fans in Ontario, particularly the lucrative and populous Southern Ontario market, followed the Expos and wanted to watch the Expos. That changed with the arrival of the Blue Jays, and much of it had to do with the way broadcasting rights were apportioned by the politburo at Major League Baseball under Bowie Kuhn, the commissioner at the time.

Kuhn ruled that Expos games would be permitted on TV in Southern Ontario all of fifteen times a season. That was the real killer. I complained bitterly to Kuhn that this would "ghetto-ize" the Expos in the Quebec market, exactly the opposite of the unifying Canadian force I wanted to create when I brought the team to Montreal. Prior to the Jays arriving on the scene, I had no idea we would be facing such damaging restrictions to our business. Kuhn couldn't have been deafer to my concerns. Thankfully, in 1984 he was replaced by Peter Ueberroth, who put forward a compromise, saying that we'd get the fifteen games, and then would have to pay if we wanted to broadcast more than that. It was a perfect business decision and I told him so. However, the hour was getting late. The team was fading, the currency issue was highly damaging, and looking at an increasing number of empty seats was depressing, not only for me, but also for the players. Why else do you go out there and play your heart out, if not for the roar of a full house?

The sport was also changing. The game I went into in 1968 was a game. In a bad year, maybe you'd lose $100,000 or $200,000. Twenty years later, you could lose ten or twenty million. It became the entertainment business, not the sports world, and I believe my views on that business are well known. As a result, in sports, the necessity to win became huge. When I left, the Expos' total revenue merely equalled George Steinbrenner's take from local broadcast rights for the New York Yankees, and there was not yet any equalization mechanism for smaller-market teams. On the currency situation, I lobbied then-premier of Quebec Robert Bourassa for a subsidy if the loonie fell below ninety cents U.S. If the Canadian dollar dropped below that threshold, we'd get some relief; if it was above ninety, the province would get the revenue. But the idea was a nonstarter. By 2001, the loonie dropped below sixty-two cents U.S., so at least we got out before the currency hit an all-time low.

The notoriety from my 1976 speech about the separatists in Quebec had, after a conversation with a reporter, resulted in me threatening to pull the Expos out of Montreal. There was such a flap that future prime minister John Turner advised me that if I were to leave, I should go to New York, under the cover of Seagram business, rather than pulling up stakes and moving to Toronto, which would result in me being viewed as a traitor at home. Neither happened, although years later I did move to New York. As for the Expos, I didn't move them any-where. Major League Baseball did that in 2004, uprooting the team and placing it in Washington. But by the late 1980s, after twenty years in the business, I was ready to pull out.

In September of 1989, my second wife, Andrea (Andy), and I had a double date with Expos minority owners and good friends Hugh Hallward and his wife, Martha, to see a game at the Big O. Before the game, I phoned Hugh and said, "Why don't we go to that Italian restaurant you like instead of the game?" When we sat down, I said to Hugh, "You know what this means, don't you?" He said yes and we drank a toast to the Expos' eventual sale. A little over a year later, in November of 1990, it was announced that the Expos would stay in Montreal under the ownership of a consortium of thirteen Quebec-based businesses. The transfer of ownership took place in 1991, thus ending my almost-twenty-three-year association with the Expos and Major League Baseball.

As Leo recounted, there was a pre-game reception in April of 1969, the beginning of our first season, and my father was in attendance. A friend approached Dad and supposedly said, "Mr. Sam, this is terrible. Charles is going to lose a million dollars a year."

"Yes," Sam Bronfman replied, "and at that rate, he'll be broke in 150 years."

For sure, the team was not really a profitable enterprise in and of itself. From a tax point of view, you could write off the losses. But never mind the bottom line, there always seems to be a buyer for a sports franchise. For a cost of ten million dollars, we ended up selling the Expos for roughly $110 million. That's damn good by anyone's standards. But that's just the economic return, not the personal return. For starters, before owning the team, I had been a shy person and often never knew what to talk about with people I was meeting for the first time. Suddenly, as the owner of the Expos, everybody would talk to me about baseball. A game taught me how to relate to other people, so even more than the money, the experience changed me and changed my life.

I had also had a success that was all my own, with nothing inherited about it. I came out of my shell and was no longer just Sam Bronfman's son. In Leo's view, it was one of the best things I'd ever done; he admitted he was wrong for advising me against investing in the Expos. I had pioneered Major League Baseball in Canada, paving the way for the Blue Jays, who would soon win the World Series, becoming the first team based outside the U.S. to do so. I was honoured when they got to the Fall Classic, because they asked me to throw out the first pitch, recognizing the fact that they wouldn't be where they were without the Expos and me having come before them.

I may have been technically finished with the Expos, but the afterglow has never left me. Even now, more than two decades after selling the team, when I'm back in Montreal, people will stop me on the street and say, "*Merci*, Mr. Bronfman, for *Les Expos*." It was also an experience that distinguished me from my brother, Edgar.

I'm not sure if he meant it, but after my 1976 speech, Edgar was always trying to get me to move to New York. In 1980, the ownership of the Mets had changed hands for the first time, when Doubleday & Co. and Fred Wilpon bought the team. But before that, around 1978, I think I gave Edgar a bit of a scare.

"Edgar, if I move, I'm going to buy the New York Mets."

"You surely wouldn't do that," he said.

Was he worried I'd steal the klieg lights from him in Manhattan, where he was the established star? I don't know, but the exchange between us hangs out there like a slow, fat pitch ready to be hit by a muscular swing of the bat.

5

DuPont: Selling the Insurance Policy

In the pantheon of business in the United States, there are certain companies that have stood the test of time. They become synonymous with the sheer might of American industry over a span of many decades, in some cases for a century or more—General Electric, General Motors, 3M, to name a few. Another member of this august group was DuPont, listed formally as E. I. du Pont de Nemours and Co. You may not be aware of it, but the company makes products that are all around you. Drive through any new subdivision and look at the houses that are half-built. Wrapped around their frames is a material called Tyvek, announced in big, bold letters for all to see. Tyvek helps prevent the infiltration of air and water, but as its manufacturer, DuPont, states, it lets water vapour escape to prevent rot and mould inside the walls. It also protects homes from wind and rain and can reduce energy bills.

In addition to Tyvek surrounding you, you probably have a Teflon product in your kitchen, while the police force in your community is likely equipped with bulletproof vests made of Kevlar. Tyvek, Teflon, Kevlar, Dacron, and nylon are just a few of the names in DuPont's lineup, not to mention a plethora of chemical and agricultural products, apparel, textiles, and construction materials.

It may surprise you that Seagram was once the biggest shareholder of DuPont.[1] As Leo Kolber said, when we owned our stake and Edgar and I walked into a room, we were Mr. Seagram and Mr. DuPont. He added that no Jewish family since the Rothschilds had ever controlled such important assets—the biggest liquor company and the biggest chemical company in North America. The scope of DuPont was staggering. When we were its biggest shareholders in the 1980s and 1990s, a *division* of DuPont would sell three billion dollars' worth of product in a year. It was, and is, a behemoth. It may also surprise you that we sold DuPont, a three-pronged mistake made by Edgar, his son Edgar Jr., and, in a strange way, yours truly. It was a mistake that would put Seagram on the path to destruction.

It's unfortunate—a couple of members of our family thought DuPont was boring. Well, I'm sorry, but my view is that you invest to make a return for a shareholder, which is the business of business, not because something is exciting or not exciting. In the case of DuPont, "boring" hit a peak market value of almost seventy billion dollars in March 2015. Seagram's twenty-five per cent stake in "boring" would be, let's see—well, you do the math, but don't forget to add in the annual dividends, which amounted to hundreds of millions of dollars a year back in the mid-1990s (about a million dollars per day), when the company opted to sell its stake to look for better opportunities—in the

---

1. On December 11, 2015, DuPont, along with the Dow Chemical Company, announced a merger of equals to create DowDuPont, a $130 billion company. Seagram's share would have been worth $15.425 billion.

less boring world of movies. That dividend, by the way, almost doubled between 1995 and 2015.

I call movie-making a "world," because it sure isn't a business. Every movie that's made is, in effect, a new business. *Star Wars* is hardly the same product as *Shakespeare in Love*. In each case, you have to start from scratch to sell the product afresh, whereas Chivas Regal, Crown Royal, or Tyvek don't change their spots from one day to the next. They're the same products, and they just keep on selling. Yes, making movies is exciting, there are glittering parties, you get lots of publicity, and there are beautiful women everywhere. But that's not what the Bronfmans did for a living. The Bronfmans sold easy-to-understand products, if you'll recall Dad's simple approach. He wanted to make something that people would see on a shelf and say, "I want that." A movie would generate customers for a matter of weeks, while a whisky would sell for generations.

Edgar wanted to get into movies for the first time in the late 1960s by buying a slice of MGM—with family money, not Seagram money. But Dad, who had a nose for nonsense, called him on it, wondering if it was really about a new way to score with women. Thus came Edgar's now-famous quote: "Father, nobody has to spend fifty-six million dollars to get laid."

The genesis of our holding in DuPont goes back to the early 1960s, when Dad made a substantial investment in the oil business. He had played around with oil-related investments prior to that but made a big leap in 1963, when we bought Texas Pacific for $280 million with a minimal amount of equity—Seagram only put up $65 million. Although leveraged buyouts, or LBOs, didn't become all the rage until a few decades later, the purchase was, in retrospect, a lot like one of them. The basic premise is that you use mostly borrowed money to acquire an asset, and use its cash flow—in this case, cash generated by selling the oil—to pay the debt.

A brilliant investment banker, Mark Millard, engineered the deal for us, using very little of our own capital, the first of three major transactions he handled for us—any one of which would have been a career high.

Dad called oil "black gold," a term from the theme song of the 1960s television cornball comedy *The Beverly Hillbillies*. Almost twenty years later, in 1980, we'd pumped a lot of black gold. By then, Dad had been gone for nine years and Edgar was fully ensconced as CEO, and I was his co-chairman and equal partner from a shareholding perspective. The decision was made to sell Texas Pacific to Sunoco, a savvy move also orchestrated by Mark Millard that resulted in us receiving $2.3 billion. That was real money in those days! It was a return of about fifty times our initial investment.

The question then became: What do we do with the proceeds? Each of us had different ideas about how the cash from Texas Pacific should be invested. I thought Kimberly-Clark, the tissue maker, would be a good place to invest. That might have been astute, but as our chief financial officer pointed out to me, buying Kimberly-Clark would only use up $800 million of the money. After that, what were we supposed to do with the other billion and a half? It was almost laughable to have that much cash available to invest back in the early 1980s. Despite my earlier joke about it being real money back then, the truth is it's still a large sum today, but at that time it was *huge*. Edgar, for his part, was interested in another consumer products business, Gillette.

Our first attempt to buy something was St. Joe Minerals,

Mother and Dad's wedding day, 1922.

With Edgar, 1939.

Dad and his boys, 1937.

Back row: Minda, Dad, Mother. Front row: me, Phyllis, Edgar.

With Mother's parents, probably in 1947.
Back row: Mother, Dad. Middle row:
Grandpa and Grandma Rosner. Front row:
Edgar, Minda, Phyllis, and me.

Dad's favourites: solitaire and a glass of V.O.
—*Photographer/Artist: Arthur Schatz*

Our family home in Montreal, 15 Belvedere, as it looks today.—*Judy Strapp*

Portrait of me as a young man of 17 by my sister Phyllis.—*Phyllis Lambert*

Leo Kolber and me at the Calgary Stampede, late 1950s.

With Dad at the opening of the Israel Museum, 1965.

My mentor, colleague, and friend, Jack Duffy, chief operating officer of Seagram Canada.

My colleague and dear friend Mel Griffin, who followed Jack as COO of Seagram Canada.

My parents, mid-1960s.

Taste testing for quality at the LaSalle plant.

The V.O. line, the heart of the company.

A Jewish fundraising dinner honouring
Ian Sinclair, chairman and CEO of
Canadian Pacific (*left*), in 1980.
Shimon Peres was the guest speaker.

The House of Seagram on Peel Street in
Montreal.

The blending room for Canada. Jack Duffy is on the right,
with Harold Abney, the chief blender.

Barbara and me with Prime Minister Pierre Trudeau at Jarry Park, circa 1970. Paul Beaudry, an Expos partner at the time, is on Trudeau's right.

With Edgar at the 1987 annual meeting of Seagram, introducing Seagram Coolers.

for just over $2.1 billion, but the company fought back. We also looked at the nickel miner Inco. The cash wasn't burning a hole in our pockets, but reinvesting it was an issue we had to resolve, in part because the whisky business was not what it once was, having peaked in the late 1970s. We liked the fact that the oil business diversified Seagram. Having done well with oil, we were looking for another way to diversify.

A year later, we would become the largest shareholder of DuPont, although it was not even a company that was on our radar. The story behind how we arrived at our holding is a great case study for a business school. Our DuPont investment was actually a by-product of another investment we tried to make, in the oil company Conoco, a firm that DuPont was bidding on as well. First, though, let's back up and get a taste of DuPont and why it was interested in an oil company like Conoco.

The family spelled its name du Pont, while the company is popularly known as DuPont. The du Ponts came to America from France after revolutions in both countries. No less than Thomas Jefferson encouraged Éleuthère Irénée du Pont to build a gunpowder mill. That's how deep the family's business relationship is with the United States. E.I. and his father, Pierre Samuel du Pont de Nemours, who escaped death at the hands of Robespierre, arrived at Block Island, Rhode Island, on New Year's Day 1800 on a ship called *American Eagle* after a hellish ninety-day crossing from France. They landed shivering and starving, finding food in an abandoned house, where, according to the company history, they left a gold coin behind. They would soon establish an empire and a corporate goliath that still stands more than two hundred years later.

Pierre Samuel had helped Benjamin Franklin negotiate

the terms of the Treaty of Paris, which ended the American Revolution in 1783. Jefferson, because he had been America's representative in France in 1785 before becoming John Adams's vice-president and then the country's third president, also knew du Pont. Gunpowder seemed the obvious business to go into, given the training E.I. had received back in France. Not only that, but Napoleon sold the du Ponts powder-making equipment "at cost." Jefferson would also enlist the du Ponts to help negotiate the Louisiana Purchase with the French leader.

During the War of 1812, DuPont sold half a million pounds of gunpowder to the United States government, and by 1816 it was the largest manufacturer of the product in America. By the second half of the century, DuPont was also in the dynamite business. As the United States industrialized, with the building of bridges, railways, coal mines, and canals, the need for explosives grew. DuPont grew along with it.

By the early 1900s, the company was making millions in profits, profits that would only grow as the First World War increased the demand for explosives by orders of magnitude. The end of that war marked a turning point for the company. DuPont had grown significantly on account of the war, an unseemly development that led to public accusations of profiteering from spilled blood. As a result, the decision was made to diversify into things like solvents, paint, dyes, rayon hosiery, plastics, rubber, and other products that would serve the American consumer rather than its war machine. This was a company that adapted and innovated to deal with changing times and has survived more than two centuries by doing so, a fact that should not be forgotten as this story unfolds.

By 1919, DuPont owned thirty per cent of General Motors'

stock, a way to participate in making products for the burgeoning automobile industry. Pierre S. du Pont, a descendant of the company founders, even became president of GM in 1920 to protect his company's holding in a wobbly car company before the legendary Alfred P. Sloan Jr. took over General Motors in 1923. By the mid-1930s, DuPont was known by its advertising slogan, "Better Things for Better Living ... Through Chemistry," manifested in products like neoprene, Orlon, Dacron, and nylon (originally called Fiber 66). By the late 1950s, DuPont had sales approaching $2 billion per ycar, and by 1962 it had earnings of $452 million.

Life changed for DuPont, however, with the fallout from the Yom Kippur War in 1973 and the first OPEC oil embargo that followed. Many of DuPont's products relied on petroleum, and after the Iranian revolution later in the decade, oil prices went up again. The feeling within the company was that it needed to "integrate backwards." In other words, DuPont should own petroleum resources itself so it wouldn't be as dependent on political vagaries and price volatility in oil markets. As a result, in 1979, it began to explore for natural gas with Conoco, broadening the agreement to include oil in 1980. DuPont's involvement with Conoco would form the roots of Seagram's involvement in DuPont. In retrospect, our investment and divestiture in DuPont would be transformational and ultimately seminal in the fate of Seagram.

While DuPont and Conoco were already doing business together in 1981, and as we were still looking for a place to invest our windfall from the sale of Texas Pacific, we learned via two top Seagram executives—president Phil Beekman and executive VP and chief financial officer Harold Fieldsteel—that Canada's

Dome Petroleum was interested in purchasing Hudson's Bay Oil and Gas, in which Conoco had a controlling interest. Dome became notorious in later years when it was hit by falling energy prices and had huge debts to several Canadian banks that badly hampered them. Prior to that, Dome was an aggressive acquirer, and its interest in a piece of Conoco via Hudson's Bay Oil and Gas yielded an intriguing market response from Conoco share-holders—high demand for what Dome was offering.

As described in *Du Pont Dynasty*, Dome issued a tender offer to buy twenty per cent of Conoco shares, which would then be swapped for Conoco's share in Hudson's Bay Oil and Gas. Anxious to sell, Conoco shareholders flocked to the offer, significantly more than the twenty per cent Dome was seeking. It was a huge clue that Conoco's shareholders were unhappy and the company was ripe for a takeover bid. It was then that Seagram decided to make a play to buy Conoco. We were not even thinking about DuPont. Phil and Harold went to see Edgar, and a date was made to see the CEO of Conoco, Ralph Bailey. At the time, I was still living in Montreal, and they called to tell me how terrific this prospect looked to them and asked if I would fly down to Stamford, Connecticut, the next day, a Sunday, to meet with Bailey. So I did.

We met in Bailey's office, and after a half hour or so, we left. Phil Beekman was a very enthusiastic guy—an Ivy League type who had gone to Dartmouth—and after the meeting, he said of Bailey, "Isn't he terrific?"

"No," I said.

"Whaddya mean?" Beekman wanted to know.

"He's saying all the right words, but there's no feeling there. He doesn't like us and he doesn't want us."

Then we found out that the Dome Petroleum people were in another wing of the building. It was pretty clear there was a bake-off about to begin, with us having to make a darn good cake for Conoco to take notice. That evening, the Conoco board convened, and Edgar gave our pitch, and it was a good one. While he did so, I was scrutinizing the faces of the board members. As we headed back to New York that night, I said, "Stone cold, those guys, stone cold." Whatever the reason, there was a chill and Edgar didn't like being rebuffed. It became a case of "if the girl doesn't want me, I'll really pursue her." Enter, once again, Mark Millard, the investment banker who had arranged the purchase and sale of Texas Pacific. He was known for his expertise in energy-related matters. On his advice, Seagram began buying shares in Conoco.

It turns out Dome was only a slice of the story, and a bit player at that. Edgar's pilots happened to hear air-traffic radio chatter that kept mentioning Wilmington, Delaware, where the headquarters of DuPont was located. It was hardly complex spadework, but it led us to the correct conclusion that DuPont was also interested in Conoco. My assessment of Ralph Bailey and the board was right. They didn't want us, and Bailey was looking for a white knight. He'd found one in DuPont, which had also started buying shares in Conoco. It was now a battle between Seagram and DuPont for control of Conoco. At the end of the day, DuPont was victorious, having bought more than fifty per cent of Conoco's stock. On September 30, 1981, the deal closed—a $7.8 billion cash and stock transaction, until then the biggest business deal in U.S. history.

But Seagram wasn't out of it by any means, and an offer by DuPont to anyone who held Conoco shares turned out to be our back-door entrance. Any party holding Conoco shares—and Seagram had a fistful—could now trade them in for DuPont shares. And so that's what we did, and we had enough of a holding in Conoco to secure, through the share swap, a twenty per cent interest in DuPont, which would make us its largest shareholder. That stake would soon grow to twenty-five per cent after DuPont did a share buyback to reduce the amount of stock outstanding, a way to increase earnings per share.

Interestingly, the du Pont family was no longer in the picture as a controlling unit. The question then arose among us: Do they really want to replace one family with another? I recall going to Mark Millard's office and saying, "They don't want us, so what do you think they're going to offer us" to go away? The North Sea division, given that Conoco had oil there? Perhaps one of the DuPont divisions, like agricultural chemicals? What will they offer to get rid of us? To my surprise, Mark said he didn't think they'd offer us anything but would want to keep us as a hedge (protection) against DuPont being bought by somebody else.

He was right. That's exactly what they wanted. Soon the call came from Ed Jefferson, the chairman and CEO of DuPont, inviting Edgar and me to visit with him in Wilmington. He told us he wanted us to agree to a "standstill," an agreement that we would not purchase any more stock in DuPont. I was in high dudgeon and grumpily said that this was a free world, and why would anyone want a standstill? I said that it wasn't in our interest and that obviously DuPont had no confidence in us. Jefferson was a Brit who had been with DuPont his entire working life. Not only was he a gentleman, but he was astute, and he told us why he thought the standstill was precisely in our interest. It came down to the fact that the du Pont family was no longer a major shareholder. He argued that DuPont employees—there were more than 100,000 of them—worked for a very traditional company and would likely be scared of newcomers. We had to earn their trust, Jefferson said, and over time we could probably become in the eyes of executives and employees the de facto controlling shareholders in the company.

Edgar and I were both convinced by what he said. John L. Weinberg, the head of Goldman Sachs at the time, negotiated the terms of the standstill, such as how many seats we'd have on the board, but one of the key points was that we would vote with management. I took on the role of chief liaison between Seagram and DuPont and set about learning the culture of the company, which was very particular. Loyalty was paramount. All the key executives lived in Wilmington, a smallish city. They were a tight group, I learned, and a lot of internal politics were glossed over by courteous behaviour.

Aside from absorbing the culture of the place, I really didn't have the foggiest about what DuPont really did. I didn't know what Mylar was, for instance. Let's put it this way: the spirits business was bred in the bone, whereas DuPont's business had to be grafted onto me. One of the ways we did the grafting: I visited several of their plants, including travelling deep into a coal mine by elevator, to study DuPont's operations.

Central to my role as chief liaison officer was being a member of the finance committee, which in Edgar's parlance was really the capital expenditure committee. If money was going to be spent on something, it went through the finance committee. It was there that I had the sheer delight of sitting next to, and getting to know, Crawford Greenewalt. He had married a du Pont, had become president of the company, then chairman, and finally chairman of the finance committee. He had also worked on the Manhattan Project, the code name for the secret assignment of scientists like Robert Oppenheimer and Enrico Fermi. Under the cloak of secrecy, they and their team had built the nuclear bombs that ended the Second World War. DuPont had worked on the Manhattan Project as well, not for profit, but rather for a symbolic fee of one dollar per year.

Greenewalt, in my view, with his great morality, wisdom, and personality, was the heart and soul of DuPont. Everyone held him in the highest regard. He never raised his voice, never cursed, and had a great fascination with hummingbirds. I once asked Ed Jefferson's successor, Ed Woolard, about people making proposals to the finance committee. "If Crawford coughs gently," I asked, "does that man or woman know he or she is in trouble?"

"Indeed, they do," was the answer.

What I did learn, however, was that DuPont was not a company that walked on water. When it goofed, it goofed big time. Case in point, the compact disc business. DuPont went into compact discs, and when we approved a particular expenditure, they projected a rate of return. I asked for a follow-up on that and we never got one (even though I asked, they never reported their internal rates of return after making projections to get finance committee approval). So we went into the CD business and we ended up selling it. I think the whole experience cost the company a billion dollars, so I called Ed Woolard and chastised him. He was chagrined. I think it was the only argument we ever had, but I wanted them to know that we were watching damn carefully. I liked them to know that, and Edgar liked them to know that.

All in all, though, our involvement with DuPont was fantastic. I was a good diplomat for Seagram with the senior people in Wilmington—others thought so, too—and they began to trust our company and me. We had five board seats filled by Edgar, me, Leo, John L. Weinberg from Goldman Sachs, and Edgar's son, Edgar Jr. DuPont also got two seats on Seagram's board. The great part of the deal was that we got hundreds of millions of dollars annually in dividends, and since the dividend was from one corporation to another, it was taxed under U.S. law at only seven per cent.

If there ever was a cash gusher for Seagram, it was DuPont. I told Edgar that our DuPont holding was Seagram shareholders' (and the family's) insurance policy against some jerk running our company into the ground. With this Edgar heartily agreed, even though the earnings were such that now a huge portion of Seagram's profits—three-quarters of them—were coming from the DuPont investment, a source outside of his direct control as CEO. That was not exactly my brother's style, but Edgar couldn't deny the cash flow or the panache provided by the DuPont stake.

At the time we had obtained our holding in DuPont, Edgar's son, Edgar Jr., was seemingly more interested in the entertainment business, and it appeared as though he wanted to forge his own path in an industry different from Seagram. He'd written songs and made films since his teenage years and seemed to be on a path that involved both of these art forms. Little did we know that path would eventually involve Seagram, and the end of Seagram. But at that time, Edgar Jr. seemed content to remain outside the family business, even though he later indicated publicly he had been destined to run Seagram.

In 1982, though, Edgar invited his son to come work for Seagram with an eye toward running it one day. By then, he understood Edgar Jr. to be disillusioned with Hollywood and wrote that he "already knew that Sam, his elder brother, would not be the next CEO (of Seagram). In fact, it was clear even when they were teenagers that the brilliant, tough-minded businessman in our family would be Efer (Edgar Jr.'s nickname). He is one of those rare individuals who instinctively understands the business world and always has his priorities in order."

My brother and I had already had a run-in during the previous decade on the subject of CEO succession at Seagram. In 1976, as Edgar himself acknowledged, I was disturbed by the company's balance sheet and the amount of debt we were carrying, somewhere in the neighbourhood of $300 million. Minda was upset as well, and it was perhaps at that time that she wanted to unseat Edgar. In any event, because of Edgar's marital problems during that period, he and I discussed looking for a new chief executive who could take us into the next century, and we went to John L. Weinberg to look into it. However, Edgar wrote that, as the months rolled by, he decided he would like to stay in the corner office to run Seagram as it should be run.

"During a quiet dinner in Montreal with Charles, I told him that I really didn't want to give up my birthright. I was enjoying life at Seagram, I said, and felt ready to guide the corporation myself. I suggested instead of looking for a CEO, we should look for a COO. Charles replied that if this was my honest intent, he would readily agree. So we shifted gears."

What a fork in the road and what a bad turn we made. Again, I had acquiesced to Edgar, a pattern that was a lifetime in the making, a pattern I couldn't shake, and a pattern that I would live to regret. The COO, or chief operating officer, we hired was Phil Beekman. Although Phil was a terrific executive, fundamentally our decision was flawed because we should have hired a non-family CEO. I was taken in by Edgar's real desire to retain the CEO position. When Edgar Jr. finally came to work for Seagram, he began as an assistant to Beekman, a position from where he'd be tutored.

The next bad turn was solely Edgar's work. In an interview with *Fortune* in 1986, without having informed the board or me—his partner—Edgar announced to the world that Edgar Jr. would eventually be his successor as CEO of Seagram. Setting aside what this meant for his eldest son, Sam, it was a clear violation of boardroom protocol.

"Edgar had no right to do that," Leo said declaratively in his book and went on to fulminate about it at length: "'Charles,' I said, 'he seems like a nice young man. But . . . [he] has no college education for the very kind of complex world we now live in. To the best of my knowledge he knows nothing about finance or money, and if you allow this to happen, you will look back someday and say it's the biggest single mistake you made in your life.'" Leo then wrote that I have occasionally reminded him of what he said. Leo deserves credit for saying what he did. Certainly the point was made that we were all shocked and deeply troubled by Edgar's pronouncement. For sure, Leo was against it—but I said to him the die is cast, let's see how he does.

After his three-month stint as Beekman's assistant, Phil thought Edgar Jr. should be the head of Seagram Europe, which is where he went, and he was successful there. Next, he ran the House of Seagram, which was the U.S. sales business, our biggest division. Although he did not have the from-the-ground-up training in the business that his father and I had experienced, to his credit he did well in the spirits and wine business. The numbers were good and he had some good executives with him, namely Ed McDonnell, a blunt, Boston Irish-Catholic who was his backstop in Europe. McDonnell, by the way, says that he had not been informed Edgar Jr. would be running Seagram Europe—until Edgar Jr. shocked him with the news on a flight to London.

"I had to hire a new guy to run Europe," Ed recounts. "And on the plane, (Edgar Jr. said,) 'What are you going to do over here?'"

"I'm going to find a guy to run the company, in Europe," Ed said.

To which, according to Ed, Edgar Jr. responded, "You are? Didn't my father talk to you?"

Asked what he meant, Edgar Jr. replied, "I'm going to run Europe."

For those who worked closely with him, according to Rod McQueen's account in *The Icarus Factor*, Edgar Jr.'s heart never seemed to be in the liquor business. I disagree. Edgar Jr. came in with very good numbers year after year when the liquor business was his responsibility. Despite running two large divisions of the company well, for me, it was hard enough to accept him in the lead role of the company. However, for a hardscrabble guy like Leo, who had come up the hard way and proven himself over decades without having the surname Bronfman, it was unpalatable.

"Edgar was mesmerized by his son. There is no other way to describe it. Edgar Jr. is a very nice man, very diffident, a good listener and not a show-off in any sense of the word. He is anything but stupid. But he had no business running Seagram, and if he hadn't been named Bronfman, he wouldn't have been," Leo wrote.

When the story appeared in *Fortune* in March 1986 saying that at some point in the future Edgar Jr. would become CEO of the entire company, I was in Florida and sat there fuming, with my stomach churning, and didn't say a word for thirty days. I should have jumped on a plane right then and there and put a stop to what became the inevitable, but old patterns die hard. Truth be told, I froze.

Tall, handsome, and soft-spoken, Edgar Jr. was just two months shy of turning thirty-one years old when my brother made the succession plan known to the world. He had been born in 1955, the year Edgar moved to New York, and would become CEO of Seagram in 1994. Of course, Edgar Jr. says that when he was just a teenager, our father, Sam, recognized him as "the one" to lead Seagram one day. He tells the story of what he remembers Dad (whom he calls "Poppa") saying to him at a family gathering. It's an excerpt from an interview with Edgar Jr. in *Whisky Man*.

He did when he was dying say something to me. And I'm not sure I ever told my father. Poppa made a toast about what he built and how he built it for his family . . . so I made a toast back to him that basically said, thank you Poppa for all that you've done for us and for the family and for working so hard so that all of us can do with our lives what we would like to do with our lives . . . But it was also a way of saying to him, not so fast. We'll decide for ourselves what we're going to do with our lives and money. When we left dinner and we were going to the library or sunroom which is where we would always go after dinner, he walked by me, and as he walked by me, he just looked at me, I remember he just looked at me and he said, "you're the one."

In addition to speaking inappropriately to *Fortune*, Edgar said the following at a public meeting: "The critical part of the job of every CEO is to train the successor. This I started doing at Edgar's birth." In 1989, at the age of thirty-four, Edgar Jr. had been named president and COO, and by 1994, at the age of thirty-nine, he was elevated to CEO. My brother remained overseer, with the title of executive chairman, while I was co-chairman, a title that turns out to have been utterly meaningless. For many years, I'd had no involvement in day-to-day company operations and stayed in Canada until the end of 1996.

By the early 1990s, the word *boring* started to come up in the same sentence as DuPont—not just from Edgar Jr., but from my brother. As Arnie Ludwick (the former president of Claridge and a Seagram VP) said, "I gotta believe those guys (Edgar Sr. and Jr.) fell asleep at the (DuPont) board meetings," adding that to stay awake, you had to be interested in chemicals, Lycra, and titanium dioxide.

It could be argued that I stayed in Montreal too long rather than moving to New York, where I would have had a better feel for where the company was headed under their leadership. However, until 1991, I still had the Expos and I also didn't think I could leave Montreal while our mother was still alive. She lived until 1995. More and more, I was peripheral, it seems. Rather than it being Edgar and me as equal partners, I now felt it was two against one. Edgar and his son were operating tongue in groove, and I would discover that my views barely merited consideration.

Aside from being boring, Edgar Jr.'s argument about DuPont was that it was old. He maintained that companies in the S&P 500 that were more than a hundred years old began to lose their edge and fall into decline. His argument might have had some truth to it. Certainly, many household names in corporate America have not lasted. As dominant as they once were, companies like Kodak and Pan American Airways have faded from the scene. But to consider a divestiture from one of the greatest names in American corporate history, you have to assess the fundamentals and how they compared with the fundamentals of the movie business. For that matter, did the movie business have any fundamentals at all? Seagram had a great connection with DuPont. It was an unassailable company which could change—and had changed—direction when necessary. To me, it was not going to be like one of the aforementioned companies that faltered.

Edgar Jr.'s other concern was that our arrangement with DuPont was coming up for renegotiation in 1997, and he was of the view that the negotiations would be difficult. I did not share his opinion. In fact, I thought the negotiations would be easy, figuring we could extend the standstill while at the same time enjoying a fair amount of well-earned influence. Put it this way: I was happy with all aspects of the arrangement we had with DuPont and wasn't going to push for anything more. I indicated this strongly in a meeting with the two Edgars.

Another situation soon arose that, in retrospect, created something of a smokescreen for the DuPont divestiture plans. In 1995, Edgar was uncomfortable about Conoco getting involved in a deal with Dubai to develop oil fields in Iranian waters, concerned that the exposure there might tilt the company toward the Arab states, away from Israel. At the very least, the optics were not good, not only for Jewish business people like Edgar and me, but also for the United States. Conoco had a business relationship with Israel through Consol—the Consolidated Coal Co.—from which the Jewish state had been buying a significant amount of coal.

To be honest, the whole thing made me nervous, too, underlined by the fact that Moammar Gadhafi nationalized Conoco's interests in Libya. However, in 1998, three years after we sold DuPont, Edgar wrote that there was no connection between Conoco's Iran deal and the divestiture. Looking back, it seemed like a decoy. The real scheming was going on elsewhere. I felt it in my bones that discussions were going on about the fate of our stake in DuPont to which I was not privy. My suspicions were confirmed when Edgar went on to write that the sale of DuPont was two years in the making and that Seagram had engaged Boston Consulting to assess DuPont's long-term prospects. Edgar wrote that Edgar Jr.'s "belief was confirmed by the Boston Group's analysis. . . . DuPont's growth would be limited by the very nature of its business: the manufacturing of commodities." I knew they were studying the efficiency of the spirits business; I do not recall being told they were looking at DuPont. This was, to my mind, a betrayal. Here I was, co-chairman, chairman of the executive committee, and chief liaison officer, and I felt like I was left out of the loop.

Although we hadn't yet moved to New York, we had a suite at the St. Regis Hotel. Edgar Jr. came to visit very quickly late on a Friday afternoon and told us he was going to Japan to talk to Matsushita, the owners of MCA, which owned the Hollywood studio Universal and other entertainment divisions, which included music and theme parks. I thought it was a lark and said okay. The fact that he was going alone should have been a red flag. With no advisors, who knows what could have happened. It's a bit like saying, "Don't worry, fellas, I'm taking the space shuttle for a spin by myself and I'll be back in a couple of days. I've never been to outer space, but I'll be fine."

The chief financial officer of Seagram at the time was Steve Banner. I strongly suspect they had asked Banner (a fine human being who has since passed away) to run all the numbers on Universal well beforehand, because obviously Edgar Jr. had an appointment. My sense is that it had gone on for more than a year. I was supposedly my brother's partner, but I had been told none of it, my opinion had never been sought. However, looking back, I should have added up the fact that Edgar had tried to get into the movie business in the 1960s through MGM, that his son had dabbled in it early in his work life, and now here they were, back at it again. However, when they finally told me they wanted to sell DuPont, I was shocked. We had had several discussions about it in which I was always against it. I asked them, "If you sell DuPont, where are you going to invest the money?" I was told straight up, "We don't know."

Edgar Jr. will say that I was informed and kept up to date continually. That may have been true, but it was by the back of the hand. Was I informed and kept up to date continually? Perhaps. But there's a huge difference between being informed and being consulted. Had the latter happened, perhaps things might have been much different. Leo described how Edgar Jr. came to Palm Beach in March of 1995 to brief the two of us on his bid for MCA, which clearly meant our DuPont holding was a goner. On April 6, 1995, it was announced that Seagram was selling its stake in DuPont. Three days later, Seagram announced it was buying MCA.

"And what did we get for our one-quarter interest in one of the greatest industrial companies in the world? A second-rate movie studio. Buying DuPont was the deal of the century . . . selling DuPont was the dumbest deal of the century," Leo wrote.

Edgar published his recollection of my conversation with him about selling DuPont in order to buy MCA.

"I thought as we got older we were supposed to get closer and be better friends," he (Charles) said.

"Well, that's what's happening," I replied.

"No, it isn't," said Charles.

"What are you talking about?" I asked.

"MCA."

"All right, Charles," I said. "Now the rules are that if you say 'no,' we don't do it. Did you ever say no?"

"Well, no, but . . ."

"Charles, did you ever say no?"

"No. I didn't want to start a family feud."

"There probably would have been one, but if you had said no, we wouldn't have made the deal. Now stop it. We've already made the deal. Let's get on with it."

✳

True, I didn't say no, and true, I didn't want to start a family war. But one might argue that my brother should not have put me in a position where I had to choose between denying him what he and his son wanted and my trepidation about starting a family war.

Edgar went on to write that the MCA purchase was to his son what the DuPont investment had been to him, "a huge, controversial deal that transformed and dramatically expanded Seagram," adding that the difference was that Seagram controlled MCA, which was not the case with DuPont. One might say my brother was also a bit too hasty in declaring the MCA acquisition a winner. He wrote that it "utterly altered the destiny of Seagram and we have Efer (Edgar Jr.) to thank for it." Well, yes, it did alter the company's destiny, but not in the way he meant it at the time. And yes, we certainly do have Edgar Jr. to thank for altering the destiny of Seagram, but again not in the way my brother meant it.

And then the capper from Edgar: "If Father were alive, he never would have approved the purchase. But things change in life. That's why when I was sixty-five, I said to Efer, 'I've had my turn, now it's yours.'" That's the crux of it. Here was the CEO of a publicly traded company saying to his handpicked successor—his son—that he could do whatever he wanted with shareholder money because *his* father hadn't let him do what *he* wanted to do.

Indeed, Dad would never have approved. There's a quote in Leo's book about just how furious Dad was when he found out Edgar wanted to get into the movie business in the 1960s.

"I don't want you in the goddamned movie business. We've got whisky. We've got real estate. We've got oil. What the hell else do you want?"

Yes, it may be said that I could have exercised my veto. And that's true. But here's what's also true. One day in my brother's office with Edgar and Edgar Jr., I said, "Okay, here's what I'm willing to do. I'm willing to sell down our DuPont stake from twenty-five per cent to twenty per cent, and I'm willing to devote the next three years of DuPont dividends to anything you want to buy—but you don't lose DuPont and you don't lose Seagram." To this day, I think that was a fair and equitable proposition. From my point of view, that was saying no. In fact, on July 24, 2002, more than seven years later and after another calamity, I wrote an email to Edgar saying, "I well recall telling you one time that the DuPont shares were an insurance policy for our family and the Seagram shareholders against someone at the helm of Seagram doing something foolish. Unfortunately, I was bang on! With all the ups and downs since that time, mostly downs, my deep regret is that I failed to make either you or Efer see that light."

My mistake was that I was trying to fight the two of them by myself. I should have armed myself with allies I had on the board like Leo, Paul Desmarais, Bill Davis, Matt Barrett, Marie-Josée Kravis, and others, knowing that the two Edgars would fight like hell.

"Charles should have gone public. There were some pretty honourable people on that board and they would have sup-ported Charles," says Ed McDonnell, who had become presi-dent of the Seagram Spirits and Wine Group. "I blame Charles for not doing enough. Charles is the only one that could have done something." I wasn't aware that I was the only one who could have done something. No one on the board asked if I was in favour of this, even though I'm sure they saw my body lan-guage. I was in a horrible state of emotional distress.

It's almost an article of faith that board members of family-dominated companies tend to vote with the family. I once asked my friend and fellow board member, the late Paul Desmarais, what he thought we should do about DuPont. I looked up to Paul, a brilliant entrepreneur and a wise man.

As recalled by Arnie Ludwick (the former president of Claridge and a Seagram VP), "Charles," Paul replied, "you've got so much more money at stake in this than anybody. Who should know what to do?"

As former Ontario premier Bill Davis, who was a Seagram director from 1985 to 1999, told McQueen for his book about Edgar Jr.'s demise, "My recollections at the board meetings was that while one might sense reservations by whoever, I don't recall ever hearing Charles say, 'I don't think we should be doing this.'" Davis was right. It was my cause to lead. Although the board members were great people and highly qualified, they sided with family. It really was a family affair, so it could only have been awkward to be a board member who was not a family member.

I could have abstained. I could have voted against. But I couldn't have voted against unless I had a majority of board members on my side. One might say I was derelict in my duty. But at the end of the day, the thought of a family war splashed all over the media in North America did me in. I voted yes. I don't think I ever said to myself, "This is the most important business decision you'll make in your life." I was a little bit lost, and I don't know why I didn't lean on Leo more. That was the time for our collaboration to really shine.

Leo, for his part, recalls he personally tried to break up the DuPont decision five or six times, including coming into my office and saying "Charles, don't you realize you have a veto?" He also recalls reporting to me that at a meeting he had with Edgar and Edgar Jr. in the Seagram private dining room in

New York, Edgar Jr. said flatly that if Charles doesn't want to sell DuPont, we won't sell it. Leo says I even set up the meeting, but asked him to go on my behalf. I don't remember this now. Did I miss these signals? Whatever the case, it seems I wasn't there when Leo was there and he wasn't there when I was there. We should have gone together.

I should have sought out Leo's help and together worked out a strategic plan and a business case for halting the sale of our investment in DuPont, explaining how it would have been the more intelligent move for our shareholders, our family, and our employees. We then should have gone to the other board members individually—most of whom I had appointed—and sought their votes at a board meeting. I would still not have avoided a family war, but the question is what kind of family war. Would Edgar Sr. have left? I doubt it. Would Edgar Jr. have left? Who knows? Perhaps by that point, Leo and I weren't as close as we had been. By then, he was a senator and was also travelling the world with retired prime minister Pierre Trudeau.

Others besides me had strong reservations about the deal but didn't come forward. I remember sitting in the boardroom when the "fairness opinion" was delivered about the sale of our DuPont shares. I had my head down between my knees and I wanted to throw up. We were selling the insurance policy. Leo remembers a meeting Edgar and his son arranged with four or five people from Goldman Sachs, including the late CEO John L. Weinberg and future U.S. Treasury secretary Robert Rubin, who was a senior Goldman executive in those days. According to Leo, the group from Goldman said it might not be a fabulous sale, but it would be an okay sale. It was hardly a ringing endorsement but enough for my brother and his son to do what they wanted. At the meeting to approve it, Leo describes going to the men's room, where Weinberg said to him in a raised voice, "Have we lost our fucking minds, Leo?"

"Have *we* lost *our* minds?" Leo fired back. "Your company did the goddamned study saying that the selling of the shares was not a bad deal—not necessarily a good deal, but not a bad deal."

I remember telling him, "Edgar, you have a fiduciary responsibility." But I couldn't bring myself to tell him I was going to the board. I just couldn't say it. If we'd had our heads screwed on, though, we should have gone out and hired the best damn non-family CEO to run the company and we'd co-chair it. That would have been rebuffed so fast, though, so I had a choice of either having a family war or of going along. And thus began the bad times between Edgar and me, bad times that lasted at least a decade.

You may wonder, aside from still being in Montreal, whether a burgeoning interest in philanthropy on my part had distracted me from what was going on at Seagram. The answer is no, never. But there's no question I should have moved to New York earlier. I wasn't like my brother, though. He was a hip-shooter and I wasn't. I move deliberately. Always have, always will.

On March 30, 1995, after DuPont had completed a restructuring, we recommended an offer to sell our twenty-five per cent stake in the company back to DuPont for $8.8 billion. DuPont agreed to take us up on the offer to reduce the shares outstanding, but also "because there was little point in holding onto an investor whose heart was elsewhere," at least according to the company's history. A year later, DuPont's net earnings set a new record of $3.6 billion, but by then, we were no longer shareholders, so we wouldn't be beneficiaries of the increase in profit. On April 9, 1995, three days after announcing Seagram's sale of its DuPont stake, Edgar Jr. led the purchase of eighty per cent of MCA from Matsushita (now Panasonic) for $5.7 billion.

A year later, MCA, which dated back to 1924 as Music Corporation of America, was reincorporated as Universal Studios, a company that produced movies, music, and television programming and owned theme parks. It was a galaxy away from Tyvek, Teflon, Kevlar, and nylon, and a universe apart from Crown Royal and V.O. Dad would have hit high C. Unfortunately, there would be much more to come.

Although I did not expressly oppose or veto the MCA acquisition, where I finally did put my foot down was over the proposed compensation package Edgar Jr. was considering paying super-agent Michael Ovitz as his new head of MCA. At its peak, what Ovitz was being offered was worth as much as $240 million. Fred Goodman, in his book *Fortune's Fool,* wrote: "Ovitz seemed unable to take yes for an answer, and negotiations dragged out as he piled on demands for stock options, planes, limousines, offices and anything else he could think of." The guy was an agent, and a damn good one, but he'd never been the boss of a massive entertainment company. What he wanted was beyond belief, and way beyond anything anyone qualified would charge to do the job. Leo and I were on the compensation committee and were both appalled.

"Charles, I don't care what you think, I'm telling you right now I'm voting against this," Leo wrote. With Leo's backing, I vetoed it. I called Edgar Jr. on a weekend and said, "You're not going to do it." Instead, he hired Ron Meyer, who turned out to be a good person and an able executive.

In the normal business of business, there's a salary scale. In the movie business, it's irrational. Let's say you're the controller of a company and you make $200,000, whereas a controller in the movie business might make $900,000. So how the hell do you compare the levels of jobs? The PR person at Universal might have been paid something like $800,000, whereas the Seagram PR person might have been making $200,000 at the time. I'm flabbergasted, however, that when speaking to Charlie Rose in March of 2001, Edgar Jr. took credit for nixing the Ovitz deal.

"It was *I* who said I can't live with this. The family was very supportive of hiring Mike—very uncomfortable with the package he was asking for, but supportive and would have gone along had I said, 'No, I want this man to run the business.'"

He was dreaming in Technicolor, as they used to say. What was it about Edgar Jr.? He was skilled at the art of persuasion. He would come to me and tell me what a wonderful guy I was and deride his father to win my approval. He had this way about him, a soft-spoken voice that lulled you, a winning demeanour, he was handsome and tall, and he gave off an air that he knew what he was doing.

Our relationship most certainly took a rocky turn when I finally moved to New York and my brother tried to keep me off our corporate executive floor in the Seagram Building, as I was not part of senior management. Ultimately, I got the office I wanted. After I was in New York a couple of years, though, Edgar Jr. came into my office and said, "The toughest part of my job is you—'cause you're against everything I'm trying to do in this company."

"In that case, young man, you've got the easiest job in the world, so get the hell out of here and go back to work," I said.

In March of 2015, DuPont shares hit a high of $80.50. We sold our holding for $8.8 billion in 1995. Had we kept that stake, it would have doubled, not counting the hundreds of millions in dividends we would have received each year for the last twenty years—meaning at least six or seven billion more, taxed at just seven per cent. That does not include the fact that the dividend almost doubled over that period. All in, Seagram's DuPont holding would have been worth well north of twenty billion dollars. Once we sold, though, the company had lost its cash cow and was then on the path to losing the farm.

Knowing deep down that the situation had changed for the worse, I refused to fly to California to celebrate the MCA deal with my brother and his son, giving up a chance to sit down with the last of the legendary Hollywood moguls, Lew Wasserman, who'd run MCA for decades. Later, however, after the deal had been done, I met Wasserman at a Los Angeles hotel and he donated five million dollars over five years to Birthright Israel, the initiative that would become perhaps my proudest philan-thropic venture.

But why did Edgar let his son sell DuPont? Did it really all come back to Edgar's refrain that Dad never let him do what *he* wanted to do? I didn't care. My view was that Dad made all the money, so let him do what he wants—not that our father was right all the time, but he had earned the right to be wrong. Edgar had this huge hang-up that our father never said those three little words—I love you. Well, Dad never said them to me, either, but I knew he loved me and I loved him. I was scared of Sam Bronfman, but it didn't mean I didn't love him. Dad was my ultimate defender, that's how I knew he loved me.

In 1939, I went to Camp Winnebago in Maine and I loved

it. By 1940, there were currency controls in Canada and I couldn't go back to an American camp paid for in American dollars. There was a teacher at Selwyn House who had a camp in the Laurentians called Lac Louis. So I went there instead of Maine and experienced real anti-Semitism at that camp. I was about nine when I called my father in tears. He came to the camp himself and picked me up and took me home. Normally, they would have sent the chauffeur. That's an example of how I knew he loved me.

As for Edgar's criticisms that Dad didn't know accounting—nonsense. He made a gazillion effing dollars. Who built the company from nothing? Who got us into the oil business? Who figured it all out? But Edgar believed, to his dying day, that Dad didn't love him. There's the clip near the end of *Whisky Man* where Edgar breaks down over not hearing those three words. That's where it's all at, and what led him to indulge his son. And yet, in a way, I always loved Edgar. When we were kids, he was my protector. When we were adults, he took on the responsibility of running the company and made a lot of money for us by selling Texas Pacific and then investing in DuPont. He deserves full marks for all of that.

As for whether he loved me, I think he did. But did he respect me? No, he most certainly did not. He didn't think I was very much in my younger years, and I wasn't, but as is often the case with family members, he didn't realize that I had grown up and had become a man. The game was over by then, though. Meanwhile, his son famously said in public at an analyst conference that he "wasn't going to be the one to piss away the family fortune." All we had to do was wait a few more years. The stage had been set.

6

Selling Seagram: Losing the Farm

———

I should have known. Edgar had flirted with the movie business in 1968 by investing in MGM. His son, however, was different than his father. He was legitimately interested in the entertainment business, particularly music, having penned songs under pseudonyms like Junior Miles and Sam Roman. Catching the bug from his father, in his mid-teens he started working on movies, living with the family of David Puttnam in England, and then in his late twenties, producing a film called *The Border* that starred Jack Nicholson. In retrospect, he should have stayed in that business and stayed away from Seagram, but he was lured into the family store by my brother. Edgar Jr. didn't go to university and tried to make a go of it in show business. That combination, along with good looks and a persuasive manner, seemed to hypnotize my brother.

"Edgar's fatal flaw was his hero worship of Edgar Jr," Leo wrote. I agree with him.

Such a spell, coupled with my brother's predilection for the glitz of the entertainment industry, should have been a huge clue to me about where we were all headed. But seeing the future and seeing the past are two different things.

It's a legendary quote from an unnamed Hollywood executive: "He's like a *piñata*. Hit him and money comes out." Another entertainment business player was quoted as saying, "The taking of Edgar is now a cottage industry." So reported *The New Yorker* in a now-famous profile of Edgar Jr. by Connie Bruck in May of 1998. It disturbs me greatly to repeat these, for two reasons. First, they're about my brother's son. Second, they're sad, but true.

Once the money from the DuPont sale was spent on MCA, soon to be renamed Universal, there were other purchases to come. The biggest came three years later, in 1998, when Seagram bought PolyGram from Koninklijke Philips for $10.4 billion. There were other smaller acquisitions as well, but the PolyGram purchase would be significant in a couple of respects. Yes, it was about music, which should have been Edgar Jr.'s area of expertise and should have secured long-term assets—if you've got great artists in your stable, their music lasts. However, few could predict the technological typhoon that would hit the music industry shortly after we purchased PolyGram.

For the record, in spite of the illegal downloading of music that would soon wallop the business, the PolyGram acquisition was one deal Edgar Jr. made that I thought made sense. We had Universal Music, and with PolyGram we would be number one in the world. Had we not owned Universal, I would not have been onside, but since we were already in that business, dominance should have been the goal. However, beyond most people's ability to forecast, something called Napster came along and changed the game forever. People were downloading music for free from the Internet, blowing a gaping hole in the industry's business model, to say the least. It was piracy of intellectual property. I remember Edgar Jr. being visibly worried about Napster, but I confess that I told him not to worry about it. I dismissed it. I told him that Napster would fail because the social fabric of the nation was that people paid for things; they didn't get them for free. I was wrong.

Then, there was debt. That was the part of the PolyGram deal that wasn't so good. As a result of the PolyGram purchase, Seagram had taken on more than four billion dollars in debt, doubling what we owed. As soon as you pile debt on, everything changes and any shocks to the global financial system—which seem to happen more and more frequently—send investors running for the cover of strong balance sheets. The acquisition took place in the same year as a couple of major scares in global financial markets, which resulted in a tightening of credit.

This was not the economy of my father's era, or even the era Edgar and I had operated in for most of our careers. It was now a tightly interwoven, electronic, global series of markets that could turn on and off like a switch. Billions moved across borders with the stroke of a key on a computer. Both the Russian debt crisis and the resulting pressures on a high-flying hedge fund that few understood led to a tightening of credit. Those with high debt loads were no longer the darlings financiers had once courted. Credit-rating agencies got out their pencils and adjusted their scores accordingly. Lower credit ratings meant higher interest payments, or in some cases, no more credit at all. The financial world had changed on a dime.

Seagram's weakened balance sheet meant we were not in a position to continue consolidating entertainment and media assets, at least as a buyer. But around us, the industry we were now a part of because of our Universal and PolyGram purchases was rapidly changing in another way. In January of 2000, as the dotcom wave was cresting, AOL and Time Warner announced plans to merge. By dollar value, it was the biggest deal in history. That got Edgar Jr. very nervous. He'd gone holus-bolus into media and entertainment and would now be a mid-sized fish when a whale was being created.

There's nothing like the fear of being left behind to make CEOs or investors scramble to respond with a deal of their own to show they're in synch with the times. But with the debt load and a technological revolution throwing the business model into disarray, Edgar Jr. had found himself, and the company, in a tricky spot. We were big but perhaps not big enough, and we certainly didn't have the wherewithal to bulk up anymore. That part of the plot had played out. The only thing to do was to merge with another company looking to get larger.

In this case, merging really meant selling our stake in Seagram for a stake in Vivendi (although I didn't really think that would mean we would get out of the liquor business). Edgar Jr.'s plan conveniently aligned with an increasing willingness on the part of both my side of the family and Edgar's side of the family to consider selling our holdings. The fact is, after DuPont and MCA/Universal, I was upset and less interested. In particular, since the sale of DuPont, I felt of no importance to Edgar or his son. I consulted my children, Stephen and Ellen, and neither had any interest in working for the company, nor did they expect their children to be interested. They too were ready to go their own way.

For his part, my brother had seven children and twenty-two grandchildren. The family had become large and more dispersed. As Edgar Jr. expressed to Charlie Rose in March of 2001, "My father has always had the view, and I think he was right, that family control was not going to survive to the next generation . . . so the notion that this company was going to survive into the fourth generation of family leadership was highly unlikely."

For my part, I say "so what" to that. I've always marvelled at the rare family that can preserve its lineage in a business for generations—in the case of the du Pont family, hundreds of years. When we first invested, the du Pont family was no longer involved in management. Professionals had taken over from family, and the decision to use professional managers was the right approach. Too bad we took another route.

All told, though, there was an argument building to sell Seagram. There was the rapid shift in the entertainment industry because of the AOL–Time Warner deal, a deal that made Edgar Jr. hear footsteps. There was the debt. And there was the happy fact that Seagram shares were floating at all-time highs as the market peaked with the first Internet craze. The questions became: To whom should we sell, and at what price?

It turns out that there was someone—there's always someone—and that someone was a deal hound like no other: Jean-Marie Messier. Messier was another young CEO—a couple of years younger than Edgar Jr.—and he too got a case of the nerves when AOL and Time Warner announced their deal. Messier's company, Vivendi, had its roots in another business (water and sewage), and he and Edgar Jr. had other things in common. For starters, they were both charmers. While DuPont had bored my brother's son, the unglamorous business of pumping water and waste had bored Messier. Edgar Jr. also liked doing deals, but Messier was described as a shopaholic. It was almost fate that they found each other. The fact that Messier was Mr. Smooth should have been a clue. The fact that he was a serial acquirer with no fear of debt—a fatal attraction if there ever were one—should have been another.

By the year 2000, after six years with Messier at the controls, Vivendi's communication division accounted for just thirty-five per cent of the company's overall business, while the environment division (water and sewage) and other segments like construction and real estate made up the rest. Just 32,000 of its 290,000 employees worked in communications and media. Turning Vivendi into what would soon become Vivendi Universal—a communications- and media-focused giant—would be the equivalent of a corporate sex change, a bit like turning a liquor business into a communications company.

To be fair, Edgar Jr. was not the only one who would fall victim to Messier's charms. His smooth talk had also seduced leading French businesspeople. This was a man who signed his memos and emails "J2M" and was frequently the subject of fawning media coverage. Messier had worked his way up the French society pole by being a key advisor on privatizations at the French finance ministry. He then moved to investment banking at Lazard Frères, a leading French firm, where he moved swiftly from deal to deal. Embraced by the French elite who attended the right schools, in 1994, at just thirty-seven years of age, he became chairman and CEO of a water and sewage utility called Générale des Eaux that had been in operation since the mid-1800s. Suddenly, someone who had never even run a *division* of a major company was running a corporation with extraordinarily diverse global operations and a workforce of almost 300,000. He was also sitting on a handful of other major boards. Messier was the French *wunderkind* of the 1990s, the poster boy for the future, the kind who could lead France's business community globally beyond its myopic French-only view of the world. It would be a couple of more years before the emperor lost his clothes.

Before that, though, Messier would change the name of Générale des Eaux to Vivendi, a more modern, Internet-age moniker. Run-of-the-mill corporate jets with copious seating for a handful of executives would not be enough for Messier. Eventually, in addition to the Seagram fleet of aircraft he would pick up, the company would also use an Airbus A319, normally purchased by airlines to fly 120 passengers. The Airbus was outfitted luxuriously for executives—shower and all. The company would also pay $17 million for a Park Avenue apartment for Messier to use while in New York, a price that didn't include seven-figure renovations to bring it up to snuff. While I certainly had my issues with Edgar Jr., Messier was in a class all his own.

The nucleus of the deal between Edgar Jr. and Messier was that Vivendi did not have the cash to purchase Seagram shares, nor did we want cash. The family wanted a share swap in order to protect itself from a massive capital-gains liability on the appreciation of stock over decades. If we took their shares for our shares, we would be exempt.

Because Vivendi owned certain Internet-related assets— specifically, a portal called Vizzavi—its shares had run up to a ridiculous height along with other companies with exposure to the dotcom world. Vizzavi, a website that didn't make any money, had been valued by analysts at forty billion euros in the last days of the 2000 tech bubble. Vivendi was therefore strutting around with serious currency in its jeans, at least in the form of share value. The family, sadly, would be seduced by

Messier and what turned out to be his crummy stock.

According to the 706-page proxy statement filed with regulators in connection with the sale of Seagram to Vivendi, the first meeting between Edgar Jr. and Messier was at breakfast in Paris in October 1999. It was a discussion about industry developments with no discussion of combining the businesses. In mid-February 2000, after a Seagram board meeting at which consolidation in the media and entertainment industries was discussed alongside our company's strategy, Messier and the chairman and CEO of CANAL+ (a French pay-TV firm and the third company involved in the deal) asked Edgar Jr. to meet them in New York. On February 25 and 26, senior executives of the three companies met. Soon after, the companies had their advisors look at structures for a stock-to-stock business combination that would provide tax-free treatment and voting rights for Seagram shareholders.

On March 22, Messier made a preliminary presentation to the Bronfman family at the Seagram building. I was neutral on him—I didn't like him, I didn't dislike him. But I was not about to veto the deal. By April, exchange ratios—the amount one company's stock would be worth versus another—were discussed. Negotiations were underway. On June 4, Vivendi and Seagram entered into a confidentiality agreement, and by June 8, the exchange ratios for the share swap had been determined, including the extent of a "collar," which was designed to protect Seagram shareholders, but only up to a 12.5 per cent drop in the value of Vivendi's shares between the time the deal was announced and the time it closed, which would be six months later.

The collar was a type of insurance policy, but with limited

range. As long as Vivendi's shares between the time of the deal announcement and the closing were within a range of $96.69 and $124.34 U.S., Seagram shareholders would have their Seagram shares valued at $77.35, the deal's much-advertised buyout price. But if Vivendi's shares dropped below $96.69, the collar was no longer in effect, and Seagram shareholders would then receive less than $77.35. Conversely, if Vivendi's shares rose above $124.34 during the period, Seagram shares would be valued at higher than $77.35. Unfortunately, Vivendi's shares began a dramatic descent, busting through the bottom of the protective collar. From its high in the first quarter of 2000 to its low at the end of the fourth quarter on October 31, 2000, Vivendi's stock value fell by roughly one-half. For Seagram shareholders, at the time the deal was announced on June 20, 2000, a value of $77.35 on their stock looked absolutely mouthwatering. Seagram's all-time high was $64.50, meaning the Vivendi offer constituted a 19.9 per cent premium—hard to resist. At the time, the C. Bronfman Family Trust, which consisted of four entities, had 41,286,760 shares of Seagram, worth roughly $3.2 billion. In addition, two charitable foundations for which I was the voting trustee and director owned a combined 3,334,164 shares, worth approximately $258 million. At that point, Edgar controlled more shares (60,104,604) through his trust. His side of the family had more than mine (this fluctuated over the years), in part because my side had sold some $400 million worth of stock in the late 1990s.

By June 13, news reports began appearing that talks were in the final stages of an agreement, leading to Vivendi and Seagram issuing press releases the next day to say that they were indeed negotiating but had not reached an agreement. On June

19, Goldman Sachs and Morgan Stanley delivered oral opinions at a special meeting of the Seagram board, stating that the exchange ratio in the agreement was fair. I cringed. We were now on an unstoppable train and Seagram was about to disappear with it. As with DuPont, it was at this point that I again put my head between my knees.

The board agreed and determined that it would recommend to shareholders to vote in favour of the arrangement. As with the DuPont sale, I did not oppose this. Transaction agreements were executed, and on the morning of June 20, 2000 (ironically, the wedding anniversary of Sam and Saidye Bronfman and the birthday of Edgar Bronfman Sr.), Seagram, Vivendi, and CANAL+ announced to the world they were combining. The purchase price of Seagram shares was 32.458 billion euros, while the purchase price of CANAL+ was 12.388 billion euros. Translated, Seagram was sold for between $34 billion and $35 billion, the price fluctuating somewhat due to currency movements and share ratios. Adding in the assumption of $8 billion in debt by Vivendi, the total deal price was approximately $42 billion. Including the CANAL+ purchase, the whole transaction was valued at approximately $60 billion. If Edgar's dictatorial announcement in *Fortune* that his son would be CEO was the "beginning of the beginning," and the sale of DuPont was the "beginning of the end," this was indeed the end, or close to it. We just didn't know it yet. When *Titanic* hit the iceberg on that beautiful night, the passengers probably had no idea that the ship was doomed.

Speaking after the announcement on June 20, Edgar Jr. said, "Today is my father's birthday and I can think of no better present that I could give to my father, his children, his grandchildren, and his great-grandchildren than this world-beating company that we are creating today."

Two-thirds of Seagram shareholders had to vote in favour of the deal for it to pass. At that point, the Bronfmans' holding amounted to twenty-four per cent of the company. The second biggest shareholder was Philips N.V., with approximately eleven per cent of the outstanding shares, a vestige of Seagram's purchase of PolyGram when Philips took Seagram stock as part of the deal. A registered shareholder could dissent and have received fair value for shares. Vivendi Universal ADSs (American depository shares) would be listed under the ticker symbol "V" on the New York Stock Exchange and under "VUE" on the Toronto Stock Exchange.

At that point, Seagram had four business segments: Universal Music, the world's largest recorded music company; filmed entertainment, which included Universal Pictures; recreation (including the theme parks); and Seagram Spirits and Wine, which would be sold. Vivendi Universal's board would be slightly reduced to eighteen directors (from twenty), five of whom would come from Seagram, including three family members as long as the Bronfmans maintained at least seventy-five per cent of our investment in the new company.

Messier had a minuscule amount of skin in the game. According to the proxy, Vivendi's directors and executive officers and their affiliates owned approximately one-twentieth of one per cent of the outstanding Vivendi shares.

Vivendi, meanwhile, was an indebted company. At the end of its 1999 fiscal year, it had U.S.$1.3 billion in net cash and almost $22 billion in net debt, according to regulatory filings. By June 30, 2000, in the pro forma financials laid out in the proxy statement, Vivendi's total liabilities were almost $52 billion, with shareholder equity of just $16.7 billion—a highly leveraged balance sheet.

Seagram's balance sheet was nothing to brag about, either. By then, in the wake of the PolyGram purchase, the company had total liabilities of close to $18.5 billion and shareholder equity of $12.8 billion. As for CANAL+, it had lost money in both 1998 and 1999 and also had more net debt than shareholders' equity. For sure, Seagram had married down.

It was also a complex deal—a three-company merger involving very different businesses, with a moving price target in a world that was getting weary of complexity. Within two years, there were two high-profile scandals involving byzantine companies in the United States. Both Enron and WorldCom would go up in smoke because of accounting fraud, making investors even more suspicious of companies whose concepts couldn't be explained or had presented mind-numbingly complicated financial reports. Vivendi Universal would report its results using French generally accepted accounting principles (GAAP), and then, for U.S. reporting purposes, reconcile those to American GAAP—one more layer for investors to scrutinize.

As for the "risk factors" inherent in the deal, they were outlined in the proxy statement and are frequently boilerplate inserted into such documents. The first one read: "Seagram shareholders may receive Vivendi Universal ADSs or exchangeable shares having a trading price *of less than* U.S.$77.35 per Seagram common share." I wonder how many of us read that and considered less valuable Vivendi shares to be a real possibility. As for the other nineteen major risk factors cited, none seemed to foreshadow the risk of an uncontrollable, deal-junkie chairman and CEO like Messier, who would go on to make tens of billions' worth of additional rapid-fire acquisitions. It's hard to believe, but the AOL-Time Warner merger in 2000 would set off a whole new level of lunacy at Vivendi. Fearful that it would be left in the dust, Messier, together with Seagram and CANAL+, were racing to stay in the communications game.

The ink was barely dry on the agreement before the hemor-rhaging began. By the time the deal was set to close in December, Vivendi's stock had fallen, and the deal price of $77.35 per Seagram share had fallen to $57. The collar wasn't enough—it only protected us against a 12.5 per cent drop; after that, we were on our own. That was both emotionally and financially important to me. We were also bound to hold on to our shares for at least ninety days after the deal closed, a period known as a lockup. By the time of the shareholder vote in December, I was a wreck, seeing the value of our holding evaporate by the day. Dad hadn't built the business to see it disappear. Hell, Edgar and I hadn't continued to build it with investments like DuPont to see the whole enterprise begin to vanish into some pipe dream.

Once the lockup expired on March 8, 2001, and we were free to sell (Vivendi shares closed that day at 72.85 euros, equal to U.S.$67.84), I couldn't bring myself to do it. For starters, the stock was below the deal price, but it was also simply too emotional for me to let go, so we did it over time, which was very painful. On May 29, though, Edgar's family sold just over a billion dollars' worth and the Claridge Foundation, associated with my side of the family, sold just under one hundred million dollars' worth at 76.94 euros per share, equivalent to U.S.$66.65 each.

After the shares tumbled, Edgar Jr., rubbing salt in the

wound in an interview with *Fortune* in 2002, said that "the Charles side of the family" had difficulty taking responsibility for its actions and could have sold all of its position at $65 or $70. True, we could have sold more then, like his side did. In fact, we did sell a large chunk of our holdings, via several transactions through the remainder of 2001, at prices ranging from almost 77 euros down to 49—i.e., from the mid-60s to the low 40s in U.S. dollars. It was, however, 2002 that hurt us the most. In a series of sales, we sold a massive amount of stock at prices between approximately 10 and 17.50 euros. We sold all the way down. I remember sitting in meetings with my family, saying, "We can't sell, we can't sell, it's going to go up." My son-in-law Andrew Hauptman—Ellen's husband—was getting advice from the late Richie Metrick at Bear Stearns, who kept telling us to sell earlier.

"Alan Schwartz (who would later become CEO of Bear Stearns) and Richie were advising the family, and Richie was calling me daily and was very vocal about selling," Andrew says. "His team had run the numbers and his team had seen the writing on the wall."

When the stock dropped to roughly thirty dollars, we were finally prepared to do so. Montreal lawyer Sam Minzberg was running Claridge at the time and had become my representative on the Vivendi board after I'd attended just one board meeting. I thought Sam could stand up for my interests better than I could. Eventually, he would confront Messier. At this point, though, Sam advised us against selling because he thought that, despite his pit bull–like questioning of Messier at meetings, things might turn around. I don't blame Sam; I could have overruled him. The decision to sell or not was ultimately mine.

The truth is, I was emotionally depressed and couldn't think as clearly as I should have. It was my fault. We should have sold sooner.

In the boardroom and in the executive offices at Vivendi Universal, there were other kinds of problems. The agreement was that Edgar Jr. would be executive vice-chairman of the newly created company—Messier's number two. On *Charlie Rose* in March of 2001, Edgar's son put on a happy face, telling the interviewer that his relationship with Messier had strengthened in the days leading up to the closing of the deal and since the closing, describing it as "very strong, we trust each other, we listen to each other, we work together extremely well."

The truth is that, right from the get-go, Edgar Jr. was marginalized. This was particularly galling given that the family was the largest shareholder in the company. The deal to buy Seagram and CANAL+ had cost Vivendi sixty billion dollars. Not long after we merged, the deal junkie was at it again, spending 2.4 billion euros to acquire a thirty-five per cent stake in the phone company in Morocco—Maroc Telecom—without telling Edgar Jr. That was wrong.

The Maroc Telecom deal was just the beginning of the deal-a-minute atmosphere, which included buying publishing house Houghton Mifflin in May 2001 and other companies, like MP3.com, picked up on the fly as more and more cash went out the door. The publishing purchase left Edgar Jr. "cold," according to authors Jo Johnson and Martine Orange in their book about Messier. "It effectively reversed his 1996 decision to quit the publishing business with the sale of MCA's general fiction arm" to Pearson. There was also the issue of culture shock, not to mention complexity. Here were two French companies, Vivendi and CANAL+, combining with Seagram, an American company largely controlled by a Canadian family or ex-Canadians. An ocean is a vast separator, not only when it comes to communications, but also in the way things are done. It was also an exceedingly intricate transaction, involving three companies, not two. In addition, it required a significant sale of assets—the liquor business. That alone is a big job, all set against a rapidly moving, technologically evolving entertainment business. To pull all of that off, you need superstars at the top. We did not have anyone close.

Messier's personal behaviour also turned us off. The Seagram art collection was a marvellous achievement, comprising thousands of pieces meticulously and studiously collected over decades, with the intimate involvement and inspiration of my sister Phyllis. Enter Jean-Marie Messier, who seemed to think he could choose from it at will. He tried to move *Brown and Black in Reds* by Mark Rothko from a public place in the Seagram Building to the apartment Vivendi had rented for him. When we protested, he put it in his office instead. J2M was soon known as J6M—Jean Marie-Messier, *moi-même, maître du monde*, or "Jean-Marie Messier, me, myself, master of the world." That stunning art collection, by the way, was auctioned off in a highly publicized event at Christie's in New York in the spring of 2003.

"The summer that I heard that Seagram was to be sold to Vivendi, I mourned all summer. I really mourned . . . I mourned to see something that was built and responsible and had a great sense of culture go up in thin air. Just be dissolved, that was why I mourned," Phyllis said around the time of the auction in an interview with *Venture,* a CBC Television business magazine program. She was right, and I felt similarly. We were Bronfmans and we were Seagram. The two were almost inextricable. From when I was a kid, I'd go into homes or restaurants and note what brands of whisky they had. It was in our DNA. And it was also a helluva business, in spite of changes in drinking habits, which wax and wane like the tides. If you don't sell a twelve-year-old whisky, it stays in the barrels, and soon it's an eighteen-year-old whisky and it commands a higher price. Phyllis sold the balance of her Seagram shares two months before the Vivendi deal closed.

Both Edgar Jr. and Messier were young to be CEOs. In Messier's case, he took over Vivendi at thirty-seven and was forty-four when he bought Seagram. Edgar Jr. was just two years older but like Messier had become CEO in 1994, when he was thirty-nine. Setting aside the basic issue of having the right qualifications and realizing this might sound like the rumination of an old geezer, there is something to be said for having a few wrinkles and battle scars. While there are exceptions, it seems logical that you should be in your fifties before becoming CEO of a major corporation. At that stage of a person's life, it's likely that being appointed chief executive would be the capstone of a career, his or her last major job. At that age, you have the accumulated experience and wisdom, but also the energy to do the work.

The arrogance and compulsiveness of youth is not to be underestimated. As one of the leading entertainment industry investment bankers, Herbert Allen Jr., told McQueen, "If you're going to run a business, you have to go through the mailroom." Neither Edgar Jr. nor Messier did. Messier was a bureaucrat, and then an investment banker. His resumé did not feature the job of running one of the world's largest corporations or having worked his way up through various positions within a company to the upper reaches of the executive team. Edgar Jr. specifically didn't have the education or experience. His father was brought up in the business, as was I, for that matter. He wasn't. That said, both Edgar Sr. and I had both age and experience on our side and should have been the adult supervision. We both failed.

For all their failings, fifteen years later, their visions look to be correct. Media convergence is in full swing. People watch movies and TV shows on their smartphones and iPads, courtesy of the Internet and services like Netflix. The problem was, they were two cocksure young men in a hurry. In business, it can be fatal to be too early, and they were almost a decade too early. It's a long time to wait to be paid, and a long time to service debt. When AOL and Time Warner combined and Vivendi and Seagram combined, very few had ever heard of Netflix. It's a bit like putting a parachute on the market before there's sturdy enough fabric and strong enough rope to support a skydiver. The business landscape is littered with people who crashed while promoting ideas that were ahead of their time.

Of course, Edgar Jr. didn't set out to wreck Seagram. Just the opposite. In his heart of hearts, he was making the company better. But he was taken in by Messier, like just about everyone was taken in by Messier. Messier's board of directors, which was populated with France's corporate high flyers, was taken in by Messier. Even Messier's top executives couldn't believe what was happening. In a famous memo sent in December 2001 and published in *The Wall Street Journal* in 2002, Messier's CFO, Guillaume Hannezo, sent a near desperate note to his boss.

"I've got the unpleasant feeling of being in a car whose driver is speeding up into the bends and that I'm in the death seat. All I ask is that this doesn't end in disgrace."

It did end in disgrace, for everyone concerned—for the

family, for me, for Edgar, for his son, for Messier, for all of our shareholders and our employees. It was the same for Vivendi. My side of the family, including the foundation, was predominantly invested in Seagram stock. We took a major bath. It was one thing for my family and me to lose money; it was another thing for the foundation to be devastated. It was the nadir of my life—my business life, absolutely.

It comes from taking a hands-off position in much of the company's affairs and not having drummed into myself that I was an equal partner and I had a veto right. But I had never used it before. You don't play major league until you've played minor league. You don't use your veto the first time on something that big, because the people you're vetoing would say you've gone crazy. If you use your veto a couple of times up along the way—not just saying no, but introducing other things in a positive way—then your veto is respected. The veto was also only as good as my relationship with my brother, and there had been a pattern of being unable to stand up to him. I guess I had been conditioned from childhood to be that way. I had not been included, and to some degree I had excluded myself and turned myself into a passive investor. It was also two against one—Edgar and his son. I can't let my brother off the hook, and I can't let myself off the hook. We all made blunders.

Incredibly, for the first time in my life, I thought I might be headed for insolvency. A bankrupt Bronfman! Now *that* would have been one for the history books. My net worth never recovered, although fortunately it's still substantial. Aside from my family's losses, there were Seagram's other shareholders, executives, or anyone in the company who had stock options. All took a terrible hit.

Believe it or not, though, the horror story wasn't over. Early in the summer of 2002, Edgar Jr. and Sam Minzberg led the charge to force Messier out—Sam did the heavy lifting—in the midst of, among other things, a liquidity crisis that left the company just ten days from insolvency, according to the CEO's replacement. I will add that even Edgar and his son eventually appreciated my envoy, Sam, on their side—although, for a time, Edgar treated him with utter contempt. Sam didn't care what all the people on the board thought of his prosecutorial questioning—he did it for us.

Messier's terms for stepping down were, as you would expect, outrageous. According to Johnson and Orange in their book about him, Messier wanted to remain honorary chairman, he wanted a say in who his replacement would be, he wanted four years' pay, his stock options, use of the New York apartment, use of company aircraft, significant charitable donations made on his behalf, all legal costs, and healthcare for his family. He had chutzpah; I'll give him that. The guy decimated a company and still wanted to be rewarded.

Universal ended up being sold to NBC, with Edgar Jr. failing in his bid to buy it back. The U.S. cable company Comcast now owns NBCUniversal. Vivendi's water business was renamed Veolia, and in the spring of 2016 it had a market value of U.S. $12.3 billion. Vivendi SA still exists as a media company and in the spring of 2016 was valued at U.S. $24.2 billion.

Messier ended up facing suits and regulatory probes, culminating in a civil fraud settlement with the Securities and Exchange Commission on December 24, 2003, which resulted in Vivendi consenting to pay $50 million in disgorgement and other penalties. Messier, who, with the other defendants, consented to the settlement without admitting liability, received a civil fine of a million dollars and was restricted from acting as an officer or director of a publicly traded company for ten years. He also agreed to relinquish his claims to a 21-million-euro severance package that he negotiated just before he resigned. The settlement was in connection with a complaint alleging fraud between December 2000 and July 2002, including false press releases, improper adjustments to earnings, and failure to disclose future commitments. The SEC goes on to detail that Messier, along with his CFO, "disguised Vivendi's cash flow and liquidity problems, improperly adjusted accounting reserves to meet earnings before income taxes, depreciation, and amortization (EBITDA) targets, and failed to disclose material financial commitments, all in violation of the anti-fraud provisions of the federal securities laws."

During Messier's tenure, the company destroyed some $100 billion of shareholder value. He is now listed on LinkedIn as General Partner of Messier, Maris & Associés, described as an independent investment bank whose website says it has offices in London, Paris, and New York.

As for Edgar Jr., he has had to live with his decisions—just as I have to live with mine and Edgar had to live with his. In fact, Edgar conceded to Brian Milner of *The Globe and Mail* in July 2002 that he and his son had to take responsibility because they badly misjudged Messier.

In fairness, I should say that, as officials of a public company, there was no intent to lose money. Business judgments were made. Sometimes they work, sometimes they don't. Edgar Jr. had done his research, the media world appeared to be changing around him by the day, and he was convinced Vivendi was the right way to go, and we all voted in favour of the transaction.

Edgar made mistakes. His son made mistakes. I made mistakes. And frankly, I'm just as frustrated with my own as with theirs. The truth is that it was the sum of all our mistakes that sank the Seagram name and the family's holding.

I only had lunch with Messier once. It was at the Four Seasons in the Seagram Building. We chit-chatted a bit. Then I told him that I was giving him two dates—March 12, 2001, and June 27, 2001. "On March 12," I said, "I will have been with the company for fifty years. On June 27, I will be seventy years old." He said March 12 sounds like a good day. Why? "'Cause it's the day I'm retiring (from Seagram)," I said.

Edgar graciously gave me a lovely retirement party. DuPont executives came, and various people spoke. Then I spoke and talked about how much I loved Seagram, and that's what cracked me. I was so fond of my colleagues in the company, and it's such a cliché, but a truism, that you don't know what you have until you lose it. I used to know who was sick, who was healthy, whose offspring were being married, who had a baby, and I would sit and schmooze with people. That was over, and tears came to my eyes. So much had been lost. Shareholders lost money and our family lost its identity. The Seagram Building in New York, which our sister convinced our father to build, no longer has a trace of Seagram or my family personally. I lost communication with most of my colleagues. Our employees lost money, while many lost positions and their place as a member of a "family" business. It was awful.

In a coda to the tragic opera, the liquor business was almost forgotten. For a time, I toyed with the notion of buying it, but I didn't try very hard. It was eventually sold to Diageo and Pernod Ricard at the low end of the range mentioned in the proxy filing explaining the Vivendi–Seagram transaction. Shareholders had been told to assume it would fetch $9.5 billion, the average of a range of $8 billion to $11 billion. They got $8.15 billion. In the denouement of all of this, I recalled my father saying, "I don't sell businesses. I buy them."

Fortunately, I sought a path beyond Seagram—a philanthropic path. Those investments have perhaps been my best, paying dividends to my soul, and I hope they continue to do so for many, many years after I'm gone.

7

Philanthropy: Finding My Métier

―――――

When one is born with a silver spoon in one's mouth, the incentive to make more money is often simply not there. Instead, I've always measured success by achievement, not dollars. My professional and business success with the Expos notwithstanding, my greatest success in life has been in philanthropy—and not just willy-nilly, but strategically, with a sense of purpose, always measuring the results as though the mission were for private enterprise. In all, through my foundation and private giving, we have disbursed approximately $325 million. I wish it could have been more. I often think of how much more I could have done philanthropically with the money lost in the sale of Seagram, because I intensely believe in the causes to which the foundation and I have given. By the time I die, though, in the spirit of Bill and Melinda Gates, Warren Buffett, and the so-called Giving Pledge, I'll have given the majority of my wealth to philanthropic causes.

As Jeff Solomon—the president of Andrea and Charles Bronfman Philanthropies—and I wrote in our book *The Art of Doing Good*, when you give, you get. And what you get is immense satisfaction. Jeff and I also shake up the commonly held negative perception of so-called do-gooders. To us, "there are few greater callings." We make it clear that "a do-gooder is as selfish as the next guy," because gratification and satisfaction come from what you do for others. As we say, "Philanthropy is not altruism; it is much closer to narcissism." While my giving has unquestionably done something for others, it has also performed miracles for me. It has nourished my soul.

Just about everything I have done philanthropically relates to who I am, at my core—and my core can be visualized by two halves of an apple. One part is Canadian, proudly Canadian. The other is Jewish, proudly Jewish. In fact, in 1948, when the State of Israel was founded, I had to do some intense soul searching. All of a sudden, at the age of seventeen, I was saying to myself, "Who am I?" Thinking hypothetically, I asked myself, "What if there were a war between Canada and Israel? On whose side would I be?" Clearly, it was ridiculous to think the two countries would go to war, so I tossed that question aside. But I came to a conclusion about what I am: I'm both a proud Canadian and a member of the Jewish people, and those two chunks of my soul have defined my charitable endeavours.

My history with philanthropy goes back to my teens in Montreal, collecting fifty-cent pieces for Jewish charities in a not-so-well-to-do part of the city. That canvassing proved to me, early in life, that you do not need to be rich to be a giver. While half a dollar was not to be sneezed at by middle-class or lower-middle-class people in the late 1940s, it was also not the kind of charitable donation that would get your name on a building. But if there's a worthy cause, people from all layers of the socioeconomic strata will contribute, make a difference, and feel good about doing so. In fact, as Jeff and I have discovered, while large, marquee donors get a lot of ink, the bulk of giving, at least in the United States, emanates from households with incomes below $100,000. It all adds up.

The charitable thinking of my parents influenced me, of course. During his era, my father was the biggest donor in Canada's Jewish community, while also being a substantial contributor to broader Canadian causes such as the Red Cross, hospitals, and universities. His operating philosophy was that if the donation was for the Jewish community, eighty per cent of what we gave would come from the family, while twenty per cent would come from Seagram through our corporate giving program. If the donation was for non-Jewish causes, eighty per cent would come from Seagram, while twenty per cent would come from the family.

As for his prominent role in the community, Dad was co-chair of the Jewish Immigrant Aid Society, president of the Jewish Philanthropies of Montreal, and president of the Canadian Jewish Congress. From a more patriotic point of view, he commissioned Canadian humourist Stephen Leacock to write *Canada: The Foundations of Its Future*, printing 165,000 copies in 1941—an enormous print run for the country, then or now. Trying to show that Canada wasn't just a nation of Mounties and igloos, he also sponsored a travelling exhibition of paintings of Canadian cities, and he led the Canadian Jewish fundraising campaigns during the 1956 Suez Crisis and the 1967 Six-Day War. In addition, he famously escorted a future president and prime minister of Israel, Shimon Peres, to Ottawa in 1951 to meet high-profile cabinet minister C.D. Howe in order to secure an order of weapons for the fledgling state. In a humorous episode as they headed back to Montreal for a fund-raising dinner, Dad stopped to buy Peres a pair of dark-coloured socks, wisely deciding Peres's white pair didn't go with his dark suit. It's a story Shimon—a friend of some sixty years—has not forgotten and recounts often.

Then there was the case of Israel's first ambassador to Canada, Michael Comay. When the diplomat and his family arrived, they had no official residence where they could set up a home. Instead, they camped out in a suite in Ottawa's Château Laurier hotel, which was half-home, half-embassy. Clearly, this was not the making of a happy, long-term situation. Dad jumped in and took it upon himself to hold a fundraiser with the aim of buying a home that became the ambassador's residence in Ottawa. While he was unquestionably a big giver, and my mother was involved in various cultural and hospital charities in Montreal, they did not have a foundation—and I didn't have one until 1985. In fact, foundations weren't at all common among the wealthy in Canada.

When Dad died in 1971, I was forty years old, and the leaders of the Montreal Jewish community came to me and wanted me to take over my father's philanthropic leadership role in the city. It was a case of "The King is dead. Long live the King." By then, it had been sixteen years since Edgar had decamped to New York, so I was now considered the leader of the family in Montreal, even though it was a position with which I was not yet comfortable. I told the federation representatives that I was intrigued, but I wanted a year to think about it, adding that I was most definitely not interested in stepping into a dead man's shoes. I wanted them to know in no uncertain terms that I was not my father, and I would never be my father. However, given that Dad expected me to be the one destined to burnish the family's reputation, my decision was inevitable. I would do it.

I'd begun attending meetings of the Jewish Federation in Montreal years before and had been flabbergasted by the amount of hot air in the room. I discovered that the first ten minutes were devoted to congratulations—to Mrs. Schwartz on the birth of her son, to Mrs. Flagelbaum on the engagement of her daughter, to Mrs. Epstein on her nephew getting into medical school. I thought to myself, *God, is that what we're here for?* Many years later, when I'd become president, that practice had long been dispensed with and we didn't congratulate anyone for anything.

I became the chair of the executive committee in 1973 and the president in 1974–75. But before I moved up to those positions, there was a president who was an old-school type from eastern Europe, and he held officers' meetings at lunch on Friday. On the agenda was the Jewish Home for the Aged, and the president came armed with a list of names. The place had run out of money and the question around the table became "Should we give Mrs. Goldberg seventy-five dollars per month and Mrs. Greenberg one hundred dollars?" The president duly called out the names of all the *bubbies* that lived in the home, and everyone voted yes, while I voted no. Name after name came and went, and I voted no to all of them. They must have thought I was a Jewish version of the Grinch. The president finally chimed in.

"Charles, do you have something against these people?" he asked.

I said, "No, but I really don't think it's up to us to play God about whether Mrs. Greenberg should get a subsidy or not."

Do we have money in the bank, I asked? Yes, I was told. So then I said, "Why don't we just send the agency twenty-five thousand dollars and let them make all of these individual decisions, because they'll have a better understanding of what the residents' needs are?" He looked at me in astonishment and said, "That's a good idea." They had never thought of it that way. To me, though, it was just common horse sense, the kind my father taught me. Not to make light of the situation; these were important decisions for the people concerned.

When I became president, not only were there no more congratulations, but meetings started at four and ended at six. No flex. The first hour was devoted to reports from each of the section heads, the second hour was set aside to deal with one policy subject, and the decision had to be taken by 6 p.m. And it was. I felt badly for the executive vice-president, the paid employee, because he had to deal with a no-nonsense character like me. The experience, though, taught me how to listen to people and their needs as well as the community's needs. If I was vehemently against something, I made my position clear and fought for it. If I was only mildly against something and the group wanted it, I had to work for something that I wasn't necessarily in favour of, which was a good discipline. It reinforced the art of compromise and that my way wasn't the only way. I also learned how to run a public meeting and how to use patience, discovering that I had to be persuasive, no matter what my last name was. After all, this wasn't command central at Seagram, with the shots being called by the family with the shares. This was a volunteer enterprise. When people are giving their time and money, you have to be a different kind of leader.

It was right in the middle of a trustees' meeting when I was handed the gavel by the outgoing president—the first test—and I had to deal with the issue of the Jewish healthcare system in Quebec. Although we fell under the provincial funding regime, we had our own add-ons, via philanthropy, to meet cultural desires and needs. The province, however, wanted to make alterations to the system, and certain people in the community worried that these changes would take the Jewishness out of some of our institutions—there wouldn't be kosher this or kosher that. Ironically, the provincial government seemed to be patterning the province's healthcare system after the way our federation was running ours, but that's beside the point. To have this as the first major item I had to deal with was a challenge. I said to myself, "You have to win this. If you don't, you're chopped liver." We won it, and that established my leadership.

By the 1980s, however, I was beginning to think differently about philanthropy, perhaps subconsciously at first, and then purposefully. I had become frustrated with traditional public philanthropy, and the notion of a private foundation had been milling around in my head. By then, I was in my fifties and my self-confidence had been boosted by my success with the Expos. There had also been a tectonic shift in my personal life. My marriage with Barbara had been disintegrating for some time and I had fallen in love with another woman. Her name was Andrea Cohen and I had been an usher at her first wedding in London, England, where she grew up as Andrea Morrison. She had married someone I'd grown up with in Montreal, David Cohen. Fourteen years younger than me, Andy was feisty, with a bit of a wild streak that contrasted with my more restrained demeanour. After their wedding, she and David lived in Montreal, where her older sister Kappy was living and still resides. They were married for thirteen years, had three children, and I would see her from time to time in the community. Barbara and I, meanwhile, had been sailing on opposite tacks for many years, and eventually one thing led to another. To make a long story short, I left Barbara, Andy left David, and she and I were eventually married.

I told Stephen, who was sixteen. As for his reaction, sixteen-year-old boys don't say very much about anything. Ellen was just eleven. She yelled, and then ran and hid in the basement. Soon after this, I remember being at a concert, sitting there in tears, thinking about all the people I was hurting, but I couldn't help myself. I remember Barbara saying, "That woman will never be in my house," and she never was.

In 1980, Andy and I began living together, and we were married in 1982. Needless to say, it was very difficult for her children and mine, although all of the kids got along well. Barbara must be given great credit for not only producing and raising two wonderful children, but for tolerating an immature me for more than eighteen years. To say the least, it was a life-changing event for all of us. The Expos' success aside, for me it began a transformation.

Like me, Andy also had to tolerate boarding schools and hated them like I had hated TCS, which immediately fashioned a bond between us. But for both of us, a dislike of school did not mean a dislike of learning. We loved learning, but not in the pedantic form doled out by stern headmasters, something that would eventually become a powerful theme in our philanthropy—informal education. Without a doubt, I would never have achieved what I have done in philanthropy without Andy pushing me past my natural limits when my reflex tendency was always to back away from things. Although she came from a prosperous family—her father owned dress shops throughout Britain—she was no dilettante, as Tom Axworthy, a former head of our foundation, has said. During the period when there were worldwide protests to try to gain freedom for Soviet Jews, Andy helped organize demonstrations in Montreal. Founding a group known as the "35s," she and other women would dress in black, appear outside of Russian events, and chain themselves to posts and fences to register their protest about the treatment of Jews in the former Soviet Union.

Andy was also part of a family with deep ties to Israel. Her father, Hyam "Scotty" Morrison, was chairman of the Joint Palestine Appeal of Great Britain (later renamed the Joint Israel Appeal) and knew everyone who was anyone in Israeli politics. Her mother, Doris, was the founder of the British Friends of the Art Museums of Israel. Later, her parents would move to Jerusalem, and Andy and I would eventually spend the summer months there and focus a substantial amount of our philanthropic work there.

Which brings me to the question of focus. There are certain charitable causes you donate to as an individual simply because you are a citizen—medical research, the Red Cross, and so on. At the company, we also encouraged employees to be engaged in community giving. It was good for them, for the community, and for Seagram. But as I said earlier, there has been, and there continues to be, a purpose to my philanthropy. You have to give a damn about something and it has to connect to you. Just throwing gobs of money at this or that can be disastrous and horribly wasteful. Who, aside from perhaps the Rockefellers, has given more money than

Bill and Melinda Gates? But look at how they have given it. Their foundation has targets, purpose. That's the way to make a difference. As Jeff and I wrote in an earlier book, *The Art of Giving*, philanthropy—or charity, as it used to be called—was in the past often about power, influence, ego, and assuaging a sense of guilt. It was rarely about impact. While my philanthropy has most certainly stroked my ego and arguably given me influence, I have been most concerned about its impact. That was the impetus of setting up a foundation, to separate impact giving from normal, citizen-like giving.

The precursor to the foundation was my giving in Montreal's Jewish community. My professional colleague when it came to that effort was Manuel "Manny" Batshaw, who during the writing of this book passed away at 101. Manny was a social worker who happened to marry a social worker and devoted his life to being a community professional. He was prominently involved in helping Vietnamese refugees, the so-called boat people, in the 1970s when they made their way out of war-ravaged southeast Asia, hundreds of thousands of them on rickety ships floating toward the promise of a better life elsewhere, an immigrant story so familiar to North American Jews. The Batshaw Centres, designed to provide psychosocial rehabilitation and social integration for displaced youth in Quebec, are his legacy. Among other things, Manny had been CEO of the Montreal Jewish Federation and worked with me when I was president. He was a seasoned executive who knew a lot about Jewish philanthropy and the federation movement in North America, particularly in Montreal. One day, my successor brought him into my office and said Manny had to retire because he was sixty-five.

"So what's he going to do?" I asked.

"He's going to work with you at philanthropy," came the answer. We had worked well together at the federation and I knew the Jewish community well, not just in Montreal. But I needed an advisor on Jewish philanthropy and I needed someone to nudge me to make phone calls. So Manny did both in the late 1970s. He used to sit in my office and dial the phone for me so I could make the *schnorring* calls that I should have been making. He got me to do things I should have been doing anyway. That helped me come to the conclusion that perhaps a foundation was what I needed in order to achieve goals in Canada and Israel—my focus, based on those two halves of the apple.

Because both Andy and I loved learning but didn't like school, we were both interested in the idea of informal education. Again, this spoke to our heart and soul and what mattered to us as people. If you set about on a philanthropic mission and it's not hardwired to who you are as a person, you'll lose interest. In advising others on how to get started in philanthropy, our president, Jeff Solomon, liked to use what he calls "value cards" to understand the essence of people's motivations. It was a way of ranking how a person truly feels. There are twenty-five "motivational values" we asked potential donors to rank in order of significance so no one was under any illusions about why he or she was embarking on philanthropy. Was the person driven by community, compassion, courage, effectiveness, and obligation—or by pleasure, power, and recognition?

The latter three don't constitute a crime, by the way. If you know why you're doing it, you're less likely to become disenchanted when things go awry, as they always do. Back when we started the foundation, we didn't go through that psychological winnowing process to help determine our path, but we would now if we were establishing one today. That said, we knew the directions we wanted to take and jumped in, learning from our mistakes.

We began calling together groups of experts to talk about what kinds of programs deserved money. These were brainstorming sessions where we'd listen and ask questions, hoping they would lead to the creation of a new institution based in Canada. There'd be ten or twelve people in the room, one of whom was Tom Axworthy. The brother of Canada's former foreign minister Lloyd Axworthy, Tom is less known to the public but every bit as accomplished. A PhD from Queen's University, he had been principal secretary (meaning chief advisor) to Prime Minister Pierre Trudeau and was intimately involved in the patriation of the constitution and the establishment of the Charter of Rights and Freedoms, perhaps two of the achievements most associated with the late prime minister. After Trudeau retired, Tom went on to teach at Harvard's Kennedy School of Government and has held many other distinguished positions (he has since led another foundation set up to honour the memory of the late finance minister Walter Gordon).

By 1985, we had set up the CRB Foundation—my initials are CRB—in Montreal. Not only had I thrown money into the pot, but so had Andy, who had family money of her own. She was both my life partner and my philanthropy partner. Our first president was an Ivy League–educated Canadian who was an expert in Israeli politics. Unfortunately, it was a mistake on both sides, although he deserves full credit for hiring Tom Axworthy and also for finding Janet Aviad to run our initiatives in Israel.

He was with us for about a year before Tom replaced him at our behest. One thing we have learned over the years in running the foundation is that, when we're hiring someone, we always like to meet his or her spouse, in part to see how the two treat each other. So Andy and I invited Tom and his wife, Roberta, to dinner at our home in Montreal, followed by a baseball game. Tom, it turns out, loves baseball. As he describes it, Roberta "fell in love with Charles and Andy right away." Tom had experienced a pretty exciting boss in Pierre Trudeau and clearly had employment options that went beyond running our foundation, but he chose us.

Although Tom is not Jewish—he and his family were active in the United Church of Canada and he taught Sunday school the entire time he worked for us—most of our money was being spent in Canada in the early years of the foundation, and his towering intellect and analytical mind allowed him to grasp and make sense of our Israeli and Jewish programs. While I've heard that our naming him as head of the foundation did not go unnoticed in certain corners of the Jewish community, it didn't matter a whit to Andy or me. In fact, on one of our trips to Israel, Tom asked if he could bring his mother, given that his father had recently passed away. I recall seeing Tom and his mom on some parapet in Jerusalem, with him explaining to her how the water system had worked in the City of David. What a wonderful mind!

Initially, we funded the foundation with $100 million, which turned out to be too much money because we didn't know what we were doing at the time. To comply with the rules, we then had to spend about five million dollars a year. In order for it to be a foundation, you either had to spend a minimum amount each year that was approximately five per cent of the capital, or you had to spend the interest on the capital.

People think philanthropy is easy. It's not, at least to do it well and effectively. One of the big problems with getting involved in philanthropic work is that there's generally been no career-development process for philanthropists. It's not like working your way up the greasy pole at work over a series of decades. A lot of people jump into philanthropy figuring the combination of their fat bank account and their know-how from accumulating their fortune are the only ingredients they need to make it work. Not so.

As Tom, who worked with us for about twenty years, puts it, running a foundation is like investment banking, but for the common weal. You're not just giving to charity, you're investing—or at least you should be, in my view. You should be concerned with addressing root causes of problems, rather than merely the symptoms of a problem. You want to invest to create solutions, not just provide a monetary Band-Aid. You also need to know how to say no. Tom's assessment is that, for every time you say "yes" to a project, you have to say "no" ninety-nine times. His take is that you also have to take risks—a novel notion for nonprofit enterprises—and we did. He says if governments take risks, they lose votes, so if philanthropists don't take risks, who will? He's dead right, and that's what we tried to do. Fortunately, a foundation doesn't have the bureaucracy of a government, so once you make a decision, it doesn't have to go to committee and then the legislature for a vote. It's ready, set, go, and you're off. Hence the Heritage Minutes, our multiyear commitment to teaching Canadians about the long-ignored history of the country, through the production of spellbinding, sixty-second movies that have illuminated everything from Sir Sandford Fleming, the inventor of standard time, to the reception of the world's first wireless radio signal by Guglielmo Marconi in St. John's, Newfoundland, in 1901.

Andy was a critical ingredient in how the foundation gelled. Beatles producer George Martin has described the songwriting magic of Lennon and McCartney in terms of cooking, saying that while Paul was the olive oil, John was the lemon juice. Using that rudimentary analogy, I was Paul and Andy was John. While we both knew how to ask hard questions and were not cowed in the presence of PhDs like Tom, I was the more trusting part of the combo, while she was the skeptic. I am also more process-driven, taking my time, letting ideas percolate, while Andy was more of a gut-feel decision maker.

"She was about the best shit detector I've ever seen," Tom says of Andy, adding that I probably needed a person like that around me. She would do the sniff test on people, while I was good on ideas. Poor Tom. He had two CEOs over his head. Add to that the fact that we had the likes of Leo Kolber hovering around the office, so when it had anything to do with numbers, there was a tight-fisted check on decision-making. I've always admitted I'm not good with figures. Thank goodness Leo was around to scrutinize them. Tom says that, in a sense, I had set it all up this way, with different types of people pulling in different directions. If he or someone else was struck by a brainwave, Leo would be there to zero in and ask how it was going to be funded, or Ann Dadson, who was our chief operating officer, would have to figure out the logistics of how to make it work. It's great to have big-picture people like Jean Drapeau was with the Expos, but you need a general to keep the soldiers moving and a numbers whiz to watch expenses. Philanthropy is nothing if you can't execute on your plan, and foundations need the same kinds of checks and balances that companies need; otherwise, the money evaporates without having any effect, a tragic waste when there's so much to be done.

The Montreal office was one thing. Israel was another. I had first been there in 1958 with Leo and his late wife, Sandra. It was the beginning of something akin to an addiction to the country, a condition that intensified in the 1980s, after I married Andy, who had even deeper ties there. At one point, I was the largest foreign investor in Israel. My family's involvement in that country goes back decades, and certainly from a philanthropic point of view, the Israel Museum is a touchstone for the Bronfmans. In the early 1960s, the archaeological wing was named for my father's seventieth birthday—a gift from my siblings and me. In addition, the pursuit of peace in the Middle East has always been close to my heart, and for many years, from a centre-left position on the political spectrum, I have been a supporter of a two-state solution. Mainly, though, I have always felt that there are two great Jewish societies—one living in Israel and one in the Jewish Diaspora, principally in North America.

At the time I was formulating those thoughts, I was not thinking about the millions of Jews who were still stuck in the Soviet Union. It was hard to get a read on actual numbers, given that religion was officially banned there. But it was always my feeling that if Israeli Jews and Diaspora Jews could forge deeper ties and understand each other better, each would be enriched, thereby helping Israelis and the Jewish people outside of Israel to flourish. To that end, while the CRB Foundation would focus on promoting Canadian heritage and identity through informal education, it would also work to foster peace in the Middle East and a deeper, more meaningful relationship between Jews in Israel and Jews in the Diaspora. The question, in each case, was how to do it. In a sense, we needed programs for each country and a business plan for each program—a lot of work.

One of the people who came to one of our brainstorming sessions was Janet Aviad, a Philadelphian with a PhD from Columbia who has lived in Israel for decades. She was trying to make an academic career there, teaching part-time at Hebrew University, but was finding that the academic world wasn't a great fit for her. Janet was invited to the sessions by Steve Cohen, our first president—not by Andy or me. She had never heard of the Bronfmans, nor had she ever been to Canada, but the prospect of sitting around with Israeli cultural figures appealed to her. It was, like many periods, a tense time in Israel, with the rise of the ultra-right-wing Meir Kahane extreme nationalist movement, and Janet was profoundly concerned about the direction of the country, which she viewed as dangerous.

Today, she talks about how neither Andy nor I would have hired her. It's a good thing someone else on our team did. She says she didn't know how to dress or how to eat at the Bronfman table, what humour was okay, what wasn't. One of the founders of the Peace Now movement in Israel, Janet was a political activist and a self-described bull in a china shop. She admits she embarrassed me a few times—and she did, by speaking through *The New York Times* about the political situation in Israel when we at the foundation had to be, at least on the face of it, politically neutral. Although I wasn't particularly a supporter of hers at the beginning (Andy was), I took her to lunch and asked if she'd work for us full-time. She agreed on the condition that she would not stop being active politically in Israel, although she promised she would do it privately and not be quoted in publications like the *Times*. For the most part, that's what happened, and she has been with us for almost thirty years, brilliantly overseeing the Israel office, its focus and its programs—informal after-school enrichment programs that have touched hundreds of thousands of children, Birthright Israel, which has touched hundreds of thousands of young adults from all around the world, in addition to support for the decorative arts and the Israel Philharmonic, guiding our interest in the Israel Museum, advocating for environmental issues, small-business loans to Arab-Israelis, and "people to people" programs between Jews and Arabs in the wake of the Oslo Accord.

Although we're nothing compared to the size of a multinational corporation, the goals of our foundation have been ambitious. And like the managers of successful businesses, we are strong believers in measuring performance. We want to know if our programs have worked and achieved their lofty goals. Did the Heritage Minutes actually excite people about Canadian history they didn't know, and if so, how well? How did we change the lives of both Arab and Jewish children in Israel who didn't have the opportunity to learn music or computer skills because the government had cut those programs? How did we improve the environment by being a critical player in getting a clean-air act passed? How did we change the view of Israel among young adults who travelled on ten-day discovery trips known as Birthright Israel? How did we change the view of Israeli soldiers about people their own age living in the Diaspora through their encounters with the groups? As Jeff and I wrote, "If you can't measure the impact of your gift, you should not make it." Here's a specific way we suggest that the question be framed:

> *If you give five hundred dollars to the American Red Cross to help the victims of Hurricane Katrina, you don't have any assurances whatsoever that your five hundred dollars generally buys five hundred dollars' worth of goods or services. That is to say, in the for-profit world, five hundred dollars generally buys five hundred dollars' worth of goods and services. In non-profits, five hundred dollars buys—well, who knows exactly?*

Any business plan, whether at a for-profit or nonprofit, involves facing up to hard questions to test whether you're really up to the task. Are you ready for the commitment required if the project takes off? Are you prepared for the risk that it fails? How much of your life, particularly your family life, are you prepared to give up for the cause? Are you prepared to stick it out for ten years, a time frame Jeff and I think is required to make a difference? Are you willing to share credit? Would you be thrilled or terrified to be on *60 Minutes*? And yes, as with any serious endeavour, what is your exit strategy? These are just a few of the questions we recommend considering and answering honestly.

The other big question, aside from whom to hire to run your foundation and execute your strategy (a whole other matter), is how to manage the funds. When you've got a big pot of money, there's no end to the number of people who will not only ask for it, but also want to help you manage it. A friend of mine who "invested" with Bernard Madoff suggested we give the Madoff fund a good look. Fortunately, we steered clear because there were several unanswered questions that resulted in Madoff, the perpetrator of a huge fraud via a Ponzi scheme, not passing our smell test. You will also encounter greed on the other side of the ledger. I was once solicited to give money to a certain cause, and when I said I would donate five million dollars, the person soliciting the donation said it was not enough and would lower the standard for what his organization expected others to give, thereby hurting the fundraising campaign. I immediately told him that I didn't want to create a problem for him and would withdraw my intention to donate. His tune quickly changed.

There are other charitable endeavours that have evolved separately for me but are still very close to my heart. One of them tackles the ghost of my ill-fated time at McGill University. It is possibly the closest thing Canada has to an Ivy League school and probably the best-known Canadian university outside of the country. Its campus on the first day of autumn 2014 was still leafy, with little evidence of the changing of the colours. As a new crop of students bustled about, a decidedly older crowd gathered in Moyse Hall in the Arts Building, which sits above a plot where the remains of James McGill are interred. The McGill Institute for the Study of Canada (MISC) assembled to hear Calgary mayor Naheed Nenshi, possibly the best communicator among Canada's political class, speak via live video link about leading during a crisis, in his case the 2013 floods, which resulted in $6.5 billion in damage, the costliest natural disaster in Canadian history.

Following Nenshi, two separate panels discussed issues surrounding civil society and public expression in a democracy. Panellists included the likes of former Ontario premier and interim federal Liberal leader Bob Rae. In the audience were some of Canada's most respected historians, including Desmond Morton and Irving Abella. It was the twentieth anniversary of the founding of MISC, as it's known, an organization I helped found in 1994 at the university I dropped out of at the age of nineteen. Cyril James, McGill's principal who gave me foolish advice, must have been rolling over in his grave, given MISC and the fact that I have an honorary degree from the school, one of six conferred upon me (McGill, University of Toronto, Waterloo, Concordia, Brandeis, and Hebrew University).

That evening, a glittering crowd, including former prime minister Brian Mulroney and his wife, Mila; my sister Phyllis Lambert; former SNC-Lavalin CEO Jacques Lamarre; and Irving Abella, along with his wife, Supreme Court Justice Rosalie Abella, joined in a warm and emotional dinner in what must be one of the most beautiful and elegant rooms in Canada, the Oval Room at Montreal's Ritz-Carlton Hotel. Canada's governor general, David Johnston, a former principal of McGill, joined us by video. My old friend, whom I've known since Selwyn House days when I was just six or seven years old, Alex Paterson, gave a heartfelt tribute and plunked an oversized Expos hat on my head. I was very moved to have been feted by this group. After supper, we settled in to hear many fine speakers, among them the former prime minister, who, I must say, knows how to poke fun at himself.

"What do I miss most about politics?" Brian Mulroney asked rhetorically in his speech. "I miss the adulation," he said to hearty laughter from the crowd.

"Bob Rae and I share in this overwhelming tide of gratitude," he added, gesturing to his fellow former politician.

Rosie Abella also made us laugh, referring to me as "Chuckie

Bronfperson." She joked about how I had applied for what had become the controversial Quebec seat on the Supreme Court, pointing out that, for one thing, I'm not a lawyer, and it had been many years since the court had heard an appeal in Yiddish. She added that in "the bar," legally speaking, we are not looking for someone with behind-the-bar experience—and that my experience with the Expos dugout was not the kind of "bench" experience they were looking for on the court.

She also humbled me. "You may not make it to the Supreme Court, but you are supreme. You may not have a law degree, but you know justice. You are our best self."

Isn't it amazing what a McGill dropout can do for McGill?

8

Heritage Minutes: I Didn't Know That!

―――――

Try walking onto a playground on the South Side of Chicago and telling the neighbourhood kids practising to be the next Michael Jordan that the game of hoops they're playing was invented by a Canadian, James Naismith, who started with peach baskets. They'll probably think you escaped from the nearest psychiatric ward. Can you imagine a time when goaltenders in the National Hockey League did not wear masks, and that it was a quirky goalie from Shawinigan, Quebec, who pioneered the idea? In a more serious vein, how did runaway slaves make their way from the United States to the freedom of Canada?

A whole generation of Canadians knows the answers to these questions because of Heritage Minutes, sixty-second TV "commercials," or mini-movies, about pieces of Canadian history that a lot of people weren't aware of prior to the Minutes being broadcast. As Ann Dadson puts it, how much of the work of nonprofit institutions like the CRB Foundation has found its way into popular culture? Not much, but Heritage Minutes have succeeded.

The genesis of the Minutes goes back to 1981, when I was inducted into the Order of Canada, the country's highest civilian honour. The ceremony at Rideau Hall, the governor general's residence in Ottawa, was a revelation. Here was a roomful of honourees, all of whom had lived lives worthy of great stories. What struck me was that most Canadians would never know their stories. Yet this was Canada; these people *were* Canada— the firefighter from Calgary, the black minister from Halifax, the Mountie from British Columbia who worked with street kids. It dawned on me that we didn't know our own country. The sum of Canada is made up of the multifarious actions of millions of people over a century and a half—everyday acts, extraordinary acts by ordinary people, discoveries, bravery, kindness, brutality, and much more. Our shared values, traditions, and sense of what being Canadian means is, quite simply, the sum of all these acts.

When I was a kid, as with most of my schoolroom experiences, I wasn't crazy about the way I was taught history. It was colourless. There was no life to it, yet *history is life*. Memorizing the dates of major events and learning which king ruled when was not a great way to stoke curiosity in any youngster who wasn't much of a student. The history that was taught—one might say force-fed—was also a very thin slice of history, dominated by the glories of the British. Our chauffeur's daughter, on the other hand, learned the same history but from the French standpoint. Although the First Nations people were obviously already here, the Anglophones and Francophones are considered the founding peoples of modern-day Canada, and the forging of their two cultures in 1867 resulted in what we know as our nation. Those histories are important. Learning about Queen Victoria's reign or Samuel de Champlain is useful, and knowing dates helps put events in context versus the evolution of society.

However, by the 1980s, a large percentage of Canadians were of neither French nor English heritage—and the truth is, whether your grandparents were from the moon or Scotland, it didn't matter. For a lot of kids, no matter where they're "from," this kind of information would go in one ear and out the other. That's because it was just information, not knowledge that translated into meaning. What was missing from history class, at least in my day, was the word embedded in the word *history*—the *story*. We didn't know our stories or myths. We didn't know our heroes or heroines. These are the things that make a successful society, make its people proud and fortify the fabric of a nation. When you asked a Canadian what he or she was, you got a non-answer.

"I'm not American. I'm not English. I'm not French."

It's astonishing that Canada didn't even have its own flag until 1965, ninety-eight years after the birth of the country. Talk about apathy or lack of confidence. The flag debate was slightly divisive in our household. My father didn't like the design of what became the new Canadian flag, while I did. He wanted it to reflect *a mari usque ad mare*—from sea to sea—with blue columns on each side representing the Atlantic and Pacific. I told him I liked the new design, the Maple Leaf in red and white. He wanted to know precisely what I liked about it.

"Because it's ours," I said.

What struck me at the Order of Canada ceremony—and the need to tell our stories—later made me remember a series of television bits I'd seen in the mid-1970s in the United States. Bicentennial Minutes ran on television from July 4, 1974, through 1976, in honour of the two-hundredth anniversary of the founding of the United States. They were, however, very different from what Heritage Minutes became. The Bicentennial Minutes were more in the realm of a lecture or report fronted by a well-known person, including First Lady Betty Ford, Vice-President Nelson Rockefeller, and even President Gerald Ford. In one of them, stage and screen actress Jessica Tandy introduced herself and told a story about an event that occurred on that same day, two hundred years earlier. The segments aired on CBS at 8:58 p.m., right smack in the middle of prime time.

Tom Axworthy, accompanied by independent Montreal film producer Patricia Lavoie, paid a visit to the Museum of Broadcasting in New York City (now called the Paley Center for Media) to see the Bicentennial Minutes. Lavoie had worked on *Sesame Street* and was one of a small group intimately involved in the birth of Heritage Minutes. They watched all of them in one day. Although they were the right length, they were not exactly what we wanted to do. They were too much like a lecture. We wanted informal education. We wanted stories told in an absorbing, engaging way as a means of enhancing "Canadianism" or Canadian heritage.

We had already spent some money supporting the Canadian Film Centre, established by director Norman Jewison, as well as youth-focused television programs that turned out to be very successful. These included *Degrassi Digest*, which supported the drama series *Degrassi High,* as well as *Les Petits Débrouillards,* a science show. As good as they were, Andy and I agreed that they weren't what we wanted. We were looking for stories that would inspire and unite. Tom recalls that I didn't say I wanted a bunch of heritage TV commercials, but that's exactly what he started calling them. Dubbing them "heritage commercials" was a wonderful way to frame the concept. As Ann Dadson has said, we wanted them to be like trailers for movies.

We started by trying to figure out how to tell the stories. Young people were not watching the CBC, nor were they rushing to the National Film Board of Canada to borrow videos. In fact, surveys we had conducted prior to the launch of the Heritage Minutes showed young Canadians' knowledge of their own history and heritage to be, in a word, pathetic. As described by Carl M. Brauer, a Harvard professor we hired to chronicle and evaluate the Heritage Project (the umbrella under which the Minutes fell), we paid for a National Heritage Test conducted by Goldfarb Consultants. Students, in Grade 10 through college, could correctly answer only twenty-nine of fifty-one questions. Seventeen per cent couldn't think of a single Canadian they admired, and only thirty-nine per cent could name three Canadians from the past whom they admired. Twenty-three per cent of young Canadians couldn't come up with a Canadian event or achievement of which they were proud.

In 1987, as Tom has documented, "twenty filmmakers, historians, and educators met in Montreal to brainstorm whether it was possible to make sixty-second mini-movies on Canadian history." One of the people who attended the session was Gerry Lesser, an education professor at Harvard. He was one of the founders of the Children's Television Workshop, the group that invented *Sesame Street*, considered groundbreaking television for preschoolers when it came along in the 1970s. Tom says Gerry believed there were only two ways to get through to children, either via music or TV, not via books. Thus we requested proposals from the broadcast media about how to achieve what we wanted. We said the CRB Foundation was interested in shows or series to educate young people about Canada. We got fifty-one proposals. Some were good, but none close to what Tom or I thought we needed. Finally, during a cab ride, Tom recalls one of Gerry Lesser's grad students, André Caron (who, along with Lavoie, had been one of the first to call for Heritage Minutes) telling him that the people in the television and film industry didn't think you could tell people about history in what amounted to commercials. Tom responded by asking, "Why don't we do it ourselves? We just asked the industry to do it and nobody came up with any ideas."

From there, Tom called entertainment lawyer Michael Levine, who said he had never taken a contract from the Bronfmans because of a family connection through the marriage of his Uncle Moe to my Aunt Freda. Tom told Michael, "It's not Charles Bronfman hiring you, it's me hiring you," and he insisted that Michael bring Patrick Watson to the project.

Patrick had come to prominence on Canadian television in the 1960s with an explosive program called *This Hour Has Seven Days*. In some respects, it was a precursor to *60 Minutes*, the long-running CBS investigative magazine program, complete with controversial stories, blunt questions, and tight close-ups of the guests feeling the heat. *Seven Days* was so explosive it only lasted a couple of seasons before CBC cancelled it, but by then, Watson was well known. Years later, he produced a landmark documentary series called *The Struggle for Democracy* that filmed all over the world. Watson later became chairman of the Canadian Broadcasting Corporation. Not only was he popular and well known, but he was an intellectual who could produce, write, and host—an unusual combination of doer and thinker. Coincidentally, he had once been a juror at a one-minute film festival. Carl M. Brauer wrote in 1995 that Watson had been enchanted with the challenge posed by such a short form. Watson also had a connection to historical programming through a series he hosted in the 1970s called *Witness to Yesterday*. In each episode, Watson would interview a well-known historical figure portrayed by an actor. As a result, Watson "interviewed" Joan of Arc, William Shakespeare, Socrates, and Queen Victoria, among others.

In his own memoir, Patrick wrote about how Michael Levine called him and said he, Watson, had to go to Montreal for a meeting at the CRB Foundation to hear about and discuss the Heritage Minutes project. Watson groaned. He was up to his navel in other epics. What did he need this for? Watson described Levine, who is a major-league salesman, telling him how he simply *had* to go.

"Listen to me. Trust me on this. You have to do this."

According to Watson, at the meeting I said that if we could use sixty seconds of television to persuade Canadians that corn flakes are interesting—or Cadillacs or tampons—couldn't we use sixty seconds to persuade them that Canada is interesting? Then someone said young people are interested in movies, so why not sixty-second movies? By the time the day ended, we'd agreed to give it a shot, and the first one would be about the Underground Railroad.

A writer and a cinematographer who Watson had worked with on *Witness to Yesterday* were hired to write and shoot the first Heritage Minute. They, along with Watson, deferred their fees to maximize what they could put on the screen, a major contribution on their part to get the Minutes off the ground.

Writing a script for a sixty-second movie is no small feat. Every syllable and pause has to have maximum impact. In his book, Patrick provided a sample of a script he wrote for one of the Heritage Minutes. It's about Alberta's Emily Murphy and the struggle for women in Canada to become "persons, under the law," something they did not achieve until 1929. The script is just 119 words, roughly a paragraph in a book. And that is likely a relatively wordy script, because it was shot with actress Kate Nelligan simply speaking to camera—much like Jessica Tandy in the Bicentennial Minute—in contrast to most, which were produced as minute-long movies in which the action tells the story.

The Underground Railroad may be one of Canada's proudest achievements and was fittingly the foundation's first Minute. As Marsha Boulton described in *Just a Minute*, the first of two books sketching the stories portrayed in our micro-films, she called it a railroad with no tracks and no engine. Rather, it was a secret network of people who helped between thirty and forty thousand slaves escape under cover of darkness and through backwoods channels to Canada, in many cases to the area around St. Catharines, near Niagara Falls in Southern Ontario. That was the base of operations of Harriet Tubman, who became known as "black Moses." Tubman alone made fifteen trips to the deep South, rescuing three hundred slaves, including her parents. It was extremely dangerous work, given that there was a forty-thousand-dollar bounty on her head as a result of outraged slave owners. Both white and black sympathizers joined in, hiding runaway slaves in barns and other structures. They had come northward to a place where slavery had been legally abolished in 1833.[2]

We on the executive committee at the foundation loved the first Heritage Minute, but there was a realization that each one would cost a significant amount. A decision was made that we needed partnering sponsors, and to get them, we needed to make two more Minutes as pilots. The initial budget was $250,000 to produce the first three prototypes. That quickly became almost $600,000. To make ten more to complete a series of thirteen, a magic number for broadcasters' schedules, the budget would be significant. Eventually, we often produced them in batches for efficiency. To make the next two, we brought Patrick on as creative director, and from that point forward, both he and Tom were the creative force behind the Minutes. Each of them knew storytelling—Patrick from his years as a broadcaster and journalist, Tom from his years briefing people like Pierre Trudeau. While we Bronfmans distilled liquor, Patrick and Tom distilled stories.

Patrick wrote that I made almost no interventions regarding content or style, but that I did insist on the topic for one of the two additional pilots that became known as "Valour Road." To this day, it is still one of my favourites. It's the story of three boys who lived on the same street—Pine Street—in Winnipeg. After the First World War, the city changed the name of the street to Valour Road. The change was made to honour the individual acts of heroism of the young men in the Great War. All three had been awarded the Victoria Cross, the country's highest award for courage.

---

2. In 1793, Lieutenant Governor John Graves Simcoe pushed to end the legality of slavery in Upper Canada. Legislation was not passed until 1833, and slavery was not abolished throughout the British Empire until 1834.

"Valour Road" was not an easy story to tell in what amounts to a cinematic blink of the eye. Sergeant-Major Frederick William Hall died at Ypres, Belgium, in 1915, while trying to rescue an injured fellow soldier. Corporal Leo Clarke died a month after the Battle of the Somme in 1916, where from the muddy trenches he single-handedly attacked twenty German soldiers, killing four after having been bayoneted in the knee by the enemy. In 1917, at Passchendaele, where 16,000 Canadians died, Lieutenant Robert Shankland crossed the battlefield alone to deliver crucial information. He was the only one of the three from Pine Street to survive a war that resulted in sixty thousand Canadian deaths, a little more than half the number lost by the United States, which did not join the fight until 1917, three years into the war. At the time of the First World War, Canada had a population of only ten million, while the U.S. had about 100 million. Many historians believe the country's experience in the Great War was a defining period for the nation.

Patrick said telling three stories in sixty seconds was "going to be nearly impossible." I asked him to do his best. Eventually, he got it to two minutes. I said, "Good progress. Keep trying." Lo and behold, Patrick found a solution.

The third of the three pilots was more in tune with popular culture, and the first of several that would focus on sports. Of course, the Minutes being about Canadian history, the sport would be hockey. Again, like "Underground Railroad" and "Valour Road," the story we chose to tell was about courage, but in this case, also innovation. Today, if you were watching a hockey game and the forwards and defencemen were not wearing helmets and the goalies were not wearing face masks, you'd think they were crazy. But have a look at old newsreel footage of games played in the 1950s and '60s. Players didn't wear helmets, and more amazingly, goalies didn't wear protective masks on their faces, let alone helmets.

The exception was Jacques Plante of the Montreal Canadiens, who also distinguished himself from his teammates by knitting sweaters and toques for himself. Plante claimed that knitting helped him relax and kept his hands supple. They were supple enough for him to win the National Hockey League's award for its best goaltender, the Vézina Trophy, seven times.

On November 1, 1959, in a game at Madison Square Garden, the New York Rangers' Andy Bathgate fired a shot that resulted in Plante requiring seven stitches from his nose to lip. The new needlepoint added to an already staggering total of more than two hundred stitches Plante had required on his face during his NHL career. After getting sewn up, Plante told coach Toe Blake that he'd only go on the ice again if he could wear the protective mask he'd made and had been wearing during practice sessions for four years. In spite of the jabs he got from the stands and other quarters, he did it, and the team went on to win the game. Plante went on to an eleven-game winning streak, in the process establishing a new norm, a practice that would eventually be de rigueur in hockey.

Once the three initial Minutes were finished, they were screened for a group in our boardroom and I looked around for reaction. People were hesitating. Making a raft of these little movies was going to cost a bundle, and they were probably thinking, *Gee, it's his money, why don't we wait to hear what Mr. B. says?* However, Leo Kolber was in the room, and Leo speaks his mind, so I asked for his view. Patrick described Leo as having "a severe exterior that conceals a sensitive and humorous mind," while admitting to being "somewhat intimidated" by him.

> *Leo Kolber rose sternly to his feet. I felt sure heavy weather was coming. His first words were "Well, I don't know what we're wasting our time for . . ." and my heavy weather now looked like a cyclone . . . "These things . . ." he went on, scowling fiercely, ". . . these are the best damn things I've ever seen in my life. I think we should just get on with it."*

I then chimed in, saying, "Let's go." Heritage Minutes were about to take off and vastly upgrade awareness of Canadian history.

Getting sponsors to join in was not easy. There was fear of controversy—no one knew what one of the Minutes might say to tick off a particular group. As well, there was a sense that Bronfman's rich. If he wants to do it, fine, he can pay for it. In Brauer's assessment, he says that Michael Levine recalled between seventy-five and a hundred rejections from potential sponsors. In one case, I was part of a delegation that included Tom, Patrick, and Leo that went to see executives of one of the big banks—including a bank that did a considerable amount of business with Seagram and companies related to our family. We showed them the pilots. They thanked us politely and showed us the door.

Although I was worried that Canada Post was too associated with government, I got over my internal resistance and the Crown corporation came in as our first major sponsor. For the issuer of Canadian stamps, there was an obvious connection to the Minutes. Also, in part due to my friendship with the late, great Paul Desmarais, Power Corporation stepped forward because Paul thought it was a good idea. We also got grants from the Secretary of State for Canada, and the federal government later contributed in a big way, as did major corporations such as Weston, Rogers, Molson, and many others.

Ann Dadson joked that here was the crew at the CRB Foundation, working for one of the richest families in the country, and they had to become fundraisers in order to make the project blossom! But that's the best kind of philanthropy, when the philanthropist can leverage his or her dollars to bring in others and make the enterprise larger than it would otherwise be. The operating principle of the foundation was to provide seed money, finance prototypes, and cover administration, but then the enterprise had to attract support of its own to be self-sustaining. The federal government was particularly keen because of continued concerns in political circles about national unity.

To touch all the political bases, Ann met with all of the provincial education and communications ministers, while I travelled across the country, meeting with all of the premiers to get another level of government excited about the project. Here I was, Mr. Seagram, who sold whisky to each of the provinces, and we never talked whisky. It was gratifying that everyone was onside with the idea. Once we got rolling, there were contests for which Minutes we should produce, and we had some great submissions from citizens who were history buffs. They were shot on 35-millimetre film, just like big-budget movies were (they have since moved to digital technology), so they could be shown in theatres. The Minutes soon became regular fare on television and were also shown prior to feature films after

Michael Levine made a deal to show them in 850 Cineplex Odeon theatres across Canada.

In 1989, Patrick Watson was appointed chairman of the CBC. As a result, that curtailed some of what he was able to do on the Minutes. To help ease the pressure, he brought in Quebec-based broadcaster Robert-Guy Scully to oversee the Minutes produced in French. Scully, who hosted programs on both French and English television networks, helped neutralize some of the concerns that this was just an English-Canadian enterprise. Still, we were criticized in some quarters in Quebec for our choice of stories and the fact that the bulk of the Minutes were produced in English and dubbed into French. The fact that Tom was so closely associated with an ardent federalist like Pierre Trudeau may have aroused a certain nationalist sentiment against us in Quebec, and the memory of my 1976 speech about the separatists may not have helped, either. But we were based in Quebec, and as a result, I believe we were sensitive to Quebec and had good support from the Francophone community, and the Minutes were shown there as much as anywhere else.

In fact, one of the most chilling Minutes ever produced was about the hanging of Métis leader Louis Riel, an event that to this day resonates for many French Canadians. There is a footnote to that Minute, however. After I screened it, I felt it was too controversial, and it was quietly withdrawn from the rotation. It was, though, made available to schools, where it could be discussed. It was one of the few times I was called in—we figured we had to show it but felt a responsibility to do so in a sensitive manner.

Ultimately, the Minutes were shown a huge number of times, but because measurement is crucial in philanthropy, we wanted to know precisely how much they were seen and what their impact was. The amount of time they aired on television is staggering. Brauer reports that in 1992, they filled eight hours per month of airtime. By September of 1993, that number had risen to nine and a half hours a month. A separate report to our board in 1998 showed that Heritage Minutes were filling a whopping forty-six hours per month of Canadian airtime. The times they'd get used the most were during weaker periods in the economy, when the networks didn't sell as many commercials, or to fill slots during the broadcast of U.S. programs (American networks were allowed more commercial minutes per hour than their Canadian counterparts). They'd just plop a Heritage Minute, which they got for nothing, into the spot where a car ad usually went. Michael Levine persuaded Canada's broadcast regulator, the CRTC, to deem Heritage Minutes as programming rather than commercials—and as Canadian content. As a result, we didn't have to buy airtime to broadcast them, and broadcasters were anxious to use them to meet their Canadian-content requirements.

Although today's teenagers are not particularly aware of the Minutes, thirty-year-olds know them. Patrick describes how he would go into schools and ask kids to raise their hands if they knew what a Heritage Minute was. About half of them, he said, would do so. Then he'd ask if any knew the story of the Halifax Explosion. It told the story of what was the most powerful man-made explosion in history prior to the atomic bomb dropped on Japan in 1945, and which is still the largest disaster in Canadian history. On the morning of December 6, 1917, two ships—the *Imo*, a Norwegian steamer, and a French munitions ship—collided in Halifax harbour. The French ship, the *Mont Blanc*, was carrying TNT, acid, and gun cotton, among other things. When a fire on board led to an explosion about an hour after the collision, it sent a plume of smoke eight kilometres in the air, and the force of the blast could be felt 320 kilometres away.

With much of the north end of Halifax demolished, two thousand people were killed, nine thousand injured, and some six thousand left homeless. Patrick says that when he asked if anyone knew the story, a student would often get up and virtually recite the script he'd written for the Heritage Minute about the accident, sometimes in detail. This was a clear sign that we'd punched through the noise. The main character of the Halifax Explosion Minute was a telegraph operator, Vince Coleman, who furiously tried to get a message to an incoming train to stop and not approach the harbour because of the impending blast. Watson calls Coleman "the Canadian paradigm of a hero. He was an ordinary guy, who when extraordinary circumstances came along, did the thing he was supposed to do. That's what we're about."

In addition to the one about Louis Riel, a few other Minutes were controversial. Although historians were brought on board to check for accuracy and sensitivity in how events and people were portrayed, Ann Dadson says that when the Jacques Plante Minute was shown, every guy in every office had an opinion as to whether the details were right, since most of them were hockey nuts who considered themselves experts. There were also the inevitable tensions between the filmmakers and the historians we hired as consultants.

We got great reviews from the *Montreal Gazette* and *TV Guide*, while culture critic Robert Fulford trashed them as "earnest" and "solemn and boring." I will agree to disagree with him. Besides, we weren't aiming for the elites. When the Minute about John McCrae's famous war poem, "In Flanders Fields," was released, several towns and their mayors claimed McCrae as their own. This was, of course, a mark of success.

Some of the episodes conveyed highly unpleasant aspects of Canadian history. The so-called Nitro Minute dealt with the Chinese labourers who used nitroglycerin for the blasting that allowed the Canadian Pacific Railway to be built. The narrator says, "They say there is one dead Chinese man for every mile of that track." The Chinese community in Canada expressed great support for that Minute. On the other hand, we encountered static from Turkey's ambassador to Canada after he didn't like the portrayal of Turks in our Minute about peacekeeping in Cyprus, a film that featured Lester Pearson, a former prime minister who is widely viewed as the father of United Nations peacekeeping efforts. The ambassador was upset that the Turks were wearing fezzes on their heads. I agreed with him and we withdrew the film from circulation, although again, like the Riel Minute, it was made available to schools for discussion.

The point is, people had become engaged in history, which was the goal. Best of all, if a kid watched a Minute like the one about the invention of basketball by Canada's James Naismith, and he could then brag to his American cousin about it, that was sweet beyond words. Clearly, not all the answers could be given in sixty seconds. You could really only catch people's attention and maybe get them to say, "Wow," or "I didn't know that!"

Even though they have, in some respects, recessed in many people's memories, there is still funding for new Minutes—for five new episodes a year at least through 2017, with the federal government paying for two a year. The newest are about the War of 1812, the centenary of the First World War, and the bicentennial of Sir John A. Macdonald's birth. Over time, as we reaped production efficiencies, the Minutes ended up costing about $100,000 to produce, with some coming in at $300,000.

Eventually, what we were doing at the CRB Foundation on the Heritage Project became too big for one foundation. In addition to the Minutes and interactive learning projects associated with them, among other things, we were also heavily involved in a program connected to schools across the country called Heritage Fairs. But between the Minutes and the Fairs, it all became too unwieldy for our foundation to manage and handle alone. Fortunately, a bit of luck intervened. Tom happened to notice a story in *The Globe and Mail* about a speech at York University business school by Lynton "Red" Wilson, who was at the time the chairman and CEO of BCE (Bell Canada Enterprises). Wilson was lamenting young Canadians' lack of historical knowledge about their own country. He thought the business community should do something about it, and he was willing to pledge half a million dollars toward changing the status quo.

Tom called me and suggested the two of us might want to join forces. As a result, I made a "challenge grant" of twenty-five million dollars to see if corporate Canada could come up with additional funding. The challenge was to run over five years, and the goal was met in three. The response was overwhelming, and the result was the formation of Historica, now known as Historica Canada. It defines itself as the largest independent organization devoted to enhancing awareness of Canadian history and citizenship, reaching more than eight million people annually. Its programs include not only the Minutes, but also *The Canadian Encyclopedia* (donated by Avie Bennett), Encounters with Canada, which brings thousands of students to Ottawa each year for themed study, and the Memory Project, in which veterans share their experiences with classrooms and community groups. Mix a great idea with a dollar here and a partnership there, and look what happens.

As for the value of learning history, Tom says it best: memory matters. It's important for citizens to know how Canada came to be, why things are the way they are, and how our predecessors coped with challenges. It's not all as serious as that, though. In the United States, the Bicentennial Minutes quickly became grist for the mill of comics, with satires appearing on *The Carol Burnett Show* and quips about them being made on *All in the Family*. That was a huge victory—you knew the project had entered the popular imagination. The same thing happened in Canada with *Heritage Minutes*. Once the comedy program *This Hour Has 22 Minutes* satirized them, Tom said, "We've made it." Patrick began slipping into movie houses whenever a new version of the Minutes was released to cinemas. People, he said, were applauding them.

Twenty-five years after the first Minute was produced, Canada is a prouder country. No doubt it tickled Canadian pride to learn from one of the Minutes that even Superman had his roots in the creative imagination of a Canadian illustrator named Joe Shuster and his friend Jerry Siegel of the *Daily Planet*, based on the *Toronto Daily Star*. So today, if you ask a Canadian who he or she is, that person may not say "a superhero," but you're more likely to get an affirmative answer.

9

Israel: Hope Over Upset

While my Canadian roots are undeniable, as a Jewish person, I have a deep emotional connection to Israel. As a
Bronfman, I have a deep family connection. In 1956, my parents paid their first visit to Israel, but they had been supporters
of a Jewish state since the 1940s. In 1945, they attended the
United Nations conference in San Francisco, where the future
of a Jewish homeland in Palestine was a central issue. In 1958,
I took my first trip to Israel, travelling with Leo and Sandra
Kolber. We met with Shimon Peres, who was director general
at the defence ministry. After our meeting, Shimon asked army
spokesman Dov Sinai to give me an escorted tour. Sinai looked
like a colonel in the British Army in India, and he took me places
where tourists don't go—squalid corners of Tel Aviv. In spite
of what he showed me, I told him Israel would survive physically, but it would have problems. Not only would there be issues
between Jews and Arabs, but there would be issues between rich
and poor, between Ashkenazi and Sephardic Jews, and between
the religious and non-religious. I don't think many tourists had
told him that, and it's all turned out to be true. I also told him

we'd see each other again, which was the case as well. A couple of years later, he became Israel's consul general in Montreal.

Our whole family met the country's first prime minister, David Ben-Gurion, in 1965 when the first wing of the Israel Museum in Jerusalem was dedicated to Dad. That gift in his honour was a contribution that helped found what has become one of the great museums of the world. As a businessman, I have also invested in Israel—making money and losing money and dealing with the nascent country's first major commercial scandal in the early 1960s. Since the founding of the state in 1948, I have known all of its prime ministers except for one (Levi Eshkol, in power in the 1960s) and have had close encounters with several.

While Canada remains one focus for my philanthropy, a significant chunk of my philanthropic work has been in Israel, from a groundbreaking informal education program called Karev involving hundreds of thousands of children (not only Jewish children, but also Arab and Druze), to projects to bridge the gap between Arabs and Jews, to fostering music through a renewed auditorium for the Israel Philharmonic Orchestra (IPO), to what is perhaps the dearest philanthropic effort of my life, Birthright Israel.

My fondness and commitment to the country would flourish after I married Andy. It was a marriage that Jeff Solomon also says parallels my love affair with Israel because of the severe pain caused by its tragic end on the morning of January 23, 2006, when Andy died after being hit by a car while walking our dog near our home in New York City. It was via Andy that I became so fond of Israel and her people, and perhaps since her passing, my involvement there has been more from a distance.

To understand her connection to Israel, you have to under-

Bronfman at the bat, West Palm Beach.

Throwing out the ceremonial first pitch at the first World Series game ever to be played outside the United States, in Toronto, 1992.

My induction into the Canadian Baseball Hall of Fame.
Gary Carter is second from left, with Pete Rose third from left.

At Expos spring training with Ellen and Stephen, 1980.

With manager Jim Fanning, after the Expos beat the Mets, winning the second-half divisional title in 1981.

Expos president John McHale, Rusty Staub, Major League Baseball commissioner Bowie Kuhn, me, and Jim Fanning.
—*Denis Brodeur*

Speaking to a Birthright group in Israel.

With Ehud Barak, former prime
minister of Israel.
—© *Robert A. Cumins, documentary
photographer*

A Karev student teaches me how
to play the drums.

Andy and me with Karev project students.

Andy and me with Birthrighters, early 2000s.

With the most respected Israeli leader, Shimon Peres.

Shimshon
Shoshani, me,
Baiga Shochat,
and Michael
Steinhardt.

With Stephen
onstage in Israel.

Talking to Canadian
Birthright participants
at the Old City wall
with Andy and our
partners, Michael and
Judy Steinhardt.

Andy, former prime minister Brian Mulroney and his wife, Mila, and me at the opening of *A Coat of Many Colours*, which Andy made happen.

With my colleague and great friend Jeff Solomon.

Israeli prime minister Yitzhak Shamir at a luncheon honouring
my mother at the Ritz-Carlton in Montreal in 1991.

Heading to the last Seagram shareholders' meeting, December 2000. Edgar is on the left,
Edgar Jr. is in the middle.

stand her parents' involvement. Back in Britain, her father, Hyam "Scotty" Morrison, had been head of the Jewish Appeal. Future Israeli political luminaries like Golda Meir, Shimon Peres, and Chaim Herzog were regular visitors to the Morrisons' home. After Scotty and Doris (a.k.a. "Sis") retired, they moved to Jerusalem. Their home in Israel became something akin to a French salon of the late nineteenth century, filled with fascinating types who engaged in stimulating conversation and debate over Saturday luncheons by the pool. It was a hothouse of thought, ideas, socializing, and warmth. Also, I'm a political junkie, and given that I'm rather obsessed with Israeli politics, whenever the politicos were in attendance I loved to pump them about what was happening.

But while my love for Israel comes flowing back in the form of satisfaction and meaning, at the same time there is sharp pain because of the ongoing conflict, which seems to become more difficult to solve each day. In my view, a deal with the Palestinians is a must, and a deal means a two-state solution, probably along the lines of the proposal put forward during talks when Bill Clinton was president of the United States, but is now further away with the re-election of Benjamin Netanyahu and the most right-wing government in the history of Israel.

The great Israeli writer Amos Oz wrote in *How to Cure a Fanatic* that it's a conflict over real estate. Oz says there are two families—the Jews and the Palestinians—who have an equally legitimate claim on the same house, and the only way to solve the situation is for each side to recognize that the other side has a legitimate claim on part of the house and then divide up the house. There's no need to be bosom buddies, just a need to make a deal, to make peace in order to stanch the bloodshed on both sides. That said, the context is beyond complicated. Another prolific Israeli author, Ari Shavit, has written in his provocative and powerful book *My Promised Land* that, within Israel, the Jews are Goliath to the Palestinian David—but in the region, the Jews of Israel are David threatened with annihilation by a Middle Eastern Goliath. Shavit writes:

> In the twenty-first century there is no other nation that is occupying another people as we do, and there is no other nation that is as intimidated as we are . . . A giant circle of a billion and a half Muslims surrounds the Jewish State and threatens its future . . . Here is the catch: if Israel does not retreat from the West Bank, it will be politically and morally doomed, but if it does retreat, it might face an Iranian-backed and Islamic Brotherhood–inspired West Bank regime whose missiles could endanger Israel's security. The need to end occupation is greater than ever, but so are the risks.

Basically, with a foot on the throat of the Palestinians, you're the villain, but give an inch in the region and you might get vapourized. From a demographic point of view, Jews within Israel are also on the road to being outnumbered, particularly secular Jews. If the present trends persist, he says, "the future of Zion will be non-Zionist."

In 1993, my brother and I sat next to each other at the White House to celebrate the Oslo Accords, the historic coming together of the Israelis, led by Yitzhak Rabin and Shimon Peres, and the Palestinians, led by Yasser Arafat. Would that the fine relationship we had that day continued. Such was not to be the case, given the sale of DuPont a few years later, the subsequent purchase of Universal, and the sale of Seagram to Vivendi. Edgar and I had many rough years during that period and after. But that day in Washington, another relationship was front and centre. The handshake between Rabin and Arafat was spellbinding.

I'm guessing that beforehand, Rabin had said there was no way he was shaking hands with that man, Arafat. But Bill Clinton, with his large physical presence and tendency toward hands-on politics, took both of them by the shoulders and drew them together. It was a take-your-breath-away moment. Two of the world's most bitter enemies had shaken hands, and Edgar and I figured everything was coming up roses. Wow, were we wrong, as were so many others. If only Rabin had not been murdered, if only Arafat had been truly willing to play, we'll never know how relations could have improved. It's another case of *if* being the biggest word in the English language.

The 2015 election results aside, it's my judgment that most Israelis simply want a deal to end the years of bloodshed. In spite of the conflict and the tragedies associated with it, Israel is too important to the identity and psyche of the Jewish people and to me personally. For a strip of land that is just slightly larger than New Jersey and with a population of eight million (New Jersey is home to nine million), Israel is one of the most dynamic, creative, soulful places on earth. Although I was born a Canadian and am deeply Canadian, I have always felt a profound bond with the Jewish people, and through that, Israel became part of my life—as a businessperson, as a political observer, and through my philanthropy. It has enriched my life.

My first immersion in Israeli life—through my first investment there in the early 1960s—turned into something of a calamity. Unfortunately, it was not a pleasant experience, resulting in the first major commercial scandal since the country was founded in 1948. The company was called Super-Sol (meaning "super store") and had been started by a group of Zionists from Detroit who knew supermarkets. Another person who was involved was a well-known Ottawa businessman named Bertram Loeb, who was in the grocery trade as well. Back then, the grocery business in Israel mostly consisted of mom-and-pop stores. Super-Sol was truly the first supermarket, and the company had just one store, in the middle of Tel Aviv. At the time, Jews in the Diaspora, like me, injected money into Israeli ventures to support the fledgling country. There was little expectation of meaningful investment returns, but I certainly didn't anticipate criminal activity.

Unfortunately, local management and Loeb were involved in cooking the books (inflating inventory numbers) to hide the fact that money had been taken from the company. The group had secretly invested in Super-Sol's suppliers and were bleeding money because they had not hedged their exposure to the U.S. dollar as the Israeli currency plummeted. To paper over those losses, they siphoned money away from Super-Sol and tried to hide the theft by overstating the supermarket's inventory. But the problem showed up when word spread that Super-Sol wasn't paying its bills—a mystery to us. In fact, the company was almost bankrupt because of all the money that had been stolen.

Given that I had purchased a lot of shares, I had been made chairman and suddenly had a lot at stake. Leo travelled to Israel on my behalf to get to the bottom of it all, hiring just about every accountant in the country to count cans of peas and everything else at the store and the warehouse. Sure enough, what was on the shelves did not match what had been grossly inflated on the books. There was a shortage and the crime had been exposed. Leo confronted one of the Israelis, who confessed, at which point the lights suddenly went out in the room, adding to the eerie, creepy nature of the situation. Later, there was a "mysterious" fire that destroyed the building where Super-Sol had its headquarters, something Leo predicted would happen.

It turns out the late Bert Loeb, the Ottawa grocery baron, was the central figure in the scandal, and the whole scheme was unmasked by Leo's hard-boiled investigation. Loeb wrote a letter of resignation to the board, and at the next meeting, at which he was present, I read it aloud to the directors. I then said I would entertain a motion to reject Mr. Loeb's letter of resignation. It was moved and seconded, and the board then unanimously voted that it not be accepted. I then said that the chair would now entertain a motion to *fire* Mr. Loeb, and Loeb was fired. He then paid us back a million dollars, which went right into the company, and he was warned that the minute he set foot in Israel again, he would be arrested. This was a man, by the way, who wanted to be head of the Zionist Organization of Canada.

As for Super-Sol, Leo returned from Israel and reported that it was bankrupt and should declare insolvency. I told him we could not suggest that because there were fifteen hundred North American shareholders who would never invest in Israel again. I prevailed, and then Leo persuaded me that he should hire a Belgian, Jacques Brin, to rehabilitate the company. Jacques had been the economic advisor at the Israeli embassy in London and became a trusted advisor to us not only on business matters, but also on philanthropy. Leo hired him, and Super-Sol recovered to become a terrific enterprise. For a time afterward, we controlled it as a public company, but we sold it in the 1980s at a profit. It's now the largest grocery chain in the country, with almost 250 stores. The whole episode, however, was a painful lesson in investing and governing a company, particularly at a distance of nine thousand kilometres away in a country I was just beginning to discover and understand.

That episode was in 1964. Things improved in 1965, the year the man who would become the legendary mayor of Jerusalem founded the Israel Museum. Teddy Kollek served as chief magistrate of Jerusalem for twenty-eight years. He had been born in Hungary and grew up in Vienna. Kollek's family moved to Palestine in 1935. In 1937, Teddy was one of a group who founded Kibbutz Ein Gev and also became active in the Labour Party. After the 1967 war and the unification of Jerusalem, he was asked to become mayor.

Who could imagine that the former kibbutznik would have the vision to found what would become one of the world's pre-eminent museums? But he did. James Snyder, who has directed the museum since 1997, says Kollek was not a museum person, nor an urban planner, but he managed to conceive an incredibly perfect museum. Snyder says that Teddy decided that Israel, which had sprouted out of the social ethos of Middle Europe, should have an encyclopedic museum just like the cultural capitals of the Western world, an institution that covers everything from the beginning of human time right up to the present. He thought Jerusalem, with its magnetic global draw, not only for Jews, should be its home.

High on a hill overlooking the city, the museum is a masterpiece, not only from the point of view of its collection, but also architecturally. Its collection includes archaeological artifacts dating from the Stone Age, the Egypt of the pharaohs, pre-historic Greece, Roman and Ottoman periods, late Islamic Art, whole interiors of synagogue sanctuaries transported from Italy, India, or Surinam, right up to works by Anish Kapoor and newly commissioned pieces by Jeff Koons. The place is a gem.

My siblings and I made the first major donation to the pro-ject in honour of Dad. Leo had been intimately involved, nego-tiating with Teddy in the years previous when Kollek was chief of staff to Ben-Gurion. The question was whether the whole museum should have the Bronfman name on it. Teddy told Leo that he could have one of two deals: for two million dollars, the Bronfman name would be on the whole museum; for one mil-lion, the name would be on a wing of the museum. Leo thought the lower-priced deal was better, and expressed his opinion to Dad. If your name is on the whole thing, if you're the guy who gets his name up in lights, he told our father, who else is going to want to give money to the place? It was a good argument, and it prevailed. The museum opened on May 11, 1965. Our whole family was there on the dais with Ben-Gurion and Teddy, two of the most historic figures in the building of the modern State of Israel.

The museum wasn't always in the glorious state it's in now. By the 1990s, it was clear it needed to be refreshed. I recall Andy, her mother, Doris, and I listening to a presentation by the then director, Martin Weyl, about how the archaeological wing could be renewed. During his tenure—eighteen years as direc-tor, thirty-two years in total—Martin really put the museum on its feet. He has been a very good friend of mine, but at the time of the renewal discussions, we weren't on the same page. In particular, Andy thought the museum should be refashioned to appeal to the three Ss—streakers, strollers, and scholars. As is often the case, less is more. You don't need thirty sarcophagi when three will do.

In 1997, James Snyder was recruited from the Museum of Modern Art in New York, where he had been deputy director. From a small town called Belle Vernon in southwestern Pennsylvania, Snyder is Jewish, secular, and had never been to Israel. He didn't speak a word of Hebrew. James succeeded Martin as director and moved the museum to its current all-star position.

"I knew nothing about this place," he says. But considering the opportunity to remake a national museum, a rare chance for a foreigner, he uprooted his wife and two children from their Manhattan existence and has been there for almost twenty years.

It was raining the day of his first visit to the museum. "Halfway up, I said this is an amazing place," he says, recounting his memory with tears in his eyes. He called his wife, Tina, and they agreed to go for it. There was one minor issue: James didn't know anything about archaeology, the foundation of Teddy's creation. Snyder's expertise was in modern and contemporary art from 1850 onward. He had to catch up on the previous million and a half years. So how does a guy from MOMA fit in with mummies?

"Everything has to do with everything. All things connect over time around the globe," comes the instant but deeply considered answer.

He's right, and with childlike curiosity, he jumped right in. It was soon clear, however, that the museum needed a remake, if not only to refresh, but to fully realize Teddy Kollek's vision.

Snyder went to work and raised U.S.$100 million after turning down a single donor who was prepared to give $52 million on the condition that the gift come with its own pre-cooked design. Snyder said the design didn't fit and bravely turned down the fat cheque.

Twelve million of that $100 million came from my children, Stephen and Ellen, and me to renew what is now called the Samuel and Saidye Bronfman Archaeological Wing. Andy and I were intimately involved in discussions with James about how to proceed, Andy more so. We had a number of meetings with him, but at one point, he said, "I get it. Leave me alone. It shall be done."

James remembers it slightly differently—"Andy could be very critical. Andy was very incisive about things"—but at a certain point, she told him, "Move ahead. I have nothing more to say." Tragically, she never got a chance to see James's magnificent achievement. Ellen, Stephen, and I were constantly consulted about the project after Andy's death. Not only is the museum a tour de force from an architectural point of view, but from a visitor's perspective, it's more effective. He doubled the size of the collection gallery to 200,000 square feet and reduced the number of pieces on display from ten thousand to seven thousand, resulting in a less overwhelming but more meaningful and enjoyable experience.

Janet Aviad speaks to James three times a week and probably puts it best. Through his renewal of the museum, Janet says, James brought to the fore the "open, universalistic side of Jerusalem" as a contrast to only the religious aspect.

"It's Jews *and* the world. Not Jews *against* the world," she says of the museum.

*

My involvement with and commitment to Israel intensified in the late 1980s with the establishment of the CRB Foundation. In addition to our office in Montreal, we opened one in Jerusalem. It's been situated in an old Arab house at 1 Marcus Street since we purchased the property at auction in 1986 from the American Friends of the Hebrew University. Surrounded by a wall, it has a courtyard with an orange tree by the steps. It is less than a five-minute walk to the house Andy and I lived in three months a year at 14 Pinsker Street, the home her parents had built when they retired. Pinsker was named for Leon Pinsker, a Zionist leader in Russia in the late 1800s (many of the streets around there are named for Zionist leaders). He wrote a book entitled *Auto-Emancipation,* which tried to persuade Jewish people to aim for national independence as anti-Semitism coursed through Russia during that time.

You can't escape history, politics, or religion when you're in Jerusalem. At times, from our house, we could hear the sounds of the Intifada near Bethlehem in Gilo, just fifteen minutes away from Jerusalem. My friend Hirsh Goodman, with whom I was partners in a money-losing but influential magazine called *The Jerusalem Report*—Hirsh was founder and editor-in-chief and I was chairman—says Jerusalem is a Middle Eastern city, while Tel Aviv, less than an hour away, is a Mediterranean city. He's right. At one point, Hirsh and his wife, Isabel Kershner, currently of *The New York Times,* became our Jerusalem neighbours. Andy had asked me to buy the house next door, number 12 Pinsker. The owners had building rights and she didn't want anyone looking down on us, so I bought it, and Hirsh and

Isabel rented it from us—for half the market rent as long as they looked after it and I didn't have to play landlord. Number 14 is on a double lot, complete with tall cypress trees and roses that Andy loved. It was gorgeous in its simplicity, and it had a swimming pool that was the nexus of parties throughout the summer.

From there, we would regularly walk to Emek Refaim, the main street of the German Colony district in Jerusalem. Fifteen minutes in the other direction and we could be in the Old City, with sites held sacred by three of the world's religions—Judaism, Christianity, and Islam. You can follow the long underground tunnels used to cart water up to the Second Temple, destroyed by the Romans in 70 A.D., with just the Western Wall remaining. There's the Church of the Holy Sepulchre in the Christian Quarter of the Old City, where it's believed Jesus was crucified, buried, and resurrected. You can visit King David's tomb, walk upstairs to the room where the Last Supper was held, and then up one more floor to a mosque—a religious triplex, if you will. One can visit the Al-Aqsa Mosque, one of the holiest sites in Islam, where it's believed Mohammed ascended from earth to heaven, and also where Abraham was ready to sacrifice Isaac. It, along with the Dome of the Rock, sits atop the Temple Mount (the Haram al-Sharif in Arabic), among the holiest sites for both Jews and Muslims.

To this day, archaeologists are still excavating Jerusalem. They are continually finding new tunnels and artifacts, adding to the already rich narrative of such a storied city.

It's my belief that it's difficult to call yourself Jewish if you don't have an emotional tie to Israel, and by extension, Jerusalem. Although there has been a marked rise in anti-Semitism and anti-Israel feeling in recent years—particularly in Europe—since 1948 there was a long period of more than half a century when "little Jew" stories faded into the background. I attribute that in part to the establishment of the State of Israel. So many of my friends and colleagues who live there are the legacy of families leaving the darkness of pre-war Europe, or those who found themselves in displaced persons' camps after the Second World War, before their families found their way to Israel. During the War of Independence in 1948, most Arabs living in Jerusalem left—some voluntarily, some no doubt by force—although they remained in Jordan-controlled East Jerusalem, the Old City. The new Jewish arrivals were people who also had ancestral or biblical ties to this land, souls without a homeland. Long before the devastation of the Spanish Inquisition and the Holocaust, many Jews were drummed out of Israel by the Babylonians and the Romans. But even then, and ever since, Jews have always inhabited the area. Nothing about the place is simple. As I wrote in 2005, one of the favourite expressions of Israelis is "It's complicated."

For several years, beginning with the Intifada, I penned a weekly blog. I wrote it to comment not only on the situation, but also to describe how we lived our lives there. Yes, there was violence, but there were also weddings on the beach. The blog started out as something simply distributed to friends. It ended up being sent to thousands of people all around the world, while I was only sending it to about three hundred. I would write it on Sunday afternoon, the first day of the work week in Israel, but a day free of interruptions from North America. Here is an excerpt of my entry for August 13, 2003.

There are so many things that can be done to ease the pain. End the humiliation. Every time a Palestinian is searched endlessly (s)he is enraged and feels like a toad in the road. End the constant barrage of anti-Israel propaganda on Palestinian TV. Encourage citizens of both sides to talk. I met with such a group during the week. These were not Peace Activists but sensible young people who simply want to live their lives . . . Encourage that. Or we'll see another Belfast!

And from June 11, 2006, regarding the criticism of Israel by the United Nations:

What the heck do those fools want? Israel gave back ALL of Gaza and told the Pals (Palestinians) to operate there in good faith, build up a reasonable economy and good luck to you. Their response was to fire rockets at a small, pretty town, then a much larger one, kill some Israeli troops, wound another and kidnap another. What, dear Lord would the UN and EU have Israel do? Suck its thumb???

As I mentioned, I have known almost all of the country's leaders since it was founded. I have also met its adversaries—namely, the late Yasser Arafat, the multi-decade face and commander of the Palestinians. Once, when I was flying over to Israel, Janet called me and said Shimon Peres wanted me to go with him the day after I landed to meet Arafat. I'm not so good with jet lag at the best of times, but that wouldn't stop me from this once-in-a-lifetime opportunity. So we drove to Gaza, and when we got to the border, another car took us to his headquarters, where we started up the steps, and there he was, in the flesh.

It was kind of otherworldly, seeing the same person I had for years become so accustomed to seeing on television, now walking down the stairs to greet us. At the meeting, Arafat was sitting on one side, Shimon on the other, and there was a chair for me, near Shimon but not next to him. That indicated I was a friend, but not part of the Israeli delegation. They were along one wall and the Palestinians were along the other. But it was a photo op for Arafat and Peres, and they were trying to make nice. The meeting was followed by lunch in the next room, and Arafat sat me next to himself, which was an honour. During the lunch, I decided to ask him a question he wasn't expecting.

"Do you have time to see your daughter?"

He looked at me and almost started crying. I don't know if he was a good actor, but it was the expression on his face that caught me.

Did he want peace, though? Paradoxically, peace is dangerous for people like that. Often behind them lurk more extreme factions. Although Arafat died from illness, people like him frequently lose power by being killed—by their own. Look no further than Anwar Sadat or Yitzhak Rabin. Both were peacemakers, both paid the price with their lives. The day Rabin was murdered, Andy and I were in Boston. We were in our hotel room when Ellen's husband, Andrew, called. "Do you have the TV on?" he asked.

I said, "No, why?"

"Rabin's been shot," he said.

There had been a political war in Israel between Shimon Peres and Yitzhak Rabin, and I was in the Peres camp—to the point that, in 1988, I was the largest funder of Shimon's campaign. In 1985, when he was prime minister, he asked me to be part of a six-person panel (which included Eli Hurvitz, the CEO of the pharmaceutical firm Teva) called "Operation Independence," aimed at making Israel economically independent. Shimon and I were, and are, close. But when Rabin was murdered, I had a meltdown for forty-eight hours. I knew something terrible had just happened to Israeli society, and unfortunately, I was right. In the twenty years since his death, the country has not recovered. It is badly splintered over which direction it should take. Even the design of Rabin's gravestone, which he shares with his wife, Leah, on Mount Herzl, in the national cemetery, reflects division. It consists of two large stone blocks: one white, one black, and no shades of grey.

Andy and I made a point of being in Israel or staying when there was trouble and violence—and our foundation has dedicated itself to improving people's lives there as well as forging relationships with the Diaspora in the hope of stronger ties. When I say "people," I don't mean just Israeli Jews, but also the 20 per cent of the total population that is Arabic (which includes Muslims and Christians), Bedouin, Druze, and Circassian. In the wake of the Oslo Accords, our foundation was asked by the Peres people to be Israel's "civil actor" and funder of people-to-people programs with the Palestinian Authority. There was a somewhat romantic idea that you could bolster the diplomatic efforts by building up contact between people in order to break down stereotypes. We matched Belgian money for joint academic research projects between Israeli and Palestinian institutions. The Israelis, with our help, gave grants to Palestinian scientists working in agriculture, water treatment, and mathematics. We matched money from Norway to put out calls for Palestinian youth educators. We ran summer camps for Jewish and Arab children who went to camp together. Many of the Palestinian kids who went had never seen the sea before that. We built a rehab centre in Ramallah for physically disabled people—Andy and I went to the dedication of the building in the heart of Palestinian territory. Our foundation was the only agency that tracked people-to people-diplomacy, post-Oslo. All of this went up in smoke with the onset of the second Intifada in the early 2000s.

Among the many programs that we've founded and built, one that will perhaps have the most profound impact on developing fully-formed children and citizens is Project Involvement, widely known as the Karev program. Karev is also the name of our foundation in Israel, and it is derived from my three initials, CRB. When you put together the three Hebrew letters that spell CRB, the resulting word is pronounced "Karev." In a happy accident, Karev also means "bring closer," which turned out to be an apt phrase.

One of the many stereotypes of the Jewish mother is that she drives her children hard so that they get a good education. Ironically, the State of Israel fell down on the job of national Jewish mother. As a result of a budgetary crisis in the 1980s, the government eliminated what it considered to be non-core courses in schools. Math and science would stay. Music, art, and the kinds of subjects that enrich minds and lives would disappear and the school day would end around 1 p.m. This was terrible, but it also created a big gaping opportunity for focused, high-impact philanthropy.

We saw a chance to offer informal education, the kind that Andy and I preferred. We also got lucky with timing. The early

1990s were the years of a mass migration of Jews from the former Soviet Union to Israel. In the decade following Mikhail Gorbachev's dismantling of the USSR, almost a million people arrived, seeking new lives, and few of these newcomers spoke Hebrew. However, many of them had valuable skills that they could teach kids without relying on the language. They were musicians, they were artists, they were dancers, they were actors, they were chess players, they were librarians, and they were jugglers.

Not only did we see the opportunity, but also in 1992 the new Israeli government headed by Prime Minister Yitzhak Rabin (he had also been PM in the 1970s) saw a solution to a pressing issue: the government wanted immigrants, but the question was how to absorb them all into Israeli society. Bingo: the government discovered our Karev program.

Rabin's finance minister was Avraham (nicknamed Baiga) Shochat. At the time, our Karev program was in just five locales. Shochat called me at my office in Montreal and asked how we'd like to expand the program fivefold. I said, "Baiga, we don't have the money."

He said, "Well, we do." He made us aware that the government was ready to step up with twenty million shekels, about five million dollars at the time. If it weren't for the post-Soviet migration, the government might not have become involved, but there was a great worry at official levels about how to cope with the tsunami of arrivals.

While Karev started as a pilot program in a handful of locales, its structure and funding evolved into a highly sophisticated model that we would later apply to Birthright Israel. Our lawyer Tzaly Reshef devised it. A Harvard graduate, Tzaly was born in

Jerusalem. His father arrived in what is now Israel from Poland in 1934, when he was eight years old, and his mother in 1940—both just in time to escape the Nazis. Tzaly comes by his sharp legal mind honestly—both of his parents were lawyers. When it became clear that the government wanted Karev to expand to fifty locations so it could sop up new immigrants from the old USSR, Tzaly said, "Okay, we'll finance the management team in all the places, and the government, municipalities, and parents will finance the actual program, one-third each."

The ministry of education collected the money from the municipalities and the parents, thereby eliminating the dirty job of us collecting from various people and entities, and then we administered it all. It was the power of leverage. Our two million dollars fed into a program with a budget of fifty million. We created the professional and educational parts of Karev and hired management so that we could maintain supervision and quality assurance. Again, bringing in partners and maximizing our dollars enabled us to make the most impact.

As of this writing, there are more than 130 municipalities involved nationally, some 800 schools, more than 4,000 teachers, serving almost 300,000 students a year with 1.5 million hours of enrichment programs, the largest education program in the country. Fifteen per cent of the program is in Arabic, evaluated by Arab educators. The program addresses one of the key goals of the foundation: overcoming economic and social polarities, or gaps, in Israel through education, with the aim of making it a more democratic, equitable society.

Among the people instrumental in helping us establish Karev as a national program was Shimshon Shoshani, a three-time director general of Israel's department of education. At the time widely regarded as the best public servant in Israel, Shimshon would later become the first CEO of Birthright Israel.

We also managed to snare another great educator to run the Karev program, something he did for twenty-five years. Nissim Matalon was born in Istanbul and came to Israel when he was just four, after the death of his father. His mother married a Jew from Berlin who lost his entire family in the Holocaust. Nissim was thus a product of both Ashkenazi and Sephardic Jews, the latter side originally coming from Spain. This mixed heritage gave him a respect for both cultures, something that would stand him in good stead while heading up an education program with children from an array of backgrounds. Nissim also got hooked on informal education during his years as a guide with the youth movement and his years on a kibbutz. He eventually became a nationally recognized principal of a high school in Arad, the desert town near Masada. After hearing about the Karev program, he took a sabbatical and joined up. He never left.

The town of Arad is where Rabin's finance minister, Baiga Shochat, had also been the mayor. Nissim and Shochat were good friends, and that's how the latter learned about the success of the Karev pilot program. Shochat told Rabin about it, and with all the post-Soviet immigration, a light bulb went on at the Knesset.

As Nissim says, the Karev program has given children the opportunity to meet experts in their fields—professional musicians, for instance—opening a window to the world that their formal teachers could not provide. From a social point of view, the program has reached out to communities that are low on the socioeconomic scale and that couldn't possibly provide the same kind of program to their kids. Ironically, the well-to-do areas saw what was happening and wanted Karev for their kids, a clear marker of its success. All the communities pay according to their means.

Sagit Klayman is director of a school called Keshet in the East Talpiot neighbourhood of Jerusalem. It's in East Jerusalem, on the other side of the Green Line, meaning it was part of Jordan prior to 1967. This is a fortunate school in the area. Of the eighty public schools in the city, only thirty per cent have the opportunity to have Karev because the municipality doesn't have enough money to fund all. Although it's an international destination, Jerusalem is the poorest city in Israel and the funding only goes so far, even though the government, municipalities, parents, and the foundation contribute. The school is also unusual in that, in the spring of 2015, it's in its second year of integrating religious and non-religious children. In this stew pot of a school, they are all mixing and learning from each other.

Amos Mendel, who is director of Karev for all the schools in Jerusalem and has been with the program for twenty years, is drawn to schools with few resources. To give you an idea of his level of commitment, he says he would like to have the words *He was a teacher* written on his headstone after he's gone. Oren Magen Cohen, the director of activities in the Jerusalem area, is cut from the same cloth. His parents are from Morocco and Iran, and he talks passionately about working with Ethiopian children. He says it was a mystery why they were doing so badly in regular school. He soon discovered that in their language, there is no word for "no." For cultural reasons, they also don't look you in the eye when you speak to them. Lowering their eyes is a mark of respect. As a result, Karev had to bring in special teachers from Ethiopia to teach the teachers. The program has also encouraged meetings between Jewish principals and the principals of Arab schools. They were amazed, Oren says, that they had the same kinds of problems—and they discovered how ignorant they were about each other.

Ironically, the government, in an ongoing state of alert about security, had deemed music a luxury in the classroom. What we found is that it can be a bridge between cultures—in this case, Jewish and Arab. It quite simply makes you a more rounded human being, one of the goals of education.

"The Arabs are the best ambassadors (for the Karev program) because they like it so much . . . It was generally in the Arab communities (where) you can't find these activities," says Nissim, adding that it's the same for the Haredim, the ultra-orthodox Jews. Their children would not have been exposed to these things without Karev. Andy was so proud of this program.

Among the honours I've been fortunate to receive—from the Order of Canada to several honorary degrees—two of the most meaningful have come from Israel. In 2005, I was asked to be one of twelve people representing the twelve tribes of Israel to light a torch on Mount Herzl in a nationally televised ceremony. To be asked to light one of these is a major honour. The ceremony marks the transition between the remembrance of the fallen in Israel's wars and the triumph of Independence Day. I was the first Jew from the Diaspora to be asked to participate, recognized for my work in education. Every bit as touching was being named, along with Andy, as an honorary citizen of Jerusalem. Few people get such a designation. It's reserved for leaders of the country or great scientists like Einstein.

The award came through our friendship with the then-mayor, Ehud Olmert, and his wife, Aliza. Later, Olmert would be elevated from cabinet minister to prime minister after Ariel Sharon's devastating stroke, from which Sharon would never recover. In fact, the night it happened, January 4, 2006, Andy and I were having dinner with Ehud and Aliza, along with other friends including Michael Steinhardt and Lynn Schusterman, my colleagues in Birthright Israel. Ehud was vice-premier at the time and Andy was sitting next to him. During dinner, one of his security guards motioned him toward an adjacent private room. There was an urgent phone call from the secretary of the cabinet. He was told that Arik (Sharon's nickname) had lost consciousness and was in an ambulance being rushed to hospital. Ehud came back to the table but said nothing. He was second in command, but Sharon had to be declared unable to carry out the duties of prime minister for Ehud to assume those responsibilities.

Aliza asked him what was going on, and he still remained silent. Half an hour later, he got a call directly to his cellphone. It was again the secretary of the cabinet, saying it looked very bad and that he should go home and wait for more news. After the call, Ehud asked for everyone's attention. He apologized and said he and Aliza had to leave immediately because the PM had lost consciousness.

"I practically became prime minister in the presence of Charles and Andy," Ehud says. Things can change fast. Not only would he suddenly become leader of the country, but also this occurred just three weeks before Andy's untimely death.

Before that, though, Andy was a friendly thorn in Ehud's side. Because she had spent so much time in Jerusalem—first with her parents and then with me three or four months of the year—she felt entitled to give her uncensored opinion. In fact, many of my Israeli friends thought of her as almost Israeli in her outspoken manner and bluntness.

"Andy would jump on me and start to yell at me. The place was dirty, the sidewalk was broken," Ehud recalls her complaining. He was, however, respectful of the fact that she had the guts to tell him what she thought without giving a damn who he was. She was someone who walked the streets of Jerusalem every day and knew it like a resident.

"I'm used to blunt people. I'm not used to blunt strangers," says Ehud's wife, Aliza, a dear friend. "She had a right to be blunt because she was part of us. When she criticized, there was pain and concern. It wasn't just an outsider coming in and telling you your faults."

The truth is, as both Ehud and Aliza will tell you, Andy got honorary citizenship not because she was the wife of Charles Bronfman. She got it in her own right. Ehud says we received it not as a couple, but for each of our individual contributions. The ceremony was held during the second Intifada and was one of the few times you saw people smiling during that very difficult period. After making the presentation to me, Ehud told the assembled audience that he now wanted to give an honorary citizenship to Andy.

"The reason I'm giving it—I want her to stop yelling at me because I can't take it anymore."

I should add that I am very sorry that, after leaving office, Ehud encountered serious legal problems. He was found guilty and was incarcerated, but that does not alter the fact that he was, and would still be, a fine prime minister. He and Aliza continue to be my good friends.

There is one Israeli leader who has been a role model and friend for most of my life. That's Shimon Peres, one of the true global statesmen of the last hundred years. A Nobel Peace Prize laureate for his role in the Oslo Accords while foreign minister, Shimon was prime minister twice and later became president. In his nineties, he is still active with the Peres Center for Peace, whose stunning offices sit next to the beachfront near Tel Aviv-Yafo (Jaffa). Born in Belarus in 1923, Peres is one of the last founding fathers of the State of Israel. He says that his first lessons in politics came while working as a shepherd on a kibbutz, trying to herd the cows and sheep back home for the evening. The beasts needed a leader to move them in a common direction. Working for Ben-Gurion after 1948, Shimon was encouraged by Israel's first prime minister to move to New York to learn English. From there, he would run the Israeli mission during the day and study the language at night.

One of his key jobs was procuring arms for the fledgling country. As Shimon explains, the United States, Great Britain, and France had put an embargo on shipping arms to the Middle East. Nonetheless, through France and a Polish agent who took ten per cent for his trouble, arms were secured illegally. Shimon didn't like the arrangement—the agent, he says, was living like a prince in the building that Napoleon had built for Josephine. He decided to look around and thought maybe Canada would sell Israel surplus arms that were left over from the Second World War. That's how he first came into contact with my father.

Almost seventy years later, Shimon still remembers the details. Shimon asked for two types of arms from Canada—cannons (known as 25-pounders) and machine guns. The Canadian government approved the sale of the cannons but refused to sell machine guns. Shimon couldn't figure out why they would sell one and not the other. He recalls that most of the Canadian cabinet had fought in the First World War, in which machine guns were assault weapons, and the Canadian legislators therefore had firsthand, frightening experience with them. Shimon says cannons weren't as well known, so the cabinet members weren't as concerned about them.

"Twenty-five-pounders—not so dangerous," Shimon says with a wry smile, describing the selective Canadian attitude.

Now that he knew what was for sale, who would negotiate? Shimon's uncle was the head of Ampal, now known as the American Israel Corporation, which had been formed in the 1940s to guarantee loans. Shimon asked him about Sam Bronfman. His uncle said, don't bother, Bronfman's a dove and he's an admirer of Nahum Goldmann, the founder of the World Jewish Congress in 1948. It turns out Shimon and Goldmann were from the same village in Belarus—and Goldmann bet him a case of whisky that Dad wouldn't meet with him. Undaunted, off he went with his handsome young assistant, Yaacov "Shapik" Shapira.

"I have a little bit of chutzpah," Shimon says with a trace of mischief in his eyes.

They went to Seagram's Montreal headquarters—with no appointment. Two tall guards asked why they were there. To see Sam Bronfman, they said. Did they have an appointment? "No, but would you please ask him if he's ready to receive us?" Shimon asked. The guard went to Dad's office and, lo and behold, came back and showed Shimon and Shapik in to see him. Shimon describes Dad as small in stature, which was true.

"(He was) the size of Goldmann, by the way, the size of

Napoleon. All of them have some sort of Napoleonic complex," he adds, which also may be true.

Dad asked him what he wanted and was informed that the Canadian government wanted two million dollars for the cannons.

"He said, 'What? It's a scandal. Surplus guns. They want two million dollars for them? How dare (they)?'" Shimon describes Dad picking up the phone and calling C.D. Howe in Ottawa. Howe was known as the Minister of Everything (at various times, he was minister of munitions and supply, transport minister, and minister of trade and commerce).

"He was known as a very fine man, a gentleman and a good friend of Israel. And before the poor Mr. Howe has had a chance to say a word, Bronfman started to attack him, like he was a small boy," repeating how it was a scandal to charge a new country such a large amount of money for something Canada no longer needed. "I'm coming to see you," Dad bellowed at Howe.

At the meeting in the Canadian capital, Shimon could hear Dad continuing his high-volume diatribe against Howe from the outer office. When Dad came out, he told Shimon he'd managed to reduce the price by half to just a million dollars. That's when he asked Shimon where he'd get the money.

"From you."

Such impudence from the young Israeli lit Dad's fuse again. He soon calmed down and called Mother, saying they'd be having a fundraising dinner that evening and dictating whom she should invite. According to Shimon, everyone who was invited came, and everybody gave. That was the beginning of a lifelong friendship with our family.

If Shimon is the Israeli leader I've been closest to, the one I've been furthest from was Yitzhak Shamir. In one of the elections in the 1980s, the two political warriors had virtually tied and agreed on a power-sharing arrangement. One would be prime minister while the other served as foreign minister, and then they'd switch roles after two years. It was certainly no secret I was a Peres supporter, but when Shamir was PM, Leo Kolber's son Jonathan and I had an appointment to see him. Normally, the prime minister would get up, greet me at the door, and then we'd all sit on a couch or comfortable chairs to talk. I'll never forget how Shamir stood behind his desk with his fists planted on it. It was clearly a stance of defiance, so I tried to defuse the tension.

"Well, Mr. Shamir, you know Jonathan and I did everything we could to make sure you're not standing where you are now. But that didn't happen. So why don't we sit down and talk business?" We did, with us on the couch and Shamir in a chair. At issue was the sale of our interest in Super-Sol. I assured Shamir that in spite of what people assumed, we were not divesting because he was prime minister and our man wasn't. I told him we would reinvest at some point. I didn't know when but guaranteed it would happen, and not just because we were nice guys, but when we saw the right opportunity.

In another instance in his office, he started in on me because he knew I was close to Shimon and he wanted to send his adversary a message through me. Shamir went into metaphor mode. He told me he was trying to steer the good ship Israel through a river that had many shoals and rocks and was doing his best to steer it to a safe harbour. "But I have a partner on the vessel," he added, leaving a long pause. I said to myself, *Display no emotion at all, no matter what he says.*

"If you have a partner," he went on to say, "that partner must go along with you, otherwise it's very difficult to steer the ship of state." It wasn't hard to decode what he was saying. Shamir wanted Peres to be truly on board, but he wasn't going to say it overtly. I was so impassive as he said this that he looked at me and said, "You do understand what I'm saying?" Obviously, I never said a word to Peres.

Shimon, though, has also been extremely close to Leo Kolber and his family, dating back to the late 1950s. In fact, Leo's son Jonathan—my godson—lived with Shimon's family in Israel for a time and refers to him as his "uncle." With Jonathan, I invested heavily in Israel in the late '80s, through the '90s, and into the early part of the 2000s, to the extent that at one point I was the largest foreign investor in the country.

A Harvard grad in Near Eastern languages (Arabic and Persian) and civilizations, Jonathan did a junior year abroad at the University of Cairo. After Harvard, he went on to Wall Street to work at the investment-banking firm Salomon Brothers, but he says he always had a dream to spend more time in Israel. His mother's grandfather had moved to Palestine from Poland prior to the Second World War, serving in the Jewish brigade in the Turkish Army in Gaza. His mother spoke Hebrew, and so did Jonathan. Wall Street culture, he discovered, didn't appeal to him, and he moved back to Montreal, where we welcomed him to work in the investment department of Claridge. Before we invested in Israel, Jonathan was active with us on a series of other deals—essentially, what's now called private equity.

In the late '80s, Jonathan and I turned our attention to investing in Israel. I had some minor investments there already but decided we should inject more, given that by then, there were viable companies and opportunities. Allocating capital there would no longer be just about supporting a struggling country trying to establish itself. As a result, we made several wonderful investments, guided by Jonathan. One was Teva, the generic pharmaceutical company that is now globally known and strides the world with a market value of more than fifty billion dollars. I was taken with Teva, as was Jonathan, but for different reasons. I was impressed with the CEO, Eli Hurvitz, with whom I had worked previously on Operation Independence at the behest of Shimon Peres. Jonathan liked the business, the numbers, and he sat on the executive committee. He's a financial engineer, while I'm an old-time investor in the Warren Buffett mould who buys and holds. Thus, when Jonathan wanted to sell and realize a gain on our ten per cent stake in Teva, I was reluctant, but we sold in 1998 and made a sizable profit. Still, look what it would be worth today! I kept a reasonable amount of shares but, unfortunately, sold them a few years later.

In 1988, we also bought out two of the families who owned the snack company Osem, one of the big food enterprises in Israel. It was a good time to buy. The Israeli economy was doing poorly, people were nervous about security, and the stock market was weak. Again, we sold for a profit, this time to Nestlé of Switzerland. Since then, Osem has gained market share and is hugely successful. But again, we made money, so I can't argue. The CEO of Osem for twenty-five years was, by the way, my dear friend Dan Propper, who remains chairman. Our third major score was with a telecom company called ECI, which Claridge sold to Koor Holdings in a fully disclosed, vetted and approved related-party transaction.

Koor was in fact our fourth major investment, and the one of the four that went sour. We got in over our heads, and frankly we got greedy. Koor was a conglomerate that had been created many years before by the Histadrut (the labour union) to provide employment, and it was Israel's largest industrial company. We bought Koor from Stanley Gold, who ran the Roy Disney family assets. Jonathan, his close business ally Danny Biran, and I became enamoured of the idea of morphing from investors to operators. And therein lay the mistake. I liked the CEO of Koor, Benny Gaon, very much. But Jonathan and Danny thought they should run Koor, and I acquiesced. Since three's a crowd, Benny left. One of the lessons is that there's a huge difference between financial engineers and corporate managers. This difference was laid bare in the running of Koor, and the company fell on hard times in part because of the tech meltdown in the early 2000s. Although Jonathan led it to a major recovery, when we sold in 2006, we took a significant haircut.

"I think they (Charles and his family) were extremely kind to me, and I worked my ass off to try to fix things," Jonathan says. "Charles's view was that in retrospect, I shouldn't have been CEO but we should have hired professional managers. He might be right."

I have purposely refrained from discussing the amount of profits and losses on each of these transactions. But suffice it to say, the Koor part of the equation led to some difficult times between Jonathan and me. However, we've now patched that up, he has a very successful investment business in which I'm a minor shareholder, and he and I are good friends. The nub of the matter is that when people work together, they have to be on the same page.

✳

It's one thing to make money—or lose money. It's another thing to do something with it. Aside from fostering educational programs or "people-to-people" programs between Jews and Arabs, or engaging in environmental advocacy to improve air quality or protect coral reefs, as we also did, philanthropic work can do so much to enhance daily life, particularly through the power of arts and culture. My work with the Expos in the field of professional sports was intended as a citizenship initiative to strengthen Canadian unity, and it inadvertently became an ego boost for me. My work with the arts has been intended to enrich the soul. Again, I have to give credit to my late wife, Andy. She made it her business to promote Israeli artists and craftspeople, determined to show they were world class, which they are.

Her partners in this were our friends Dale and Doug Anderson. Although their surname doesn't sound very Jewish, they are. They're sophisticated glass collectors who know everyone who's anyone in that world. It's their life. But I would frequently chide them for never having visited Israel. One night at a dinner in New York, Andy and I were talking about our next trip, and Dale piped up and said they'd join us. She and Andy got the brilliant idea to lure glass and craft collectors to Israel, knowing that most of them had not been there. Unfortunately, the Intifada disrupted those plans. But as an alternative, Doug knew the entrepreneur who put on *SOFA*—Sculpture, Objects, Functional Art—in Chicago and decided to take Israeli artists there instead. That show donated excellent space where artists could display their wares, and thus an organization called AIDA, the Association of Israel's Decorative Arts, was born. Doug still runs it and does an outstanding job.

Also involved in the establishment of AIDA was Andy's

dear friend Rivka Saker. Through AIDA, during the last five years of Andy's life, Rivka and Andy were extremely busy exposing Israeli craftspeople to galleries in the U.S. Andy supported Rivka's initiative to have an Israeli art week in New York, which later expanded into a month and then a full season. Rivka is the child of Holocaust survivors; her parents were originally from Poland, and at the end of the war, the Americans liberated her mother from the Nazis' Bergen-Belsen concentration camp. Her mother and father met in the so-called American zone and came to Israel in 1949.

Rivka is chair of Sotheby's Israel and also founded Artis, which promotes Israeli visual art. Like us, Rivka and her husband, Uzi, lived part of the year in New York and part of the year in Israel. When they were both in New York, she and Andy would walk early each morning in Central Park. At one point, I told Rivka I wanted to create a special prize in Andy's name for her sixtieth birthday, something we could do locally in Israel, and in doing so, make a difference for an artist every year. Franklin Silverstone, our esteemed curator, joined us in this effort. We kept it a secret. In the summer of 2005, we were with Rivka at an art fair in London and I told her, "We'd better tell Andy," because by then there was a risk she'd hear about it. We were all in a cab coming out of the fair when I told her. She started to cry.

"Wow, this is the nicest gift I could have ever gotten," she said. Andy, of course, jumped into the deep end, getting totally involved in what would be called the Andy Prize, which included a cash gift to the artist, an exquisitely produced catalogue, and an exhibition at the Tel Aviv Museum. Also, one of the artist's works was purchased for that museum as well as for the Israel Museum in Jerusalem.

In a cruel twist of fate, the first winner was chosen the day Andy died. Rivka and the jury were gathered in Tel Aviv, deliberating. Andy knew a winner was to be announced. Around three o'clock in the afternoon, Tel Aviv time, Rivka called our apartment in New York, figuring Andy would be back from walking our dog, Yoffi, in the park. She left a voicemail. Andy never heard it. A birthday present would suddenly become a memorial prize, although we would phase it out after the summer of 2015. Her children are planning something new as a commemoration.

Rivka and her husband, Uzi Zucker, would draw me into another arts initiative in Israel, one of which I am particularly proud. Uzi was an investment banker at Bear Stearns for thirty-eight years, and he and Rivka are significant supporters not only of the visual arts, but also of the Israel Philharmonic Orchestra (IPO), for which they donated a significant sum to build a chamber music hall. The venue for the IPO since the late 1950s, the Frederic Mann Auditorium, was not the best. The great conductor Zubin Mehta used to say that if you wanted to hear how the orchestra sounded, go hear it perform in one of the concert halls of Europe, like Lucerne or Berlin, but not in Tel Aviv. That's changed.

We had been involved in the Friends of the IPO, and Andy and I gave a significant donation several years ago to fund "Concert in Jeans," an informal one-hour concert at 10 p.m., which included a presenter who mediates the event in a fun, non-educational way. Not only that, but there's a free bar and party after. To help Zubin, we also gave money to buy violins for the musicians. But it was clear the Mann Auditorium needed a renovation, particularly in the acoustic department. The design was already underway when I had dinner with Uzi and Rivka in New York. Uzi said the IPO was having trouble finding a lead donor and asked if I would be interested in being that person. As I thought it sounded intriguing, I said yes, provided the terms were right. This would require a significant contribution. Fortunately, Uzi did all the negotiating for me.

In my view, there are two wonderful, world-class cultural institutions in Israel: the Israel Museum, with which I've had a half-century association, and the IPO. You might recall the difficulty my mother had in getting me interested in the symphony when I was young. Well, I grew up and became a Beethoven fan, particularly of his Fifth and Ninth Symphonies.

The hall is actually property of the Tel Aviv municipality, and because it had been declared a UNESCO Heritage Site, the exterior could not be touched. The inside, however, was fair game and required a total reworking. The IPO hired Yasuhisa Toyota, the acoustician who worked on the Walt Disney Concert Hall in Los Angeles, to give the auditorium a twenty-first-century sound.

The renovation was only half-funded, and therefore, the orchestra was looking for a donor who might want his or her name to be associated with the renewal. Tali Gottlieb, the executive director of the IPO Foundation, says that they hadn't looked at the contract with the Mann family of Philadelphia—the original donors—in years. For starters, the document couldn't be located. Was the original gift made in perpetuity, or were there time limits? After contacting the family, the IPO was told it could rename the hall under certain conditions. Frederic Mann, the patriarch, had to be remembered on the donor wall with a special column dedicated to him. Second, a room would be created in the family's honour as an original donor. And third—

the sweetener—the Mann family would be paid $300,000, the nominal amount of the donation in the 1950s. As a result, that created a naming opportunity.

Uzi insisted that the IPO and the Tel Aviv Municipality handle the Mann family. He wouldn't say it, but methinks Uzi's old financier's mind came up with the latter, creative part of the solution—which, by the way, has since been done for the remaking of Avery Fisher Hall at Lincoln Center in New York. The Fisher family has been paid more than fifteen million dollars to allow its name to be removed from the building to make way for a new donor, music mogul David Geffen, whose name will adorn a renewed facility.

None of my major philanthropic endeavours had been named for me until recently. You had to decode Karev to figure out it was derived from our foundation, and most people in Israel have no idea what it stands for. But I decided that I wanted my name associated with the IPO, given its pre-eminent stature in Israel—and perhaps the fact that I'm getting on in years. As a result, the foundation is giving ten million dollars (over eight years) toward the renovation. The building is now known as the Charles Bronfman Auditorium. The Tel Aviv municipality, however, stipulates that the "initial commemoration period" is for forty years, at which point the "naming family" or donor may be asked if they would like to cover the cost of additional renovations. If they decline, another potential donor may be approached, thereby opening up new naming rights, but the initial donor would still be recognized for his or her earlier contribution. As a professional fundraiser, Tali says she "choked" when she heard about the restriction, but she has come to the view that it's a wise way to proceed, with which I agree.

Surrounded by the warm tones of wood, the listener in the audience is enveloped by the rich yet nuanced sounds of the orchestra. From the delicate touch on the triangle, to the sweetness of the woodwinds, to the full force of the timpanis, to the crescendo of the entire ensemble, the music soars with Zubin, elegantly outfitted in tails, conducting the IPO three times a year—at the opening of the season, the closing of the season, and sometime in the middle. In March 2015, it was Bizet's *Carmen,* its thick, well-worn score in front of a passionate maestro who looks more like sixty years old than he does close to eighty. On election night, when the rest of the country's citizens were on the edge of their seats, waiting for televised results of a bitterly fought campaign in a divided nation, more than two thousand people chose instead to be transported by an orchestra that finally has a home with the acoustics and ambience it deserves.

Israel is a wonderful, cultured, technologically advanced, robust democracy. The ratio of research and development investment to gross domestic product is huge compared to the average OECD (Organization for Economic Cooperation and Development) country. Just look at the number of Nasdaq-traded Israeli companies, given the size of the country. It truly lives up to its nickname of "Start-Up Nation." Tel Aviv is a Mediterranean beach city, a party town, with surfers, great food, and great wine. Jerusalem has enough history, meaning, and singularity that you can never be bored.

And yet, while there is great beauty, there is also an ugly reality. The flip side of Israel is not comfortable at all. When Bibi Netanyahu spoke to the U.S. Congress days before the March 2015 election, bypassing the president of the United States, I, like many others, thought it was an insult to the leader of the country that has been Israel's greatest ally since its founding almost seventy years ago. To me, one just doesn't do that. The election itself—which Bibi won—made me feel sad because it pushed the two-state solution further away. Thus, my sense of upset.

However, as a Canadian or an American (I am a citizen of both countries now), I believe I can love my country but have the freedom not to like its government and what it does. That's how I feel about Israel right now. I love the country and its people but certainly have issues with the incumbent government's policies. My view is that, more than ever, it needs both the understanding and tough love of the Diaspora. It also needs to understand the Diaspora. I've always believed in cross-pollination between the Diaspora and Israel. It's the simple concept of "united we stand, divided we fall." Which brings us to Birthright Israel, a reason for hope.

10

The Magic of Birthright Israel

———

The view from Michael Steinhardt's office in New York City shoots straight up Fifth Avenue, cutting along the east side of Central Park, with the gracious tower of the Sherry-Netherland on the right and the top of the Crown Building on the left. It is, of course, a corner office, with windows on two sides. Old habits die hard for former hedge-fund types. There's a Bloomberg terminal on his right, its customized screen flickers with its trademark orange letters and numbers. Although he retired from actively managing money for clients in 1995, he still dabbles. On this particular day, he was anxiously awaiting drilling results for oil exploration in the Golan Heights. One of the original hedge-fund gurus, he launched his fund in 1967, making him a pioneer in what has become an industry of staggering size and scope. He says when he started, there were only eight or ten funds.

"Now they're at eight or nine thousand."

The term *hedge fund* can apply to many things, but in essence, it is a financial vehicle that features alternative styles of investing. Typically working for high-net-worth investors, hedge fund managers employ many strategies that are vastly different than the approach of mom-and-pop investors. The best of them do intensive research before making their wagers. For that, some have been rewarded with enormous returns. Many others have been wiped out. Michael is from the first camp. He grew up in a lower-middle-class neighbourhood in Brooklyn. Money was scarce, so he was motivated. Working exhaustively at trying to beat the market, by the age of fifty-five he had made pots of money. He is truly a self-made billionaire. But when Michael retired from the hedge-fund world, he was still young and was looking for what he calls a "practical application" for some of his fortune. He wanted to invest in something meaningful.

"When I decided to retire, I said to myself, 'I'm going to do something from this point in my life which is ennobling and virtuous.' I decided to devote basically full time and effort to what I called the Jewish future." He began to deploy his analytical thought process to the notion of youth trips to Israel as a means of "enriching and deepening" the long-term staying power of the Jewish people.

Although by coincidence he says he had managed money for CEMP—the trust set up by Dad for my siblings and me—Michael and I didn't really know each other. Also by coincidence, around the time he retired, our foundation was funding and thinking deeply about youth trips. Excursions to Israel for young people existed, but only in small numbers. Perhaps a few thousand went each year, sponsored by traditional Jewish organizations, and they were typically youth who were strongly affiliated religiously or culturally. The trips were also costly and required payment from participants, or as Michael calls them, discounted trips.

None of Michael's dreaming about youth trips to Israel had anything to do with religion. He says he's an atheist, having questioned how a good and just God could allow something like the Holocaust to occur. He says he never received a satisfactory answer. Although, like him, I am not religious, both Michael and I are culturally Jewish.

"Israel was, early on in my life, the Jewish substitute for the religion. I loved Israel. I idealized what it was. I have a house in Jerusalem. I go there two or three times a year. I think Israel is the great secular Jewish miracle of the twentieth century," he recalls.

The notion of Michael and me working together is its own miracle. Jeff Solomon calls us the "odd couple" of philanthropy. I'm thin, Michael's not. I'm an inheritor, Michael is self-made. I'm a long-term brand builder with a twenty-year time horizon, Michael is a trader with a ninety-second attention span. I'm an optimist, he's a pessimist. And as others would add, I'm the establishment while Michael's the rebel. It's that creative tension, Jeff says, that made Birthright Israel what it is. Although we came from vastly different backgrounds and approach things differently, we had something in common. Michael was concerned about assimilation in the North American community, the fact that most Jews in the Diaspora had not visited Israel, were disenchanted with traditional linkages to the culture like religion, not to mention the Jewish organizations that had perhaps become rather long in the tooth in their approach to an evolving world. As Michael says, "The average American or Diaspora Jew would as readily go to all sorts of other places before they'd go to Israel. They'd go to Italy, Ireland, and India. Just other I's. And there wasn't any deep interest in Israel."

Our motives were different, but they converged. I wasn't concerned about assimilation. I held the view that if the Diaspora and Israel could come closer together, we could indeed become one Jewish people and realize the dreams of our ancestors, including my grandparents, who had given up so much to find a place in the world. For me, it was simple: united we stand, divided we fall. I had alluded to this theme in a 1990 convocation speech at the Hebrew University of Jerusalem.

"Indeed, we dare not allow ourselves to grow apart. It is precisely the relationship between Israel and Diaspora Jewry that creates the modern compound called Jewish identity. The more intense the interaction, the stronger that identity," I said, wondering aloud whether we needed a new mechanism to create that interaction. Michael and I both felt it was high time for a new mechanism that would allow Jews in the Diaspora to get to know Israel and allow Jews in Israel to get to know those in the Diaspora.

I, of course, had been bitten by the Israel bug early on and kept going back, deepening my commitment during my marriage to Andy. As well, at the foundation there was a twin focus. Enhancing Canadianism was one, while the other was aimed at Jewish identity and Israel. The latter focus was the bull's-eye when it came to conceiving Birthright Israel. More broadly, the intent of the latter was threefold: to be happy you're Jewish, to identify with the Jewish people, and to have a positive emotional relationship with Israel.

So how did Michael and I come together on this? He and his wife, Judy, are intimately involved in the Israel Museum in Jerusalem and were instrumental in recruiting James Snyder as director. Judy, in fact, speaks with James several times a week. In

1998, Michael and I were both at an Israel Museum gala along with a few hundred other people. It was a lovely June evening, and after dinner, the two of us were on the terrace. If there is a metaphorical bed where Birthright Israel was conceived, it's there. We sat on a wall overlooking the Valley of the Cross. Michael explained his idea of a totally free ten-day trip to Israel for young adults—a gift from one generation to another as a way to learn about heritage and culture and to build a connection to the Jewish homeland.

"That is very audacious," I apparently said to him, a line he quotes to this day.

"And after saying it was audacious, he (Charles) said he would be my partner, and from that moment on until now, we've had a very solid, committed partnership, haven't seriously disagreed about too much, and I think we've really come to like each other," he says.

The CRB Foundation had been involved in youth trips since 1986 and into the early '90s with a program called The Israel Experience. Tom Axworthy recalls that it began with me talking about Israel and what it meant to me. At one point, I recall banging my fist on the table and saying every Jewish kid in the world should have an opportunity to visit Israel. I wanted to do youth trips. Why? People are sensitive or impressionable at certain ages to certain things. In a memo to Andy and me written June 19, 1992, Tom wrote, "*The* best single button to push, the *key* connection between North American Jews and Israel, is the trip. What you don't know, you can't love. And to visit Israel is to love it."

Other organizations—religious and Zionist—had been organizing youth trips since the early 1960s. Grade 11 students would go for six weeks at $5,500 a pop. For most people, it was a lot of money, so if you didn't have enough, you would be subsidized, and we contributed to that. But we also began putting money toward training Israeli guides and animators and began experimenting with incentives in Montreal's Jewish community. By 1991, we had an annual budget of $1.2 million aimed at youth trips. It had become the largest single expenditure of the foundation. The idea built and built, but as Tom remembers, it quickly became apparent that it was beyond our resources. It had to be bigger and it required major partners. In Jeff's words, it had been a "noble failure." Funding partners didn't always pony up and trip organizers did things the way they wanted rather than adhering to any strict set of standards. Most important, the number of participants did not increase, a sure sign the program wasn't going anywhere. We realized we were amateurs. Our partners were the UJA, the reform and conservative religious movements, and the Jewish Agency for Israel, JAFI. We were too innocent to understand that those bodies were not interested in increasing the number of participants. It seemed to us that those groups were more interested in using the profits to fund their own youth programs than they were in increasing the number of high school kids going to Israel. So by the time I met Michael in Jerusalem at the museum, the timing was ripe.

Before there was a glint of Birthright Israel in Michael's eyes or mine, there was Yossi Beilin. For more than thirty years, Beilin has been at the centre of Israeli political life. Born in Israel a month after the country declared independence in 1948, Beilin served in the cabinets of three prime ministers—Rabin, Peres, and Barak—and has been justice minister and economy minister, as well as deputy minister of finance and foreign affairs. He has been intimately involved in peace talks with the Palestinians, in particular the secret talks that led to the Oslo Accords. Beilin strongly believed in the need for trips for Diaspora youth. I asked him where he would get the money. He said from the Jewish Agency—shutter it, Beilin said, and use its $300 million budget to bring every Jewish seventeen-year-old from outside of Israel on a trip there. His reasoning was that JAFI's money was going down the sewer anyway. I said, "That may indeed be the case, but we both know it's not going to happen because the government will always protect it."

JAFI pre-dates the establishment of the State of Israel. Ben-Gurion headed it before independence, a kind of government in exile. After 1948, it stayed in existence as a body to deal with absorption of immigrants, as the link to the Diaspora and to get money from the Diaspora. For decades, the Bronfmans were among the largest donors in the world to the agency, giving many, many millions. I joined the board in 1980 and went to two executive committee meetings—my first and last—in 1983. After concluding how badly it was run, I resigned in frustration. I told Beilin that his JAFI scheme was a scheme to bankrupt the Jewish world. But he was on to something.

Meantime, a series of experiences with the organized Jewish community in the United States crystallized how I could best approach that side of my philanthropy, and Birthright Israel in particular. At the end of 1996, Andy and I moved to New York because Seagram's de facto headquarters was there and because it was the nexus of the Jewish Diaspora. It was also happenstance that the three major Jewish organizations in America—the United Jewish Appeal, the United Israel Appeal, and the Council of Jewish Federations—were in merger negotiations.

I had been intimately involved in the organized Jewish world in the 1970s through the federation in Montreal, but also in a larger context while I was on the board of the Jewish Agency for Israel in the early 1980s. The United States, I discovered, was a vastly different story. The U.S. was a series of fiefdoms, each run by very powerful lords. Consensus was a foreign concept. Case in point: the merger negotiations had been going on for seven years.

After just completing a successful chairmanship of the first General Assembly of Jewish Federations ever held in Israel, I found myself charmed by Max Fisher, a legendary figure in the American Jewish Community, into becoming chairman of the freshly minted United Jewish Communities, or UJC. Its birth, however, was torturous. Even agreeing on the name was rife with dissent and accusations. The issue was that the federations were virtual city-states, with the most influential being New York, Baltimore, Cleveland, Detroit, and Chicago. Whenever I tried to institute something, one or more of them would object; thus, every one of my initiatives went nowhere. As a result, I refer to my two-and-a half-year tenure at UJC as "my incarceration."

This was also around the time we were launching Birthright Israel, so I had my hands full. I had naively thought the funding for Birthright would have ended successfully by that time. But there I was, the chairman of UJC as well as co-chairman of Birthright. And even though I recused myself from any negotiations, the chairman of the executive committee of UJC was asking federations for one-third funding for Birthright Israel. Many of the power brokers at UJC considered that a conflict of interest. And in a way, I couldn't disagree.

All told, my experience at UJC was a mess. I hadn't realized the heads of the federations in the U.S. were so strong. I recognized that the federations had a role to play but decided I could make a bigger contribution to the Jewish world through our foundation.

After Andy and I moved to New York, the CRB Foundation morphed into ACBP—Andrea and Charles Bronfman Philanthropies—and it would be run out of New York City. We hired Jeff Solomon to run the foundation. When describing Jeff, I have been known to say that "we finish each other's sentences." Jeff comes from a family that left Germany as refugees in 1938 and moved to New York City. His father was a butcher and ran a deli in the Gramercy Park area. As a kid, Jeff worked in the restaurant, slicing meat, making sandwiches, stocking shelves, and making deliveries. When he was seventeen, one of those deliveries was to a social-services agency that was doing work in Harlem, and he was asked if he wanted a summer job with the organization. And so began a career.

Combining the street smarts of working behind a deli counter with the academic credentials of a doctorate, he brings an extraordinary intelligence and creativity, a robust intellectual curiosity, and a quality that should not be underestimated—a sense of humour—not to mention a taste for the finer side of life, such as single-malt scotch and cigars. When I first saw Jeff with his Beefeater moustache and beard, I jumped to the unfair conclusion that he was aloof. Wrong again. What you get with Jeff is warmth, exhibited by being a natural mentor and someone with whom I share fundamental values. Basically, what I lack, he has, and vice versa. The chemistry just works between us. I think it's also probably fair to say that anyone who climbs to the level of chief operating officer at UJA Federation of New York has a reasonably thick skin. As well, that posting brought great connections—Jeff knows everyone who's anyone in the Jewish world of New York. And not to mistake warmth for being a pushover, he also knows how to run a foundation like a business.

Jeff brought all his considerable qualities to us just as the first vapours of Birthright Israel were beginning to gather. When he arrived at our shop, he took a good, hard look at our Israel Experience trips and went into top-down management mode. As he would say, we built Birthright Israel on the "noble failure" of the Israel Experience trips. The big changes were the age group, the length of the trips, and who ran the trips. We focused on the eighteen-to-twenty-six-year-old group so we only had to market to that generation, not their parents. It was also becoming clear that identity formation was occurring later in life. Second, we went to a ten-day trip versus six weeks, which was way too long. Third, we changed our approach to the trip organizers. We outsourced, building a franchise model that had all the elements of the best franchise models. The trip organizing would be market-driven. And like all our philanthropic work, evaluation would be a core principle and be built into the budget.

Although Yossi Beilin's idea for funding differed from ours, we all wanted to end up at the same place. It was just a question of how. Michael and I began holding consultations with educators about how to set it up and soon began negotiating. Our two presidents joined us. Jeff represented me, while Yitz Greenberg, an orthodox rabbi and a leading Jewish theologian, represented Michael. You might ask what an atheist like Michael was doing hanging out with an orthodox rabbi. Personally, I think that Michael, an old hedge-fund manager, was hedging his bets. In the parlance of the market, he's long atheism, but maintains a position with the orthodox crowd as a hedge, just in case. Jeff's read is that Michael is simply drawn to *shtetl* culture. Whatever the reason, Yitz was his man.

For about a year, we worked out the details, but one issue almost capsized the whole enterprise. Michael and I fundamentally disagreed about whether the trip should be free or not. Michael pushed for free. Jeff and I thought there should be a nominal charge of $250 or $300, an amount within reach of most young people. My reasoning was that you only get what you pay for, the kind of life lesson my Dad would have imparted. To break the impasse, we hired a research firm to sound out how potential participants felt about the question. Most thought that if the trip was free, there had to be a gimmick. The research report was presented, and Michael might as well have opened the nearest window and tossed it out. He basically said he didn't give a damn what the research said, the trip had to be free. "It couldn't be another Jewish discount," he said. "It had to be a gift." It's too important to the future of the Jewish people, he said.

The atmosphere in the room was tense. I had said to Andy beforehand that I was afraid I was going to have to go to war with Michael, but I didn't want to because I liked him too much. She said, "Why don't you tell him that?" So I did, and he said he felt exactly the same way. So we agreed on a saw-off: participants would put down a deposit of $250 that would be refundable if they completed the trip. But Michael was right: the fact that the trip is a gift—all expenses paid—quickly became its signature.

Once we were a united front, we needed other philanthropists to get behind it and began asking people for a million dollars each year for five years. As Michael says, it wasn't easy to get those commitments, but we managed to get fourteen of them, including Edgar, who I have to say was very supportive (although at first he said no). Michael, for one, wasn't crazy about asking people for money, but he did. One problem was that the donors wouldn't get their name on a door. For their million bucks a year, people would think it was all Bronfman and Steinhardt. But they gave anyway. Once again, as with the Karev program, we were looking to leverage our contributions. He and I each initially contributed ten million dollars, but we needed much more to get it up and running properly. Specifically, we wanted significant contributions from Jewish organizations and from the Israeli government. Our lawyer, Tzaly Reshef, recalls a meeting before we knew how much we would get from the Israelis:

"I said, 'Charles, you can't do it, you're taking a risk.' He said, 'Look, I thank you for your advice. I'm jumping into the water.' And he jumped into the water. My advice was 'Don't do it,' but he did it anyhow. The only way to start it was just to do it. He said, more or less, 'It's my money, I'm taking the risk.'"

Then we needed someone to run the show, a show that would recruit participants, get plane tickets, buses, and hotel rooms, and have a full slate of activities. Janet said we should interview Shimshon Shoshani, who had been deeply involved in the expansion of the Karev program when he was director general of the ministry of education. At the time we called, he was director general of the Jewish Agency for Israel. Shimshon came to New York for an interview, but it was he who interviewed us. Ultimately, he was brought on as the first CEO of Birthright Israel because of his great track record as an educational administrator. A true mensch, the program would never be what it is without him. He relished the job because it got him out of the bureaucracy of the government as well as the bureaucracy and stasis of JAFI. Although meticulous in his approach, Shimshon is so anti-bureaucracy that he didn't even read a McKinsey report that we'd commissioned. It didn't matter. He knew what to do and he was CEO for almost ten years.

Shimshon remembers the meeting that Tzaly described a bit differently. According to Shimshon, Andy and I, as well as Michael and Judy, had arrived at our office in June of 1999. Tzaly was there, as was Gidi Mark, a former diplomat who had been recruited by Beilin as our marketing person and first employee (he's now CEO). As Shimshon says, up until that point there had been a lot of talk. There was also talk of another war in Israel in the summer of 1999. He says he told us that this was the moment of truth, and in order to plan properly for the first trip in December of 1999, we had to make the decision to go ahead, otherwise "the blah, blah will continue."

Shimshon says he'll never forget our faces. I looked at Michael, and Michael looked at me. Michael's face got red. I moved from one side of my chair to the other. We each looked at our wives, and all of our heads were down. Shimshon says we weren't used to the Israeli, non-polite style, a direct way of putting the issue on the table. He felt he was taking a risk, that he could very well have been thanked and dismissed right then and there for dictating to two rich philanthropists. Instead, he recalls that I piped up and said, "Michael, we are going to do it, aren't we?" And that Michael said, "Yes, we promised." As Gidi Mark says, even though ninety-five per cent of educators were against us, we went ahead anyway.

"Luckily, they (Charles and Michael) were both blind and

deaf," he said wryly.

Other critics started banging the table, right from the get-go. The so-called Jewish institutional world felt threatened. Our concept was dismissed as "Bronfman's blunder and Steinhardt's stupidity." Community organizations were already running trips, but trips that cost participants money. Here were two rich guys, coming along to offer totally free excursions.

"Suddenly, there's a new guy in town (and) he looks like a sexy guy," recalls Tzaly.

We made them look bad, and they reacted accordingly. Some started dissing the idea with questions like "What can you do in ten days?" That's true, to an extent. But as Michael says, what you *can* do in ten days is "create a spirit, create an intensity, an emotional response that might be in the end more important than the learning aspect for young people," because it sticks with you.

Among the early supporters was Benjamin Netanyahu, who was also prime minister from 1996 until mid-1999, the year Birthright Israel launched. He had signed a letter of support but was no longer PM when we sought funds from the government. It was crucial that we get government money, given the scope of what we were trying to do. We needed guides, we needed standards, and we needed security. We needed buy-in from the top.

That wouldn't be easy, given that the country had never spent a dime to fund programs for young people in the Diaspora. It had its own problems that required cash. The feeling among some in government was, "Why should we spend money on Diaspora kids (read: rich American kids) when our own kids need looking after?" The head of the Jewish Agency went before the Knesset finance committee to argue against any funding. JAFI considered itself the only legitimate interlocutor between the government and the Diaspora. In the same way, the American Jewish Federations rebelled against what they considered to be two rich bastards telling them what to do. They could gripe all they wanted, but the monopoly on dealing with the Diaspora was about to vanish.

Bullheaded, we didn't look back. Tzaly (and his partner Jonathan Schiff) put together the structure of the company, based on the Karev model of one-third philanthropists, one-third government, and one-third Jewish organizations. A steering committee was formed, because the government was not permitted to sit on the board of directors of a company. So in this case, the board took instructions from the steering committee, which was the real power behind the throne. The key was to allow the new organization to be entrepreneurial. The fourteen million dollars a year given by the philanthropists was supposed to be matched by commitments from the government as well as JAFI and the federations in North America, to give the project a starting budget of approximately forty million dollars. Again, the model was devised with a small management group, with the actual tours outsourced to both NGOs and for-profit organizations. Our mantra was "let the marketplace decide." In effect, we were a franchisor and the trip organizers were franchisees, all of whom had to abide by very stringent standards set by Shimshon and his team.

"This is the only way a small organization can bring forty-five thousand students (a year)," says Tzaly.

By the end of 2015, more than 500,000 participants had come from more than sixty-six countries, although roughly three-quarters came from North America. Dealing with the airlines became a major part of it, something Tzaly handles, mostly with El Al. By negotiating, he was able to significantly reduce the airfare. If you're transporting forty thousand participants a year, he reckons you're probably paying sixty million dollars in airfare alone, meaning every percentage point you save is a major difference and has an impact on the number of participants who can travel. In order to bring that number of kids to Israel, we couldn't really do it without an agreement with El Al. Unfortunately, El Al is almost a monopoly, which made negotiating difficult. However, the benefits weren't just one-way. It was good for El Al, too, so we came to an understanding. That did not, however, stop Tzaly from using other airlines—around twenty-five in total.

Ehud Barak was prime minister when the program received its first support from the government of Israel—seventy million dollars over five years. The money comes with a very detailed fifteen-page contract, not including attached documentation on standards, budget, and other matters. Barak, however, the former chief of staff of the IDF (Israel Defense Forces) and an ex-general, tended to trust only the guys from his elite commando unit. One of them was Loni Rafaeli, who was also one of Barak's chief aides during the election campaign. We knew Loni because he would lead our walks—often long hikes—on Saturdays. I took him with me to a meeting in Barak's office in the summer of 1999. Barak, Loni, and I talked about the proposed funding formula for Birthright Israel. I was pushing the Israeli government for a third of the budget. Barak then did a very strange thing. From behind his desk, he summoned about five different people, one after another, to ask them whether the government should fund Birthright Israel. We were sitting there. What choice did any of them have? They all agreed.

The funding for Birthright Israel was the first time the Israeli government had publicly announced its support and commitment to fund participants from the Diaspora, in order to ensure the existence of the Jewish people. At one point, though, funding from the government was suddenly cut to a mere $400,000—when Bibi Netanyahu was finance minister in the early 2000s. Michael and Shimshon had gone to meet with Bibi to ask for a continuation of funding, and both left convinced the millions would be forthcoming. They were astonished when the amount was cut to just $400,000, part of severe cutbacks to everything. I went to see Bibi and told him how much the trips were doing for the Israeli economy. He said, "Yeah, but none of it goes to the treasury."

I said, "Yes it does—through the taxes people pay."

"It's not enough," he said. The gap was filled by the Avi Chai Foundation, to whom we will always be grateful.

What the groups would see and hear on the trips was developed with great care. First of all, the trips had to be fun. My view was that if people enjoyed what they were doing, they would learn. Second, there had to be absolutely no coercion to become religious, non-religious, to embrace Judaism or not to embrace it. The idea was to leave a lasting impression, with the goal of doing something similar to the Heritage Minutes, to get the disinterested interested.

Two people who have been integral to the success of Birthright are Professor Leonard Saxe of Brandeis University, who has conducted our research, and Barry Chazan, who designed the original education program. As they outline in their book *Ten Days of Birthright Israel: A Journey in Young Adult*

Identity, the trip had to be more than just a tour. It required rich emotional and intellectual content, the framing of which was crucial. It would most certainly not be overt indoctrination, nor would it veer into propaganda or present just one political viewpoint. It would also not just be about historic sites and the Holocaust, but would strive to show that Israel is a modern, contemporary society. Not only a litany of tragedies and defeats, but also a country of victories and successes.

As well, the participants would have a chance to listen to speakers ranging from former prime ministers to academics, to business leaders, to writers; vastly different from the kinds of Jewish authority figures—mostly rabbis—they might have been accustomed to listening to at home. Guides were to be officially accredited by the government, and it was hoped that by travelling together on buses of forty people, there would be a bonding experience over the course of the ten days. There was always the question, though: Should Birthright Israel simply be a trip, as many believed, or should it have serious educational value? We insisted that if it were to be a gift, it required a sound educational foundation. Barry Chazan led the task force on creating that educational experience. Due to his dogged determination, against all odds, we prevailed in the view that education was critical.

A few years into the program, thanks to the army's then head of education, General Elazar Stern, for five of those days members of the IDF would join the groups for a so-called *Mifgash*, or "shared encounter." Stern and I had negotiated over how many days it would be—he said three, I said seven. We sawed off at five. This, I'm proud to say, is now the most meaningful part of the trip. I had promoted the idea with Shimshon from the get-go, but it was delayed due to a lack of funds. It was designed to eradicate stereotypes on both sides, a subject close to Andy's heart. The soldiers would discover that their peers from the Diaspora weren't just spoiled, entitled kids, and those from the Diaspora would discover that those in the IDF didn't have horns. Saxe and Chazan wrote that the "Mifgash experience enables participants to see themselves in the mirror: to imagine what they would be like if, at least metaphorically, their grandparents had ended up in Tel Aviv rather than New York City." The whole idea of the trip is experiential learning and for the participants to be left with "an overwhelming emotional experience."

Let's face it: as I've said, it also had to be fun. You're not going all that way just for a lecture. Interpersonal bonding on the buses over an intense ten-day period is a huge part of the deal. You make fast friends or intensify existing friendships. There's lots of staying up until three in the morning, natural for that age group. That said, the historic sites in Israel are not to be missed or diminished—the Western Wall and Masada are the top two destinations for trips. Yad Vashem, the profoundly moving Holocaust Memorial, and Mount Herzl, the national military cemetery that rises above it, are also key stops and tend to silence most participants. As you walk through the angular structure and untreated cement of Yad Vashem, the temperature gets colder, the passageways narrower. You learn how Hitler came to power, how a community that was full of life in the pre-war years was almost completely annihilated during the war in a diabolical, planned manner. At the end, you're asked by the guide to remember just once face. "They" can't remember, you're told, but we can. As you exit, you walk into sunlight and a view of Jerusalem, proof of the survival of a people. Afterward, a group consisting of young nurses, a young psychologist, and a producer for a modelling agency—part of a reform movement trip from Long Island—sat outside in the sun, teary-eyed, decompressing, trying to process the experience. As Zohar Raviv, the international VP of education for Taglit Birthright Israel, says, we try to push participants into a zone of discomfort, showing that Israel is more complicated than they believe. A generation of Internet surfers arrives, he says, with low levels of knowledge but high levels of opinion. Raviv says most find the trip humbling.

Our target market was—and is—the least engaged Jewish youth, those who never wanted to go on a trip to Israel. The zealots had already been or would go. Most Diaspora Jews, in fact, had not been to the country. Among youth in North America (the first trips were only from North America), at best about thirty per cent had travelled there. Of those we were targeting, Israel was not even in the top twenty destinations of the countries they wanted to visit. Applicants had to self-identify as Jewish and have at least one Jewish parent. The early advertising that appeared in college newspapers verged on the irreverent. We wanted something edgy. In one ad, there's a mohel with a knife, poised to perform a circumcision, with a line that says, "Sometimes it's hard to be Jewish." Then there's a picture of a group of smiling young people bobbing in the Dead Sea, accompanied by another line that says, "And sometimes it's not."

We honestly didn't know how many would apply or whether the enterprise would flop out of the starting gate. The day the applications were due, we were nervous, pacing our office, waiting for the log-ons. The response was overwhelming. For the first trip, there were twelve thousand applicants for eight thousand spaces. Interest was so intense, there was a lottery for the spots, and it wasn't long before there were substantial waiting lists. What that also did for us was create a natural control group for evaluation afterward—we had a group that went, and a group that didn't. They were all the same demographically, so we could examine the impact on the ones that went versus the ones who did not. As Gidi says, the timing was fortuitous because the launch and early years coincided with the era of online communication. Everything before that would have taken hundreds of hours more to organize. We had absolutely no trouble spreading the word. The first planeload arrived at Ben Gurion Airport on December 24, 1999. Birthright Israel was a go.

A huge boost to the program came with the addition of Sheldon and Miriam Adelson as major funders. In fact, next to the government, they are the biggest donors. A highly controversial figure in certain circles because of his support for right-wing causes, Adelson is a self-made billionaire, the man behind Las Vegas Sands Corporation, which operates, among other properties, the Venetian Resort and Casino in Vegas. His net worth in 2016 was estimated by *Forbes* to be more than $25 billion. We do not share the same political persuasion, but we both love the Jewish people and are united in believing in Birthright Israel.

Jeff and I met Sheldon in the bar of the Plaza Athenee Hotel in New York on the Upper East Side. We talked for quite a while, with him even suggesting we should own our own planes and hotels. It was quite the discussion, but soon enough I said to him that I was sorry, I had an appointment and couldn't be late. He then asked what we wanted. We asked for fifty million dollars: half for operations over time and the other half for the endowment. Jeff recalls that Adelson made it clear he wouldn't give a dime for endowment but might give annually for some time, without indicating a commitment. Trying to close the gift, I asked for one million a year for five years. Adelson said he doesn't play for peanuts. So the first few years the Adelsons gave ten million dollars a year, then thirty million, then forty million. I guess he figured I hadn't done my homework to find out how wealthy he was. Nobody else we'd solicited had given more than a million a year, so I figured that's what I'd ask of him. Politics aside, he has been an unwavering supporter. Both he and Miri love Birthright Israel and are totally on board with the educational platform.

Of course, terrorism would rear its ugly head on occasion. In September of 2000, barely a year after the first trips began, the Second Intifada erupted and resulted in the deaths of thousands on the Palestinian and Israeli sides. All of a sudden, we were faced with a very big decision. The Reform movement had cancelled its trips and the question became what to do with ours. That was my most stirring time with Birthright Israel. By then, we had seventeen philanthropic funders, so Shimshon and I convened an emergency meeting of everyone by teleconference. He gave his report and recommendation—not to cancel the trips. Even though many people were afraid to come to Israel at that point and even Israelis were afraid to take the bus, Shimshon thought the program should continue even if participation was low. His view was that if we stopped, it would be tough to restart because we were a very young and untested operation. To quit now would be disastrous. As well, the government of Israel had decided that school trips would continue throughout the country. Shimshon didn't believe the government would make such a decision if the situation were so dangerous. He said that if the government's decision changed and it cancelled its own trips, he would support cancelling ours.

I was steadfast in my support for Shimshon and for continuing. I also thought the decision was of such importance that, rather than just hearing everyone say "aye" together, I wanted to go around the imaginary table and hear everyone's vote, so that no one could hide behind someone else. As each funder said yes, I couldn't hold back the tears. Shimshon had totally taken the responsibility on his shoulders, and it was an awful responsibility. As he says, if something bad had happened, he would have been the one standing in the police station or the courthouse. You're talking about lives. Aside from Shimshon, we were all probably targets for lawsuits, since those who sue aim for those with deep pockets. Fortunately, in more than fifteen years, we've never had an incident. The approach to security is airtight. There is a protected room at the Ministry of Education—a bit like a situation room—so if there were any terrorist trouble, the bus drivers would know about it. The drivers report into the room each morning and keep their communication lines open all the time in the event they are instructed to alter their routes. It's like air traffic control, only more complicated because we also need beds. There are forty to fifty people per bus and many buses travelling around the country at once, all being tracked at the ministry.

When you ask Michael if he lay in bed worrying about sending youth to Israel during the Second Intifada, here is what he says: "I did not. Maybe I should have. But I did not." He says he thought about all the Israelis who get up every morning, get in buses or cars to go to work, and try to carry on a normal life.

He thought it was ludicrous that those living in comfort outside of Israel—who would only be visiting—didn't have the courage to do so for just ten days.

The financial crisis of 2008 and 2009 created a mini-crisis for Birthright Israel as well. Although donors were wealthy, few were left unscathed by the meltdown. Gidi had just become CEO a few months before the collapse of Lehman Brothers and everything that went along with it. Suddenly, we were looking at a twenty-seven-million-dollar deficit. We convened a meeting of key funders. Although many have described me as a soft person, Gidi says it is a mistake to paint me that way. Within an hour, after putting six million dollars of my own money on the table, we'd managed to raise similar amounts from others to wipe out the deficit.

Ultimately, we would like to have 51,000 participants a year. Why? Because the cohort of Jews born outside of Israel each year is approximately 100,000, so we'd eventually like to engage just over half of them. Right now, the budget is about $140 million per year, with an all-in cost of $3,000 per participant. Outside of the $38 million contributed by the government of Israel (a huge jump from the $400,000 it had contributed earlier) and the $40 million from Adelson, $45 million more comes from the Birthright Israel Foundation, $7 million from the Jewish Federations of North America, $5 million from the Jewish Agency for Israel, and another $7 million to $8 million from fundraising worldwide.

The goal of the foundation is to get it to $100 million per year in addition to what the Adelsons do. The key challenge is to break the myth that there are billions in the foundation. Potential donors react by saying, "What do you need any of my money for when you've got Adelson?" But because of the Israeli government's contribution and the contributions of Jewish organizations (although they agreed to "best efforts" to raise the money, they haven't ever reached the one-third funding target), we try to persuade people to understand that a trip is "a gift of the entire Jewish community."

We strive for continuous improvement. My father believed that if an organization is not moving forward, it's moving backward. I agree with that philosophy. So we're now looking at niche trips for foodies, physicians, scientists, and environmentalists, as well as extended trips of four or five additional days that will involve hiking or high tech and better logistics. We already have some niche trips paid for by the CRB Fund, set up by Andy's children and their spouses (Pippa, Moira and Tony, Marci and Jeremy), for which they have my lasting gratitude. We also now have two schools, one in Israel to turn tour guides into tour educators, and one in Chicago for North American Birthright "counsellors," two of whom accompany the participants on every bus. The goal is to ensure the meticulous educational program is compellingly taught to all participants.

But for those who worry about the essential future of the program—that it's not evolving, therefore sliding—I don't agree. Nor does Jeff. For some who have been around the program or know of it from the beginning, maybe it's become repetitive. But that's more about them than the participants. For the young participant, it's still a new and amazing experience. Bar and Bat Mitzvahs have been around for a long time, but for the youngster and family experiencing it, it's a big deal. Besides, how many people get a free trip anywhere, let alone to Israel? Over the years, we've received thousands upon thousands of notes from participants telling us how the trip profoundly affected them. For most, it was the largest financial gift they'd ever received.

As we've made clear, evaluation of all our philanthropic programs is an essential component of what we do. From the get-go, we've engaged respected researchers from Brandeis University to assess the impact of Birthright Israel. Essentially, we wanted to know if the trips were any good and whether we were reaching our target market. The answer has been a resounding yes on both counts. A study published in 2012 based on interviews with nearly two thousand respondents who applied to go on a trip between 2001 and 2006 resulted in some remarkable data. Again, we were able to compare those who applied and went with those who applied and did not go. Participants were forty-two per cent more likely to feel "very much" connected to Israel versus those who did not go. They were twenty-two per cent more likely to indicate they are at least "somewhat confident" in explaining the current situation in Israel compared to those who did not go. They were also forty-five per cent more likely to be married to someone Jewish.

While it's undeniable the program has changed many lives in the Diaspora, it's also changed Israel. In the spring of 2015, an article in *The Jewish Week* by Israel's consul general in New York talks about the importance to the country.

"For the first time in Israel's 67 years of existence, the conversation surrounding the Jewish state has changed. Rather than seeing Israel as a place of conflict, young people are now looking at it as a place of opportunity," writes Ido Aharoni. He says that via social media postings, Birthright Israel experiences are now reaching an audience of 250 million people globally. He cites an Ernst & Young study that tabulated the

Edgar and me in the 1990s.

With Andy's kids—Moira, Pippa, Marci, Jeremy, and Tony—at my seventieth birthday.

Early days with philanthropic colleagues: Roberta Axworthy, Arnie Ludwick, Janet Aviad, me, Andy, Barry Chazan, Ann Dadson, and Tom Axworthy.

With Stephen and Ellen.

With Janet Aviad in Jerusalem, 2012.—
Angela Forster

Stephen and Ellen with their grandmother,
Saidye Bronfman, on her ninety-sixth birthday.

A penholder with busts of Edgar and me.

With Rita on my
eightieth birthday.

Andrew and Ellen at
my wedding to Rita,
2012.

Election night in
Canada, October
2015, with Stephen,
his wife, Claudine,
and our new prime
minister, Justin
Trudeau.

With Andrew, Ellen,
Claudine, and Stephen, 2004.
—© *Robert A. Cumins,
documentary photographer*

With Rita, her daughters,
Andrea and Jessica, and
their spouses, Andrew
and Eman.
—© *Manon Boyer and
Pierre Arsenault
(www.bmwlm.com)*

This photo of yours truly taken by
David Rubinger, *Time-Life* photogra-
pher in Israel for thirty years.—*David
Rubinger*

Andrew, Zack, Lila, and Ellen Hauptman, 2014.

Danielle, Scott, and Talia Cohen,
2014.

With Stephen and Claudine's children—Isabella, Alexandra, Sam, and Olivia—in 2015.
—*Barbara Stoia Chevallard*

With Rita, March
2013.

With Rita on my eighty-fifth birthday.

Follow-through after a mighty blow! I am a contented man.

impact of the program on the Israeli economy, directly and indirectly, from 2000 through 2012. The figure is $825 million. Today, it has hit a billion.

In my quest to build the best nonprofit in the world, we've just seen the Birthright Israel Foundation listed as one of the fifty best places to work among the million and a half nonprofits out there. Not surprisingly, other groups of people— non-Jews—have taken notice of what we've done and put together their own Birthright-style trips. There's now something called Birthright Armenia, as well as free ten-day trips for kids from the Irish Diaspora and one to send young Greeks to Greece for ten days. Birthright Israel, a gift from one generation to another, is viewed as the most successful education program in the history of the Jewish people. Among the thousands of letters we get, we're struck by the extraordinary impact the trips have had. At the end of a fundraising dinner at the St. Regis Hotel in Atlanta in November 2015 with four hundred people in attendance, six participants got up and recounted vignettes about their experiences. Each one said, "The trip changed my life." That's echoed by the huge majority of the more than 500,000 young adults who have exercised their birthright.

11

Family: Love, Loss, Regret, and Pride

———

While the sale of Seagram and the disintegration of much of what the Bronfmans built was the nadir of my *business* life, the nadir of *my life* would be reached on January 23, 2006. Joan Didion famously wrote in *The Year of Magical Thinking* about the death of her spouse that life changes in the instant. It's true. Life changed for me irrevocably on that morning—not like the multiyear drip of Seagram going down the drain, but in an instant.

It was raining terribly that morning in New York. Andy took our dog, Yoffi, for a walk at about six thirty or twenty to seven. I had begged her not to go out, to let the dog do its business on the patio, but she was stubborn. Typically, she would walk Yoffi (a black Canaan, weighing about forty-five pounds) in the morning and I would do so at night. It was still dark when she left. She wore black running clothes, a black hat, and the dog was black.

I was in the shower when the intercom rang, and I let it ring. I thought her trainer had arrived early. I was still in the shower when the intercom rang for the third time, and so I got out. It was the doorman calling, and he said, "Your wife was hit by a car." She had been crossing the street, and yes, she had the light. I ran downstairs, and when I got to the elevator, there was Yoffi, shivering, with part of her leash in the elevator. When I went outside, there was an ambulance on 65th Street and the police had the street blocked off. I asked the police officer what had happened, and he said a car hit Andy. Apparently, a vehicle came around the corner and didn't see her. She had been knocked down by a black limo, and then another car came along while she was on the pavement. The second car didn't see her either, and the driver said he felt something and stopped the car and saw it was a woman. He took his raincoat off and put it over her. I asked where she was and was told she was in the ambulance. I said I wanted to ride with her, and the officer said, "No, you're not. We'll follow." I told him I was on the board of Mount Sinai Hospital, so we should go there. He said that if you dial 911, you go to the closest hospital, which was New York Hospital.

At the hospital, I was told Andy was in a room on the ground floor and that her injury was not life-threatening. I went into the room and spoke to her. She mentioned something to me about Yoffi, whether Yoffi was okay. To busy myself in a time of shock, I went over to register her, and then I heard shoes running down the hall. I went back into the room, and there they were, the trauma team. I asked what was wrong. They said that her blood pressure was low and they were going to operate. I then went up in an elevator with Andy and the trauma team, and they let me off on the next floor, where a doctor led me to a waiting room. I sat in there and waited. The doctor said he'd be back in an hour. I called Jeremy and Pippa, Andy's kids who lived in New York (they had already been called), and they came to the hospital.

Her son Tony in Toronto wanted to come, but we said, "It's not life-threatening. Wait until we really need you." She had broken bones, and we told him she would be confined for a number of weeks.

I started to get nervous because an hour and a half had passed, then two hours. Then a doctor arrived with an assistant. He was not the same doctor who said he'd be back in an hour. They ushered us into a little room off the waiting room. The assistant had three bottles of water. The doctor spoke, explaining that they had tried this and they had tried that.

"And the patient expired," he said.

"What?"

"I said the patient expired."

"Are you telling me my wife just died?"

This is how the news was delivered, in total monotone. And then they gave us water. Who needs water at a time like that? I said, "Let's get the hell out of here," but where would we go? I said the one place I know where we will get total compassion and love is at the office.

Jeff and my wonderful longtime assistant Angela would very quickly go into overdrive making arrangements. Andy wanted to be buried in Jerusalem. Just a few years before, she had been pestering me about buying plots, and we had arranged to purchase two on the Mount of Olives. In spite of our relationship being chilly for a number of years, my brother, Edgar, was the first one to arrive at the office to be with me that day—and he stayed the whole day. The only person I reached out to that day was our friend Blane Bowen. The year before, he called us after his wife, Sally, who was best friends with Andy, died in a motorcycle accident in India. Now, it was I making the call to him.

There would be two services—one in New York, one in Jerusalem. The next day was the first—at B'nai Jeshurun, Andy's favourite synagogue in Manhattan. I didn't speak. I forget who did. Jeff says Bill Clinton's office called to ask whether he should come to the service or to the Shiva. The Shiva was Jeff's suggestion, but at eleven thirty at night, Clinton said he wanted to come to the service. He sat at the back with family friend Martin Indyk, the former U.S. ambassador to Israel. President Clinton couldn't have been more gracious.

Andy was just sixty years old. She had died on my son Stephen's birthday. Her loss was both incomprehensible and incalculable—to her children, our family, our friends, our communities, and of course, me. Her contributions were too numerous to count. One of them, however, speaks to the compassion she had for others and is just one of the things for which she should be remembered: her response to those who suddenly faced the loss of loved ones, the families of the victims of 9/11. After the tragedy, she said to Jeff, "What's going to happen to all those widows and orphans once the hysteria is over?" Along with Andrew Tisch, Andy spearheaded The Gift of New York, an outreach to those who had lost family members in the attacks.

In an effort to help thousands begin living again, some 65,000 tickets were made available free of charge to theatre, concerts, sporting events—the kind of balm that could help families rediscover how to have fun again. There was unanimous participation from 261 New York-area arts, entertainment, and cultural institutions. In addition to the tickets made available over eighteen months so that families could use the program at their own pace, thousands of free-admission passes were made available at museums, zoos, and botanical gardens. The recipients were anonymous amongst the crowds. In Canada, Andy was the initiator of the very successful exhibition *A Coat of Many Colours: 100 Years of Jewish Life in Canada,* which toured the country, Israel, and the Jewish Museum in New York. In Israel, she introduced a program called Sunday Culture in the Army, so those members of the Israel Defence Forces who were returning to their posts after a weekend at home could enjoy theatre, music, or other forms of arts and culture while they waited to take the bus back to military duty.

To be honest, everything was a blur at that point. But after the service, I invited Edgar Jr. back to the house, where I motioned for him to join me in the laundry room.

"Look, whatever happened (to Seagram), you didn't mean it to happen, so welcome back to the family." It was clearly not a time for anybody to argue, so we shook hands, that's all.

After an abbreviated one-day Shiva in New York, we flew through the darkness to Jerusalem. In Israel, Shimshon and Janet made all the arrangements. It was raining the day of the funeral. There was a service in the park—Gan Hashoshanim—next to Andy's family home, which had become our Israeli home. A fund set up by Andy and her sister, Kappy, after the death of her parents, supplemented by me, continues to help keep the park's garden tended, administered through our foundation.

Shimshon used his clout to procure a huge tent and chairs. There was, of course, an overflow, so some people stood in the rain. There were white orchids, set in stones in front of the dark blue shroud, all under a canopy of white, flowing fabric. Stephen sat on my right, Ellen on my left, with her husband, Andrew, next to her. Tony, Pippa, and Jeremy sat next to Stephen. Their spouses, Moira and Marci, sat behind Jeremy. In the front, but off to our right, sat Shimon Peres, Ehud and Aliza Olmert, Ehud Barak, and Isaac "Bougie" Herzog. There were six eulogies. First to speak was Andy's sister, Kappy, who talked of the mark Andy left on Israel, "where she was happiest," a mark left by someone "a mere five feet, two inches with a push." Shimon Peres, without notes, gripped the lectern. He spoke so slowly and surely, it was as though he'd sculpted each word. Shimon talked of knowing both Andy's family and mine, describing the welcoming Morrison home in London. "When you knocked on the door, the family would meet you with warmth, readiness, and generosity for any Jewish need, for the needs of Israel."

A teary-eyed Janet Aviad talked of her twenty-year friendship with Andy dating back to a wintry visit to Montreal, "a meeting of values and ideas which transcended different background and style." She also highlighted Andy's spunky, complicated, often demanding ways as well as her notes full of exclamation marks.

"Who else came in the middle of the Gulf War?" she said, speaking of her commitment to the country, "without ideology, without nonsense."

Andy's friend Rivka Saker talked about being left speechless by her sudden death, a hole left in her heart. Her daughter, Pippa, spoke about how she and Andy's other children knew they were "her top priority." Acting prime minister Ehud Olmert said of Andy, "You lived here when it wasn't easy and when many of the great lovers of Jerusalem would call long distance."

It was almost like a state funeral. Afterward, we drove over to the Mount of Olives, and there was a graveside ceremony. The view of the wall around the old city and the Dome of the Rock is spectacular from where she is buried. In Israel, everyone except for soldiers is laid to rest in a shroud on a board or stretcher. I remember that when Andy's father was buried in that fashion, it was a bit too rough for my liking. I recall directing the men who lowered her in to be very, very gentle, and they were.

We sat Shiva at the King David Hotel for a week and unveiled her headstone—Jerusalem stone—thirty days after the funeral, as is the custom in Israel. On it, there is a quote from Churchill: "We make a living by what we get. But we make a life by what we give."

I did not want to go to the trial. Andy's kids didn't want to go, either, so I had a lawyer observe. The first driver got off with a fine for hitting a pedestrian. The second driver was a decent man.

I also debated whether I should sue the hospital or not.

In the years preceding the accident, Andy had struggled with breast cancer that had spread to her liver, ultimately leading to part of it being removed. Eventually, a brain tumour was discovered, although it was not cancerous. After Andy was killed, I got a call from an oncologist we had seen at Memorial Sloan Kettering. She said she wanted to give some advice.

"I don't know if you want to sue the hospital or not, but make your decision quickly. And if you do decide to sue, you stay out of it; otherwise, you will get sick yourself."

I was so upset with the way the situation had been handled from a human point of view that initially I wanted to write a letter to the hospital. After consulting with Andy's children, we decided not to sue the hospital and I decided not to write its president that letter. None of it would bring her back, and it would just prolong the pain. As for the cause of her death, a main artery had been ruptured in the accident and they couldn't sew it together. Could they have done better? Could they have saved her? We'll never know.

What I do know is that I loved her deeply and she made me a better and more effective human being over the twenty-five years we spent together. Quite simply, she built me a backbone. I don't think I had an appreciation of what my last name really meant to people and the influence it had. Andy taught me not to run away from that. We also had very different styles. I'm slow and process-driven, with an inclination to hold back. She was a gunslinger, which was both a blessing and curse. Andy's close friend Rita Mayo—who came to Israel for the funeral—said that Andy was my greatest challenge and I was Andy's greatest challenge, adding that I would not have achieved what I have without her and vice versa. She taught me how to think about myself and how I could accomplish things through the foundation. In fact, the day before she died, she gave Jeff and me hell about the Birthright Israel Foundation, telling us in no uncertain terms that it wasn't good enough. She was right, and in the hours after she was killed, we vowed to make it the best not-for-profit organization in North America. She used to say she was small but mighty, and that was true. Andy also deepened my involvement and commitment to Israel, because of her own family ties to the country.

Unfortunately, the last few years of our marriage were difficult and there were things that were left unresolved, in part due to the stresses surrounding her illness, but also because, in spite of my nice-guy facade, I still carried a certain anger from my youth that hadn't fully dissipated. She would say to me on occasion, "I love you, but sometimes I don't like you very much." We used to joke, when either of us left to go on a trip, "You're leaving me." It was all in jest. And then she really left me, big time.

After it was all over, Andy's daughter and daughters-in-law went to the Jerusalem house (and later to our New York apartment) and removed her clothes and her things. The house in Israel basically stayed empty for the next four years. There was no going back.

"When they decided to sell the house, it was like a liquidation of a chapter in his life, a very meaningful chapter in his involvement in this country," Aliza Olmert says. She also describes me as being very lost and very needy after Andy's death, which was true. It was during this period that my assistant Angela became a good friend. She went to dinner with me, kept me company, spent time with me just going through the condolences and managing the calls. She also came to Israel with me that first summer, working in the office in Jerusalem and helping me go through the house at 14 Pinsker, methodically selecting items I would give people as mementos. Many of Andy's stunning earrings we had made into cufflinks and gave to close friends and family members. Again, Andy's daughter, Pippa, and her daughters-in-law Moira and Marci made most of the decisions.

"There was a sadness about it, seeing this house wrapped, like an abandoned palace," Aliza says. But letting people have things that were there was my way of sharing something of my life with Andy—with them—one last time.

Rita was one of those who volunteered to comfort me afterward. She had not only been at the funeral but was also at my seventieth birthday party aboard a private chartered ship called *Sea Goddess I* in the Mediterranean that carried seventy of my near and dear. It was a sumptuous affair secretly organized for me by Andy after an already lovely celebration with friends in Israel, which as far as I was concerned was the best birthday party I'd ever had. For me, it had been more than enough, with the subsequent bash on the yacht feeling over the top, an unfortunate situation that led to friction between Andy and me, something I deeply regret.

Rita, who had recently divorced, had been apprehensive about coming to the party, where she'd be stuck on board a ship, but Andy made sure that her friend was looked after the whole time and that she found convivial company. On both sides of Rita's cabin, Andy had placed people Rita knew and liked.

A Montrealer most of her life, Rita was born and raised in Lima, Peru. After Andy's funeral, she told me she went to sleep very late at night, so if I couldn't sleep, I could call and talk for as long as I needed and she would help put me to sleep. That probably went on for ten days. As the weeks started going by, though, I found myself terribly alone, and at one point, I couldn't believe the sounds I made in the night as I lay by myself. With Andy's untimely death, I came to realize I couldn't be by myself. I'm the kind of person who needs companionship, even if it's just the radio. Within a short time after Andy's passing, even though I was still in a state of grief, I struck up an alliance with Angelica Berrie. For many people, it would be much too soon, but I couldn't help myself.

"He was in such a state after Andy died, he was wild, he was lost," Stephen says. "And he's such an old-fashioned guy, he needs to be married." So much so, that after Andy died, Ellen says she called my assistant Angela and told her "you'd better book breakfast, lunch, and dinner" for me because I had never lived a night on my own. It's basically true.

Someone had brought Angelica to the Shiva after the service in New York. When I returned from Israel, she had left a teddy bear at my apartment. Her late husband had been in the plush toy business, so it seemed a natural, warm-hearted, comforting gesture. I subsequently took it upon myself to invite myself to her home in New Jersey for *Shabbat* dinner. I had never met her prior to Andy's death, and she was about twenty years younger than me. Her husband had died a few years earlier. It just happened that she was open to my needs and I was open to hers. The attraction was that she was someone the likes of whom I had not known before. Solicitous, quiet, and beautiful, she lived in another orbit.

Angelica's also very interested in philanthropy and has her own foundation. The fact that we'd each lost a spouse was a bond, for sure. I remember her telling me at dinner, "You'll be safe here," which meant she wasn't after me. It wasn't a pursuit, it was just one of these things that happened. We dated and eventually ended up living together—on weekends at her place in Englewood, New Jersey, and then at my place, and then more at my place. A Filipino who had converted to Judaism from Catholicism, Angelica is a very kind woman. I have nothing but praise for her. But after a year and three quarters, we parted. I totally mishandled the parting, after which she told me that I should really learn how to do exit interviews.

After we broke up, I called my friend Michael Steinhardt and told him I was single. Michael loves arranging matches and said there was a woman I might like to meet. Her name was Bonnie Roche—did I want to meet her? I said, "I'm not going out with anyone by myself." So he said, "You have a book party tonight."

As it turned out, I was throwing a book party for David Rubinger, the photographer for *Time-Life* in Israel for thirty years. Michael added that he couldn't attend but his wife, Judy, would be there, and Bonnie would be there. That's where I met her. I knew it was her when she came in and I went over and stuck out my hand and said, "I'm Charles Bronfman." I think she was the last to leave.

In the winter, she and Yoffi and I would take walks together. We started dating. Bonnie was sixty-two and hadn't been married previously. She was an architect, had renovated some buildings—halls and things of that sort. Nothing about her conjured up Andy, and perhaps that was the attraction—so I wouldn't be reminded of what I had. We married in 2008—it was a major mistake for both of us. For my part, I hadn't really understood who she was when we got involved, and we were not compatible. She was artsy, spontaneous, and independent. I'm not. A lot of my calendar is booked a year in advance and I need a companion. Both of us were unwilling to compromise—our worlds were simply too far apart. Neither wanted to admit the mistake and the end was inevitable. Aliza Olmert, who is still friends with Bonnie, says that she wasn't right for the job. For his part, Stephen says Bonnie was wonderful to sit next to at a dinner party—attractive, fun, but not in synch with me. After two and a half years, Bonnie and I divorced in 2011.

Aside from the passages in my married life, there were other significant personal watersheds. My sister Minda passed away in the mid-1980s of cancer. It was a shock to all of us because she hadn't told anyone except for her husband and sons—keeping it from her siblings and our mother. Much later, she told Andy and me in Palm Beach that she had beaten her cancer except for one tiny speck that was left. Two days later, she had lunch with a doctor friend. During their meal, she had a soup spoon in her hand and dropped it. He said, "Minda, you're getting on a plane right now and going to Detroit" (where she was being treated). He knew it was brain cancer. We didn't know about her dropping the spoon or that she'd gone to Detroit. We were in Jerusalem when Johnny, her older son, told me on the phone that Minda had a week to live. So I started inquiring about flights to Paris and called him back to say we were coming. But during the conversation, his voice changed, and I knew she had just passed away. Minda died on July 1, 1985, at just sixty years of age. The only thing I could think of was to get to the Western Wall. My father-in-law (Andy's father) asked if he could come with me. I stood there, so pissed off. Looking up, I said to whomever the Supreme Being is, "What the hell do you want me to say to you? Thank you for taking my sister?" I cried some and I left.

Stephen was in Eilat. He, Andy, and I flew all night to Paris. Minda's husband, Alain, invited us to lunch. We were sitting in the living room, having a glass of champagne, and he said, "Well, let's go up and see Minda and we'll have lunch." It was all quite freaky. There was Minda in her bed, looking quite beautiful. I don't think we ate too much at lunch. The next morning was the funeral. They brought her coffin in, and you've heard about putting a nail in the coffin. They do it. And when they do, oh boy.

She's buried in the de Gunzburg crypt in Paris. After the funeral, there was a lunch back at the house with lovely cutlery and butlers serving—I guess you could call it a celebration rather than a Shiva. I was thinking about how I'd called her to see how she was doing and how she had probably lied and said that everything was fine.

I flew back from Paris to Jerusalem and was really angry. I went to the King David Hotel to have a drink with my good friend Irwin Field, whose wife had died of breast cancer.

"Why are you so upset?" he asked.

"If she'd told me earlier, maybe I could have helped."

"Let me tell you something. You weren't the one dying. She was. Anyone with that terrible disease chooses the way to deal with it. She chose her way and all you can do is bless her."

That was the lesson, and I got over my anger very quickly. As for childhood memories, I remember sitting on her bed. She was lying there, looking very sophisticated. Minda was six years older than me, so it was not as though she was some sort of mother substitute. But I found in her a lot of compassion, a lot of understanding. She also had a sense of humour. Although her French butler would make a production over her and say, "*Madame la Baronne est servi*" when a meal was ready, she poked fun at the Parisian pretensions. Phyllis claims she put on airs, but Minda jokingly referred to her husband, Baron Alain de Gunzburg, as "Al Ginzburg." Her son Charles became very close to us after his mother passed away. He regularly came on family trips and became like a second son to me.

Although she was upset with me for divorcing Barbara, Minda was the sibling to whom I was closest. She had also unsuccessfully tried to unseat Edgar as CEO of Seagram, so when she was gone, I lost not only a dear sister, but an ally of sorts in the family. Edgar and Phyllis were close. They understood each other, Phyllis says, and she seemed to take delight in the fact that Edgar was something of a bad boy. After Minda was gone, I was a bit more of a third wheel. Why Phyllis didn't get along with her is a mystery to me. But she says Minda didn't treat her nicely when they were kids and later disapproved of her lifestyle, particularly living "out of wedlock" after she divorced her husband. Phyllis also says that being second daughter was "pretty awful." Not that she felt she didn't count, but she recalled Dad complaining to Mother that "you're only going to give me four girls like your mother gave your father four girls." Being second, though, is something I can perhaps relate to as the second son.

"I think that he always played second fiddle to Edgar all his life," Phyllis said of me. As for Edgar's frequent lament that Dad never said he loved him, she says, "He (Dad) had nothing but eyes for Edgar. He adored Edgar. He lived, breathed (Edgar). Edgar was his successor, Edgar was his brilliant boy, Edgar was his terrific kid." It sounds familiar—just like Edgar was besotted with Edgar Jr.

Still, being a second son to Sam Bronfman carried more heft than being a daughter of any rank. When Dad divided up the spoils, Edgar and I each got more than Minda and Phyllis.

"I think it's incredible (unfair)," says Phyllis to this day. "And recently I said to Charles something about okay, it's forty/sixty, and he said, 'Oh, can't we drop that,' and I said, 'No, we can't' (laughs)." It wasn't fair, but Dad did it for business reasons, to give Edgar and me, who would be at Seagram and on the board, the heft to protect the family's stake—and it took him two years to decide the issue. If he'd split it equally four ways, we might have had another sort of family battle. In the end, Phyllis probably did better financially than me anyway. After being advised not to have all her eggs in one basket, she sold a quarter of her stake well before the Vivendi deal, and then the rest in the autumn of 2000. Phyllis says she'd never even heard of Vivendi until, over lunch in Venice, a European reporter told her about its involvement with Seagram.

Looking back, we were really not a very close family, our parents and my siblings. Some of us were close to others, but we were never a real group. Maybe it's because the girls had their nanny on their floor and we boys were on another floor. Dad was also away so much in New York and had that fearsome temper, which perhaps made each of us look out for ourselves. Still, each of us individually did well and contributed to society in meaningful ways.

Mother was still alive when Minda passed away, a crushing blow for a parent, even if the child is well into adulthood. One of the reasons Minda kept her illness a secret for so long was to protect Mother from the emotional pain. She outlived Minda by another fifteen years, reaching ninety-eight-and-a-half years of age. Until a year before, she was in very good shape, but then her body started going. The discussion with the doctor was whether to keep her comfortable, in which case she would die sooner. Either way, it would only be a matter of months at the most. We said keep her comfortable. She chose to die in between the day her daughter died and the day her husband died—Minda on July 1, Dad on July 10. Mother died July 6, 1995, twenty-four years after Dad passed away. At the time, Andy and I were on a cruise of the Mediterranean with Minda's son Charles and others. The day of her funeral I found myself in the study at home, in tears. A rabbi friend came to the house to check on me and I asked him why. She led a great life and was almost a hundred years old, I said. He looked me in the eye.

"It doesn't matter how old, or young, or healthy, or sick. We all only have one mother."

When Dad died, we never said our goodbyes or had that moment to tell him how much we loved him. There was none of that. You just didn't want to believe certain things. With Andy's dad, he had us all come over to Israel to say goodbye, one group at a time. He knew he was going. I didn't believe he was dying, and then a couple of months later he passed away of emphysema. In spite of the visit with Andy's dad, in truth, I haven't really had the chance to say goodbye to anyone—not to my mother, not to my father, not to Andy's parents, not to Barbara's parents, not to Minda. I saw Edgar the day he died, but we didn't think we were saying goodbye. And of course with Andy, it was so sudden and unexpected.

Edgar's death was expected and unexpected all at once. He died in December of 2013 at eighty-four years of age. During the last several years of his life, he did not enjoy good health. However, it was during that period that I feel as though we finally became real brothers. After a number of years of barely talking, lunching maybe once a month and tacitly agreeing not to talk about Edgar Jr., we had set aside the rancour and bitterness associated with the end of Seagram.

The last time I saw him alive was at noon on the day he died. We had been told that the end was near and we went, expecting things to be grim. However, when we got there, he was sitting in a chair in his study and appeared totally normal. The two of us chatted for a bit, nothing too profound, just shooting the breeze for five or ten minutes. He had asked me to bring our mutual friend Gerry Goldsmith to see him, and I did, and Gerry spoke with him. Both Rita (whom I married in 2012) and I were then speaking with Edgar's wife, Jan, in the small study they had. In his last twenty years, my brother had finally found a true soulmate. Jan is an artist and a wonderful person. She's politically on the left, meaning she occupied a different spot on the ideological spectrum than Edgar, who was more of a centrist, but the relationship worked very well.

We decided we'd go back to Florida the next day because it had been a false alarm with Edgar. That afternoon, we went to a movie and then for dinner with Angela. While she and Rita went to the restroom, I happened to look at my iPhone, and there was a message. One of Edgar's sons had left a voicemail. I'm not entirely sure which one of my nephews had called because some of their voices sound similar on the phone.

Edgar had died at 7 p.m. We rushed back to their apartment. I went over to the bed, kissed him goodbye, and cried. In spite of everything that had happened between us for eight decades, he was still my brother, with all the intimacy that goes with that. We'd had our good times over the years, like our hockey games or the six-week, cross-continent road trip we took together in 1949 in his Chrysler New Yorker—Montreal to New Orleans, Colorado, Vegas, Los Angeles, and Vancouver. There, we put the car on a train and flew back east in a noisy North Star, stopping in Winnipeg to visit our grandparents.

On the day of his funeral, there was a torrential rainstorm. It was a graveside service at a cemetery outside of New York City. The rabbi who officiated, Andy Bachman, used to work for our foundation and used to work for Edgar—the poor man was soaking, while the rest of us were under umbrellas. I joined in reciting the *Kaddish*, the customary prayer recited by mourners. Oddly, Edgar had wanted to be cremated. For a man who had found and embraced Judaism late in life, it was a curious choice, given that cremation is traditionally frowned upon in the faith. But the synagogue that performed the service was not the one to which he belonged, so he was buried. He was a very sick man, but he had ample opportunity to decide which way he wanted to go. He faced the reality that was facing him. Although I loved him and believe he loved me, the nature of my relationship with him is the major regret of my life.

At one point after the sale of DuPont and the sale of Seagram to Vivendi, I convinced him to join me in a session with a business psychologist I knew. He admitted during the visit that he didn't think much of me in my younger years. I had yearned for his respect but hadn't done what was required to earn it, at least in the business realm. I know he admired what I did with my philanthropy, particularly Birthright Israel, just as I admired what he did in unmasking Kurt Waldheim and exposing Swiss banks for profiting from victims of the Holocaust. He had also faced down world leaders like Mikhail Gorbachev, pushing the Soviet Union to allow Jews to move to Israel. And while giving President George H.W. Bush a tour of a Tropicana plant (Seagram owned the juice company) in Florida, he successfully lobbied for the 1991 repeal of UN Resolution 3379, which declared that Zionism equalled racism. In addition, he had his own foundation (named for our father), wrote books, and had a hugely attended memorial service at Lincoln Center in New York, where, among others, Hillary Clinton spoke.

In later years, though, he confessed. He and former Seagram executive Ed McDonnell lunched frequently in Sun Valley, where both had homes. Ed says that he lost out on fifty million dollars when Vivendi's shares plunged and that Edgar had advised him *not* to exercise his options and sell, even though Ed says my brother sold the very next week, explaining that he was diversifying his holdings. Ed says he was also present the last five days of Edgar's life. Over lunch in Idaho, though, in 2012, Ed says Edgar was coming to terms with himself and expressed remorse over his decision about succession at Seagram. "I stood up and shook his hand," Ed says.

Edgar also confessed to me that he'd made mistakes, including the serious one of not listening to his brother. Even though it was too late, this was important to me. If Edgar Jr. was his blind spot, I was his deaf spot.

In an email he sent me on July 22, 2002, Edgar was once again contrite: "I too am terribly upset about Vivendi Universal. As I look back, I realize that the basic premise was incorrect— content doesn't need broadcast control, it just needs quality."

After noting that the whole business had left Edgar Jr. "quite devastated," he concluded that "I should not have agonized so much about selling Seagram and should have spent more time investigating Vivendi."

Although my brother had verbally apologized to me for what had gone on between us, he went further in print than he ever did with me personally. In the spring of 2016, he posthumously published his last book. Here is Edgar, in his own words:

> *"Although the growing divide between us was not technically either of our faults, I acknowledge that as a young man I did little to make it better. After our father died, I became Seagram's chief executive officer, and Charles was my partner. At times, I treated him poorly, neglecting to consult with him on major decisions. Naturally, he resented it. Because*

I did not fully consult with my brother or engage him on critical decisions, I sometimes misjudged or avoided business deals and investment opportunities. Years later, when Charles and I were on good terms again, I apologized to him. That apology required complete honesty. Life would have gone on serenely for both of us without the apology, but sometimes doing nothing is as wrong as the act itself. I knew deep within myself that I needed to make amends."

We grew up in that same house together, with those same remarkable parents, in rooms across from each other, with the same DNA. It wasn't possible to be physically closer, unless we had been twins. Yet there was a gulf between us and something in each of us that prevented us from being emotionally closer, the true partners we were meant to be—and *actually were* when it came to our equal shares in the company. On my desk, I still have a beautiful black-and-white photograph of the two of us in short pants. In my office in New York, I have a penholder on my desk that Edgar had made for Dad. On it are busts of our heads, the two brothers. I was also touched by his dedication of his book *Hope, Not Fear* to Andy and me—and his handwritten inscription in *Good Spirits* about how he had tried to be honest in his memoir. In response to one of the many condolence notes I received on his death, I replied, "My grateful thanks for your message. Edgar lived a full life. He was a successful business leader, and yet his profound accomplishments were in the field of philanthropy. His passionate presidency of the World Jewish Congress saw him take on giants and bend them to his will for the benefit of the Jewish people. I loved him and miss him and will continue to miss him. As ever, Charles."

As for Edgar Jr., my relationship with him remains fractured. After his father's death, I was touched by how solicitous he was of Rita and me. He made an effort. I also extended a hand. But too many differences remain between us.

So that's where it stands. I have to admit that, had my side of the family sold at sixty-five dollars a share when the Edgar family did, it would have been the intelligent thing to do. I'm responsible for trying to hold out for more. I was too despondent to think sensibly. I should say that both Stephen and Phyllis are sympathetic to Edgar Jr. Phyllis philosophizes about how Dad loved the business, how our brother, Edgar, didn't really love it, "and by the time it got to Edgar Jr., I'm sure he didn't love it at all," more or less indicating he had inherited a family burden requiring all of us to be understanding of that.

"I never *did not* talk to him. And I feel very badly for him," Phyllis says. "He (Edgar Jr.) must have nightmares about that (Vivendi) every day." Frankly, *I, Charles,* still have nightmares. Instead of Edgar Jr., though, Phyllis blames the board, which included me.

"I'm not (furious), because he (Edgar Jr.) has to live with this stuff every day. That's the punishment he gets," Stephen says. "I feel badly for him, rather than anger. Sometimes you make bad calls. And you know, part of the failure was at the board level. Part of the failure, unfortunately, was Dad not putting his foot down and saying, 'Hey, we're not doing this.'"

Ellen feels more like me. Seagram was the big, warm blanket that enveloped us and protected us, wherever we went around the world. To have that blanket ripped away was traumatic. The roots of her assessment come from her childhood in Montreal. She was very close to my mother, whom she describes as "angelic," and says not a day goes by when she doesn't think about her Granny Saidye. In fact, Ellen was married in the garden of her grandmother's house while my mother was still alive and present. As a result of this deep connection, she says she grew up hearing stories of her grandfather—my father—working so hard in the business that the notion of selling Seagram and what happened to it is profoundly upsetting.

"I go into a bar and I see a bottle of Chivas Regal and I feel sick. To this day. And my husband feels the same way," Ellen says.

Their sentiment did not come out of the blue. Not only had both Ellen and Andrew been urging me to sell sooner, but previously, at a meeting with Edgar Jr. and me, Andrew asked him a series of very pointed questions. Afterward, when we'd left, I told Andrew that he'd been too tough on Edgar Jr. and advised him to back off. Part of it may also have to do with the fact that, in 1995, Andrew accepted a job offer from someone he greatly admired, the chairman of MCA's Motion Picture Group, Tom Pollock, for a position he wanted in Los Angeles. Then, by sheer coincidence, Edgar Jr. decided to buy MCA, which became Universal. Suddenly, Andrew was looking at the prospect of working for Edgar Jr. rather than Tom, something that wasn't exactly in his career plan. Ultimately, he did not accept the position. Later, he and Ellen moved to London so he could work for Tom there, but again Edgar Jr. made a decision that happened to scotch those plans, and Andrew only stayed for about eighteen months.

"Edgar (Jr.) and I found ourselves a little bit at loggerheads," Andrew says.

As for Ellen, she had also been in a big fight with me about my decision to put Stephen on the board of Seagram when he turned thirty-five in 1999.

"I'm blunt," she says.

Her view at the time was that Stephen wasn't ready for the responsibility of being a director of Seagram. Whatever the reasons, Ellen and Andrew wanted me to sell soon after the deal with Vivendi, and I should have listened. Ellen also feels that as long as my mother was alive, things were okay and the family more or less held together. However, after Mother passed away, Ellen believes the family bonds weakened.

"I felt like my grandmother kept us all together. And then it was like, the minute she was gone, no one cared."

On May 13, 2002, Ellen wrote a blistering letter to her uncle Edgar, saying that he and his son "have sold our family heritage down the river, have tarnished our once well respected family name, and have caused huge personal rifts."

There was most certainly a chill between Ellen and Edgar, but at Stephen's wedding a couple of years later, she describes my brother looking at her and saying, "Truce?" She shook his hand.

"It was my brother's wedding—what am I going to do?" she says. "He treated my dad terribly. And he didn't let my dad have his way. He made him look terrible in the press." Still, Ellen confesses to shedding a private tear in her hotel room the day of Edgar's funeral.

One of the unintended consequences of the losses associated with the demise of Seagram was that it freed up my kids from some of the burdens and responsibilities associated with it. At least that's Stephen's view.

"What that brought me was my own freedom in my life. So in a way, (it was a) terrible thing to lose because it was really sort of what we were. We were Seagram. The Bronfman family was an internationally known family. Powerful. I used to travel to different countries, and the Seagram representative would meet you and take you to the best places. It was like living in royalty. But it was also very, completely out of reality." When it collapsed, Stephen says, the real world came into focus and he realized he had to find a path for himself.

"I remember when I was in my twenties and we had these family meetings, and everything was one success story after another. Oh, this was up hundreds of millions. And then all of a sudden, *pfft*. That has all stopped. The machine is gone. And it was sad because it was the glue that kept the family together," he says.

Stephen reckons that we lost half of our assets. I think it was more like two-thirds, while Andrew says about fifty to sixty per cent. In spite of it all, we're clearly still a family of some means, and I know Stephen considers the impact of wealth on his own children.

"It was hard growing up as a Bronfman kid in Montreal, you know, having so many choices and not being too driven," Stephen recalls. "Scared about how you're going to fill these amazing shoes of (your) grandfather, father, uncle. Where is your place going to be? Scared of that stuff. Then, having some self-doubt, also never having excelled academically. So I think that was very similar with Dad. The self-doubt part and the lack of confidence early on," he says. "I loved my big house, but I hated bringing people there. I see that actually with my daughter, you know. (She says), 'I'm embarrassed to take friends, it's such a castle.'"

Ellen doesn't express the same anxieties about growing up

a Bronfman in Montreal. For her as a child, it was more about seeing her father's name in the newspaper because I owned the Expos, which has a certain symmetry to it, given that Ellen was born the year the Expos launched. However, she did move away from Montreal—and the family—while Stephen stayed. Her husband is an American whom she met at Yale—she always wanted to go to college in the U.S. But it's not as though Ellen felt like she was running away from her family, even though she's lived in New York, Boston, London, and now Los Angeles, while Stephen spent time away at school but then settled in Montreal.

Compared with Stephen, as a child of a very prominent, very wealthy clan, Ellen seems to have simply accepted that her surroundings were her reality. She wasn't quite blasé about private jets and being ferried by helicopter, but she accepted them as facts of her life, all while being aware that such a lifestyle could be off-putting to others. She didn't flaunt it. There's still a bit of the humble Canadian in her.

As children, both Ellen and Stephen had kidnap threats against them after Edgar's son Sam was abducted (I also had assassination threats against me). She did her best to accept the security guard who patrolled and drove her to school, at least until she was fourteen or fifteen, the first time she took the bus. She and her friends would look through the window of the school at the patrol car and joke about whether the guard would even knew who she was if they dangled her out the window.

In many ways, though, Ellen's had a tough run. She had thyroid cancer. She had a stillborn child. And she did not have a good relationship with Andy, who was perhaps too tough with her.

"She just gave me a hard time. She wasn't easy-going," Ellen recalls. "It's not that we didn't get along. We had an understanding. I was very polite. It just wasn't all that comfortable."

It took a year and a half or so for Andy and I to finalize our divorces, and then, at a family dinner, we announced we were getting married. We asked all the kids—hers and mine—if there were any questions. Ellen says she was the only one who put up her hand.

"I just wanted to know if they were going to have more kids," Ellen says. "They giggled and said, 'Yeah we're going to have another kid, and its name is Duke.' I was glad to find out that it was going to be a dog."

The plus was that she and Stephen grew up with Andy's three children and they remain close. They all respected each other's parents because Andy's kids had a different father than them. Ellen adds that she appreciated that Andy made it clear what was expected of her and was very, very kind when she lost the baby and was stricken with cancer, emphasizing that Andy was there for her whenever she was having a hard time. Stephen's relationship with Andy was cordial and polite; underneath that, I don't know. He was sixteen when Andy and I started living together.

"It was a tough five years, for sure," Stephen says. "I'm supposed to love this other person. No, it was tough; for sure, it was tough. I ended up loving Andy, but it took a long time," he says. "But she was great for Dad. She was a strong woman. She was really responsible for a lot of the great stuff he did."

What I do know is that Barbara did a terrific job bringing up Stephen and Ellen, and for that I am indebted. And you can't separate Ellen's difficult relationship with Andy from her love of her mother, Barbara.

"She was the hurt one in this situation. She was the one who was left," says Ellen, citing Barbara's remarkable ability to rise above what had happened while continuing to be a good mother to her and Stephen, always encouraging them to maintain their relationship with me.

I was also involved in raising our children, but not to the extent Barbara was. She and I would argue, however, about how to bring up Stephen. He would push right to the edge, and Barbara feared he would go over. I always knew he wouldn't and preferred to play him like a fish—letting out the line until he tired. I was convinced I could read into his mind and soul. I was the disciplinarian, playing the usual role, but I also used to play with both of them, skiing and skating, or playing catch with Stephen.

He was a tough kid to bring up. Ellen was easy to bring up—nice, kind, smart. Before I split from Barbara, Ellen would choose my shirt and tie every morning, a heartwarming ritual. Growing up, she was the responsible one of my two children, and at Stephen's fortieth birthday she jokingly introduced herself as his "older, younger sister." And she was a good student in high school. Stephen was good at junior school but, like his father, had educational problems in high school. With energy to spare, his natural habitat was not a schoolroom. He should have gone to a high school where that energy could have been expended positively on sports, given that he was a fine athlete. At college, he had his challenges. He went to Williams College for two years, then did his junior year abroad at the University of Southampton in England, then back to Williams for a year, followed by courses at Concordia in environmental studies and geography.

In high school, Ellen liked working on theatrical productions, but behind the scenes. Later, among other things, she worked as a film buyer for Cineplex Odeon, a company we owned, although she never lorded that fact over anyone. Ellen and Andrew oversee their holding company, Andell Inc., and are the owners of the Chicago Fire Soccer Club. They live in Los Angeles with their two kids. Stephen lives with his wife, Claudine, and their four children in Montreal, working out of my old Claridge office. Now that my two children are adults and just five years apart, they are very close. After recognizing their divergent styles and experiencing a few scrapes, Stephen and Ellen made the wise decision not to do business together.

"We love each other so much . . . We got into some disagreements about business, but it was not worth it. We made the decision that we'd rather invest together by choice rather than being tied together. And I had seen what had gone on with my dad and my uncle," Ellen says. Smart kids. It was a decision I applauded.

While some might think that reducing life to an accounting concept is ridiculous, the balance sheet isn't a bad framework for assessing the pluses and minuses of one's time on earth. I have most certainly laid out my own personality liabilities. My assets, however—and I'm not talking about financial ones—are as strong as oak. In spite of my splintered relationship with Edgar Jr., my principal assets are my family and friends. They are the emotional assets, the most important of all. When it comes to family, my children are at the core. As adults, they are both major philanthropists, which makes me proud. They're not working for Seagram, but in my view, they have carried on the family business.

Ellen and Andrew have the Hauptman Family Foundation, which supports a number of organizations in areas including education, the arts, and the environment, as well as health and civic engagement. They are passionate supporters of City Year and in 2007 co-founded City Year Los Angeles, which Ellen describes as an urban Peace Corps. Volunteers between the ages of seventeen and twenty-four work in high-poverty urban schools as "near peers" to help at-risk students stay on track to graduate high school. These "near peers" could be Harvard grads or even former gang members who serve full time for a year, spending time with students to keep them on the rails. Since they founded it nine years ago, City Year L.A. has directly served twenty thousand students in the L.A. public school district and supported a hundred thousand with after-school programs and schoolwide events.

To hear Ellen and Andrew, you know they've poured their hearts and souls into it. For me, there's an echo here, recalling my own difficulties in school and my subsequent interest in informal education. Ellen is also a supporter of the Israel Museum.

Stephen is very involved in environmental issues and has been on the board of the David Suzuki Foundation for twenty years. The foundation is the largest and most influential environment-focused, nongovernmental organization in Canada. When he was just four or five years old, Stephen loved watching *Mutual of Omaha's Wild Kingdom*. When he was nineteen, he visited Israel, where, after spending time with a park ranger, he was smitten with the idea of improving the environment.

"I realized how much of a connection I had with nature," Stephen says. "My pop knew his boy pretty good, and that connection was one of the most important connections in my life in terms of personal understanding and growth."

That led to our foundation supporting the Green Environment Fund in Israel, run by Sigal Yaniv out of our Jerusalem office. The GEF was integral in getting a Clean Air Act passed in Israel, protecting coral reefs, establishing sustainability education in Jewish and Arab schools, successfully fighting for the preservation of the Jerusalem Hills, and winning environmental concessions associated with the construction of a major toll road. Stephen has also carried on the family tradition of being involved in the Jewish community. In fact, he brilliantly chaired the annual Montreal Jewish Federation fundraising campaign. He's also deeply woven into other causes in Montreal—getting wayward kids to camp, for example—both with Jewish and non-Jewish philanthropies. Stephen's now intensely involved as well in backroom politics as one of the key supporters of Justin Trudeau, who was elected Canada's twenty-third prime minister on October 19, 2015. Stephen is chief revenue officer for the Liberal Party of Canada.

Stephen and Ellen's mother, Barbara, must have been a brave young woman. When we were married, I was a wreck with a bad temper. She was always kind, even though she might have been terrified of me at the time. Minda was quite angry with me when I left her for Andy, because Barbara's such a fine person—she got along well with my mother and with Minda. Although she's originally a New Yorker, she chose to stay in Montreal. Today, I'm very pleased we're good friends and we can laugh together—thanks partly to Rita, who put out a hand, which Barbara took. Since marrying Rita, I now see Barbara again. She actually got in touch when Andy died—in spite of her feelings about her stealing me away—and came for the memorial service. She felt badly for me. Barbara has always held me in her heart, which is wonderful of her. Ellen says there is only one good thing that has come from Andy's passing—that her parents are now close again. It's true. When Barbara and I are together now at family occasions, we sit, read the paper and magazines, talk politics, and kibitz like old, old friends. She is genuinely happy now and she sees me happy with Rita, which is very generous. And she would definitely not want me back.

12

Reflections of a Contented Man

Part of reaching a state of contentment is coming to terms with one's regrets and demons. As I've said, my greatest personal regret involves my relationship with Edgar. Although we reconciled in his last years, it's those years beforehand I wish I could have back to play over again. Some might ask, why bother analyzing what happened? Those people will say it's not going to change anything, but I beg to differ. An informal, introspective forensic examination, something I've gone through via hours and hours of interviews for this book, has actually been a therapeutic experience. The truth is, I've been searching. I've been trying to get to the bottom of the problems I've had in life and the mistakes I've made and make peace with them. I've also been trying to put them into context, given all the successes I've had. After all, each of us is on an odyssey, and although some of us may be able to point to well-considered plans, most of us probably make it up as we go along and just hope to do our best in spite of our flaws—whether we've inherited wealth or not. Perhaps the more money you have, the more you lock horns within families.

Even though Edgar was arguably a more successful businessperson than me, I believe I had better judgment and I may have been more successful at escaping the shadow of our father, even though I stayed in Montreal until I was in my sixties. The Montreal Expos were the key to that—a huge ego boost—followed by my philanthropic endeavours, which have given me an enormous amount of satisfaction. Yet, while my successes with the Expos and philanthropy are evidence of my ability to be proactive and innovate, there remained a passive side of my personality that came to the fore in my dealings with Edgar.

While I struggled to bolster my confidence, Edgar struggled to shake off a father who couldn't let go of the business. My searing emotional experience was witnessing Dad's treatment of Uncle Allan, imprinting on me the notion that I should avoid a family war at all costs. Edgar's searing emotional experience was being unsure whether his father loved him—and having a father who did not let him run Seagram the way he wanted to when he became CEO.

As for DuPont, I wonder what it was in my lifelong friendship with Leo that prevented me, and us, from going to the barricades on the sale. Had the relationship diminished over the years because I'd moved to New York and he remained in Montreal? Was he forever resentful about the sale of Cadillac Fairview? Had his appointment to the Senate and travels with Pierre Trudeau pulled him in another direction? He and I have talked about it, and neither of us has the answer. Or was it simply me, paralyzed, as I had been in the exam room at McGill, unable to find the voice within me to say no and to hell with the family consequences?

Maybe it was a bit of everything. Or maybe it was just the

natural order of things. As W.B. Yeats wrote, "Things fall apart; the centre cannot hold." Things fall apart—how elementary is that? Was it simply a fundamental law of physics and human nature that Seagram was destined to eventually fall apart? Family relationships disintegrated over time, and business interests disintegrated alongside them.

In spite of everything, through it all, Edgar deserves credit for some major transactions. He sold Texas Pacific at the right time and he bought DuPont at the right time. Although I would have vastly preferred to keep it, he sold it for almost nine billion dollars.

Phyllis is my only living sibling. During the process of gathering material for this book, she brought to my attention a beautiful portrait she painted of me in 1948 when I was just seventeen. She said I told her at the time that I didn't like it, apparently hurting her. For that, I'm sorry. I must have been on Pluto when I made that insensitive remark. I love it now.

As Phyllis says, she and I work at our relationship these days because we were not naturally close like she and Edgar were. I'm also grateful because I think she respects me now. I'm proud to say that she and I are the only brother and sister to receive the Companion of the Order of Canada—she in 2001 and me in 1992—the country's highest civilian honour. Edgar received the Medal of Freedom, the highest civilian honour in the U.S., from President Bill Clinton. Interestingly, Phyllis says she's amazed I survived our father. Even though I lacked confidence as a kid, my siblings seemed more terrified of Dad than I was. Phyllis even talks of being hit across the face by him, claiming Edgar got the same treatment. It seems I'm the only one who was left with warm feelings toward him. In my view, Dad was a great man, a business genius, but like all of us, a flawed man as well. His famous saying to us about the primacy of family—that "blood counts"—may be the most flawed part of his worldview. A tantalizingly simple notion, it is also grossly simplistic. While I was still at university, I interned at Seagram New York with the eastern division manager. I recall telling Dad that I thought I was as intelligent as the man who ran the division. He looked at me, totally shocked.

"You're my son. Of course you're smarter than he is."

I loved my dad deeply, but how egocentric a remark was that? Edgar and I could not possibly have duplicated what our father did simply because we shared his DNA. Even Edgar challenged the notion, bringing up the fact that Dad's brothers couldn't match his drive or business acumen, while they too shared the Bronfman bloodstream. Still, they were marginalized or cut out of the business. How could that be explained? Yet while Edgar voiced skepticism about whether blood counted, he defaulted to exactly that modus operandi in choosing Edgar Jr. as his successor. Clearly, blood counts sometimes and doesn't count at other times. *Which blood counts, and when?*

To be fair, I too succumbed to the belief that blood counts. My inability to stand up to Edgar and his son when it came to major issues in the company was rooted in not wanting to cause a family feud. Blood clearly counted for me in that equation. I was arguably too concerned about being a peacekeeper in the family, keeping the blood together. Conversely, blood most certainly did not count when it came to Edgar's view of me. If it did, he would have taken my views into account. Blood counts, but only to a point.

As for the taint of bootlegging that haunted Dad all his life

(Phyllis maintains Edgar was deeply ashamed of what happened during Prohibition), one question that has never been fully answered for me is why the Bronfmans got so blemished while others, like the late Harry Hatch of Hiram Walker-Gooderham & Worts[3] did not? Canadian Club, a Hiram Walker product, was extremely popular in the United States—in the 1920s. How exactly did that happen? In fact, a flotilla of vessels that went back and forth from Windsor, Ontario, to Detroit was known as "Hatch's Navy," named for Harry Hatch, my father's archenemy. And what about Molson and Labatt? As the eminent historian Michael Bliss wrote, Molson kept "product flowing" during Prohibition, and Labatt "collected handsome dividends" during Prohibition. How often do you hear the word *bootlegger* associated with those two Canadian icons? Never. Bliss goes on to say, in no uncertain terms, "There is little foundation for the stories of the Bronfmans selling rotgut whisky or having been bootleggers." He says we were simply better at what we did than our competitors.

Perhaps Bliss is being overly generous, but if this is true, how unfortunate that Dad had to wear the bootlegger label all his life. Without it, would he have been a less angry man? If he had been less angry, would he have been more likely to let Edgar operate the business as he saw fit? And if Edgar had been given more of a free rein, would my brother have been so quick to give his son carte blanche when it came to running the business? Phyllis maintains that Dad's temper clearly played a role in setting the stage for the unravelling of Seagram. As for

---

3. Albert Gooderham, the former managing director of Gooderham and Worts, was knighted in 1935.

the impact on me, if he had been less likely to fly into a rage, would I have had more confidence? All speculation, all armchair psychology. History is nothing if not a game of "if."

What's clearly apparent to me, however, is that *new blood counts*. In recent years, there is another person who has been part of my life, and is now the nucleus of it—the beautiful Rita Mayo. In 1970 at the age of twenty, she moved to Montreal after a coup d'état in Peru. She studied art history at the Université de Montréal, where she earned a BA and went on to pursue her master's with an emphasis on Russian Constructivism. Rita completed the course work for her MA, but with the birth of Andrea, her second child, she was unable to finish her thesis and went on to raise a family.

By the time Andy died, Rita was divorced and would go out to dinner with Angelica and me. After my relationship with Angelica ended, she would join Bonnie and me for dinner. She was a good friend. Later, though, I told her that I thought of her more romantically. For quite a while, unfortunately, that was a nonstarter. She didn't want a relationship with me; she was quite concerned about the difference in our ages—nineteen years. As she said, I was getting into the difficult years—code for old! She also didn't want to take a chance on losing a friend. All of this put me through the hoops, emotionally. As for the late-night calls after Andy died, that was a thoughtful gesture of friendship on her part.

The stars began to align with Rita, though, before Bonnie and I got divorced. Rita was coming from Montreal to have dinner with us in New York. She got to the airport, but her flight was cancelled. I suggested she go home and fly in the next day, but she stayed at the airport in Montreal, got a flight, and landed in

New York around 7 p.m. Then Bonnie bowed out of dinner due to a headache, so I picked up Rita around eight fifteen, two blocks from where I lived, and we went to Cipriani's. I told her how desperate things had become with Bonnie. I also asked her how she was faring.

"I'm not unhappy," she said.

"That's an interesting way of putting it," I replied.

The next morning, I showed up where she was staying. She had a terrible hangover and claimed I got her drunk. The next time I was in Montreal, I called and she invited me for coffee. I thought I was going to hear the same nonsense I'd heard before, but nonetheless I sat down on the couch. She also sat down on the couch.

"You know, I've been thinking," she said.

"Oh, you have?"

"Yes, I have. Why don't we give it a shot?"

So that summer, the summer of 2011, I was in Israel and I called her in Canada and said, "Why don't we spend a week together somewhere?" She said, "Okay, where?" I suggested Forte dei Marmi in Italy, one hour north of Florence, on the seashore.

"You know I was there a month ago?"

"Why don't you want to go back again?" I asked. "Doesn't your best friend live there?"

I knew that was the case and had an ulterior motive for suggesting we go there. I wanted to be inspected by her dear friend Rossella to get the *Good Housekeeping* Seal of Approval. So we visited Rossella in Forte and in Florence. From Florence in my rental car, we soon got lost, ending up in Pisa. I had only been to Pisa once, when the tower was closed because they were trying to reduce the angle of the tilt. This time, it was open, so I said to myself, "I'll show her I'm not so old," and I climbed the 294 steps of the Leaning Tower of Pisa. She thought I was going to die on the way up and that my children would kill her, but we both made it to the top. Then she illustrated what kind of a person she is. After we walked down, we went to a tea room where there was a sour-faced waitress who seemed to be ignoring us. I suggested to Rita that we'd never get served.

"Well, let's see about that," she said. Rita started talking to her in Italian, and suddenly the woman had a smile on her face and served us nicely.

"What did you do?" I asked.

She said, "You have to understand. This woman got up early in the morning and has been here all day. She probably gets very small tips and has to deal with demanding people like you, so why should she have a smile on her face?" She said she had asked the woman about herself and might have been the only person that day who treated her like a human being.

Still, it was a rocky start. A few nights later, while we were still in Italy, Rita couldn't sleep and was sobbing.

"I can't go forward," she said between tears.

After a couple of questions, I realized she wanted to end our romance. She was still very worried about the age issue. It was a real problem for her. "If you were fifty and I was thirty-one," she said, "that would be one thing, but you're entering the time of life when you'll start falling on your head." It was looking grim. So I decided to take a page out of my father's book about being in a tight situation. I suddenly got very calm and said to her that Dad told me if you really, really, really want something, you fight and you fight and you fight till you get it. And then I told her, "Rita Mayo, you aren't going anywhere. Nor am I."

The next day, she agreed to think about it and said she would tell me at dinner. To help resolve the issues, she decided she needed another perspective and should visit the therapist she'd seen while she was going through her divorce. Her appointment back in Montreal was set up for exactly the same time as I was leaving Israel to fly to New York. From there, I was to fly to Montreal on a private plane. But en route from Israel, I'd slept overnight in Milan and left my cellphone behind. I asked Angela to get me a new one and put it on the plane that would take me from New York to Montreal.

The main reason I was going to Montreal was that my daughter-in-law Claudine was having a C-section on June 15, 2011, to have her fourth child with Stephen. I had asked Rita not to leave me a message on the phone but said I would call her when I landed in Montreal. In the meantime, Angela had the new phone sent to the private plane. I opened it, and lo and behold, there were two emails from Rita Mayo. One said, "I love you." The other said, "Couldn't be better." That was the beginning of a new beginning.

Rita is the world's most wonderful woman and has made me an extremely happy, calm person. And she's made me younger. She has boosted my ego, and for the first few weeks and months, I realized the only surprises I was having were happy ones. She is very caring, loving, thoughtful, and efficient and runs a great home. She loves her two daughters and is very fond of my children, grandchildren, and stepchildren, having become part of the entire family. When it comes to many things, we have exactly the same tastes—in decor, clothes, and other people. At dinner, we often order the same things and we both enjoy golf and tennis. We're at a time in our lives when we don't have to worry about what most people worry about, like schools for kids, the day-to-day nitty-gritty stuff you struggle with when you're younger. The only condition she set, and I happily agreed to: she'd go anywhere in the world for ten months a year, as long as we spend the summer in Montreal. That's a pretty good arrangement.

Dad was certainly right about blood counting when it comes to love for the next generations, who also keep me young. Stephen and his wife, Claudine, have four children, while Ellen and Andrew have two, so between them, I have six biological grandchildren. And then there are my three stepchildren via Andy, plus three more grandchildren from that side. I must say that I consider Pippa, Tony, and Jeremy my children as well. When Andy and I married, they were young, so as a result I had a major hand in raising them. While it took some getting used to on both sides, we've always been close and have become closer since Andy's death. We celebrate each other's achievements, are in constant communication, and console each other in times of loss. And now there are two more stepchildren in my life, Rita's two daughters, Andrea and Jessica, and Rita's new grandson.

What hits me in the gut, though, is the gift Stephen and Ellen have given me. In 2004, they set up the Charles Bronfman Prize. Every time I think about it, I get choked up. Each year, $100,000 is given to the person or persons under fifty who have made a difference to humankind. Their work is inspired by Jewish values and is of universal benefit to all people. However, it is a major job to choose the winner out of the forty to fifty applicants annually. The work that goes into selecting the finalists and the debates that occur among the judges—major figures like the former president of the World Bank, a former deputy prime minister of Israel, a former American ambassador to the European Union, and a Canadian Supreme Court justice—is significant. The executive in charge of the prize, Jill Collier Indyk, has taken it to heart and does everything to make it what it is—from recruiting the field of candidates to keeping the family of prizewinners connected.

"What have we got ourselves into?" Ellen jokes. "We should have given him a tie or some golf clubs."

The first winner set the bar for what's expected. Jay Feinberg was just twenty-two when he was diagnosed with leukemia and was told his only hope was a bone marrow transplant. When immediate family members were ruled out as a match, the search went global, with more than fifty thousand people of Ashkenazi Jewish extraction being tested because the best chance for matches falls within your own ethnic group. The size of that pool, however, was drastically affected by the Holocaust. Eventually, the last person tested on the very last drive to find a donor was a teenager in Milwaukee. There was a match! That donor saved Jay's life, and he has since dedicated himself to convincing people to join bone marrow registries around the world. He is the founder and CEO of the Gift of Life Bone Marrow Foundation. As of mid-July 2015, there were more than 240,000 registered donors. That's led to more than 12,000 matches and facilitated close to 3,000 transplants.

To give you examples of the calibre of the winners since Jay, in 2014 it was Sam Goldman, the founder of d.light, a solar energy company delivering affordable solar power designed for the two billion people in the developing world—households and small businesses that don't have access to reliable energy. In 2004, when Goldman was a Peace Corps volunteer in Africa, he witnessed his neighbour's son suffering from severe burns as a result of an overturned kerosene lamp. In far too many cases, people in the developing world have fumbled about in the dark with kerosene or diesel lanterns or candles, resulting in fires and painful, debilitating accidents. There are thousands of deaths per year associated with kerosene fires in places where there's no reliable electrical power. For children in certain parts of the world, a clean and safe source of lighting means the ability to study in the evening without the risk of being burned by oil lamps or harmed by toxic fumes. Sam's company has now sold some eight million solar-powered lights in sixty-two countries. The lamps are ten dollars each and pay for themselves in a matter of weeks.

Then there's Dr. Amitai Ziv, a former fighter pilot in the Israeli Air Force and another winner of the prize. He learned to fly jets with the help of simulators. When Amitai moved into the medical sphere, he wondered about a very simple, basic question: Why does a new doctor have to "practise" medical procedures on a real person when he or she starts out as a doctor? Why can't medical students practise on simulators, so when they "graduate" to real people, they've at least gone through virtual practice runs? At Chaim Sheba Medical Center in Tel Aviv, they do just that. There are simulation dummies that "experience" cardiac arrest, there are simulated knees on which a future orthopaedic surgeon can do arthroscopic surgery, there are simulated eyes on which a future eye surgeon can remove cataracts, and even actors who play the role of a furious patient in the hallway waiting for a bed, forcing a medical student to learn how to deal with a volatile, emotional situation.

"This is a place to learn and reflect on your errors," he says. In medicine, "we're too tolerant of errors," citing that in 1999, there were 100,000 deaths in U.S. hospitals from medical errors. The numbers he quotes come from a NASA scientist who lost a son to a medical error in Dallas.

And there's Karen Tal, a teacher's teacher and another winner. With the help of a thousand volunteers, including some of the most successful businesspeople in Israel, she has turned around eighteen at-risk schools, including two Arab schools. These are poor schools, on the periphery, with children from North Africa, Russia, Arab communities, and orthodox Jewish communities. In fact, Karen cites the fact that there are more than 800,000 at-risk children living below the poverty line in Israel. Their parents frequently have to work two menial jobs to keep up, which means there's no one at home.

A Sephardic Jew born in Fez, Morocco, who came to Israel as a little girl, Karen's view is that you need "haute couture" learning for each child, a made-to-measure educational approach. In fact, she and her band of committed teachers map out the strengths and needs of each and every child. If there's a lack of clothes, they get them clothes. If they need glasses, they get them glasses. If they need psychological therapy, they get them therapy. There are even sandwiches available by the door of the school because there's often nothing in the fridges in many of the children's homes. And it works. Grades go up, a lot, and the children love coming to school. When they compare it to home, there's no comparison. Every year there's a Jay, a Sam, an Amitai, or a Karen honoured for their work, all of them originals, changing the world for the better. What greater honour could a father receive from his children?

The other child in my life has been my foundation. And like a child, it has provided immense satisfaction, pride, and joy.

But unlike a child, I made the decision some time ago that it wouldn't be forever. In 2001, after what befell Seagram, it was clear there would be only so much money left. The foundation was badly wounded by the episode, with most of its assets consisting of Seagram shares. After robust conversations between Andy, Jeff, and me, we made the decision that in 2016, the foundation would close and in the final years there would be a "spend-down." It would also be the year I would turn eighty-five, and it was clear that my children did not want to take over running the foundation—they had their own philanthropic interests and I didn't want to force mine on them after I'm gone.

"Charles did not want to be the cold fist trying to rule from the grave," Jeff and I wrote.

The philanthropic interests Andy and I shared were an expression of our values, experiences, and interests. As we anticipated entering a less-engaged chapter of our own lives, a spend-down became the obvious answer.

In 2011, Jeff and I published a letter explaining the spend-down, likening it to the successful landing of a plane. As of the publication of the letter, we had granted more than $325 million, with two-thirds of that going to strategic giving. We also stated that we were "committed to creativity and innovation, not to perpetuity for the sake of perpetuity. The next generation of philanthropists and board leaders will be tomorrow's investors."

In December of 2015, with the sunset of the foundation less than a month away, I gathered forty of my closest colleagues for a dinner in the private dining room of a restaurant in the Gramercy Park neighbourhood of New York. These were most of my indispensable partners in philanthropy over three decades—from Israel, the United States, and Canada. After cocktails, a meal, and high-decibel conversation among good friends, I stressed to everyone how we'd all worked so collegially for so many years and how each of them had made me look good. What speaks volumes is that so many of them worked by my side for such a very long time. *They stayed.* Those who did and eventually moved on to other things did so only after we'd spent many years together. Yes, our foundation was a fine place to work—and to change for the better that part of the world in which we were engaged.

The evening was filled with warmth, humour, and intense emotion, like the gathering of a truly close family. In fact, that's how Jeff referred to the group when he expressed his and my appreciation to all for allowing our work and innovation to occur in such a magical way. He also fittingly described the dinner as bittersweet, reminding us that it was almost ten years since Andy passed away and that the foundation was so much a part of her legacy. How true. It has, after all, been ACBP—Andrea and Charles Bronfman Philanthropies—with her name first.

For me, I kept getting choked up. While Seagram may have been the beginning of my working life, the foundation was my true career. It was truly a marvellous journey. After the phasing out of the foundation, along with help from Jeff and Janet, I continue my own personal philanthropy, an extension of the values that led us to it in the first place.

Philanthropy is really about the future. In Canada, Historica and the McGill Institute for the Study of Canada will continue to enhance and preserve Canadian history and heritage. Birthright Israel will continue to nurture the unity of the Jewish people, and a gift we have made to the Mount Sinai Medical

Center in New York is designed to help people everywhere. The Charles R. Bronfman Institute for Personalized Medicine aims to use information about a "person's genetic make-up to customize strategies for the detection, treatment and prevention of disease." In essence, we're all different, yet we're more often than not given a "one size fits all" treatment when we need a tailored, bespoke approach. Thirty years from now, my hope is that when you go to a doctor and need treatment, you get a medication or a therapy that's designed precisely for your own genetic composition. I also hope that by having a map of your body's exact genetic characteristics, you and your caregivers will be able to head off disease before it takes root. I want my grandchildren and everyone's grandchildren to benefit from this.

Aside from family, the Expos, Israel, and philanthropy, the other part of my life that has given me great pleasure and satisfaction is art. Although works by the masters are often de rigueur among people like me—and yes, I have some of those— what's really been fun has been collecting the diverse work of an array of Canadian artists. At its peak, my Claridge collection amassed a body of some three thousand works. My partner when it comes to art has been Franklin Silverstone, a wry Dubliner whose specialty is eighteenth-to-twentieth-century European paintings, drawings, and watercolours. He says that he would "die of starvation in North America if that's all I did." Frank and I met around the time of the recession in the early 1980s in Montreal. We have been art partners ever since, so much so that he feels extremely proprietary about the collection.

"It's mine too. We've been together thirty-three years. Screw him," he wisecracks.

After Frank signed on as our curator, he spent two years

travelling around Canada, finding people in the various cities who knew the local art scene, and then he would set up studio visits. He would select works and have them shipped to Montreal, where a few of us, including Andy, would view them on a Monday in a closed gallery, like something out of a Roman circus, giving the thumbs-up or thumbs-down to what we saw. While there's clearly an emphasis on great art and beautiful objects, there is also a place for humour and the light touch. If you wandered through our office in New York, you'd find the latter creates a playful, friendly atmosphere. With me, buying such works of art hasn't been for investment purposes. I buy what I love.

"Charles will pay fifty dollars for something he loves and love it just as much (as a masterwork). He loves it for what it is, not for what it's worth," Frank will tell you. He also introduced Andy and me to glass collectors Dale and Doug Anderson, and as a result, there's a great deal of spectacular glasswork in our homes. And after Andy died, Frank created the most beautiful keepsake for friends and family, a "memory box." Small, grey, and wrapped with a red ribbon, each box contained a sheaf of papers, with each page bearing a personalized note about Andy written by someone close to her. These were lovingly distributed to all of those who wrote.

Alas, like the foundation, the Claridge collection has been in sunset mode as well. In recent years, chunks of the collection have been auctioned off, with the proceeds going to Historica Canada. And as Stephen is now ensconced at Claridge, with his keen eye, he is building the Claridge collection, Phase Two, with a much more modern bent, which is appropriate.

As for Israel, I worry greatly for its future, and by extension the future of the Jewish people. I'm concerned that the countries surrounding Israel look upon it as an appendage to the Middle East. Often times, when the body fights long and hard enough, the appendage is removed. Concern about such matters runs deeply through our family history. On a trip to Europe in 1932, my parents had Sunday lunch at the country home of—of all people—Joachim von Ribbentrop, who would later become Hitler's foreign minister. In her book *My Sam*, my mother describes how she and Dad had just come from Vienna, where they had seen extremely upsetting things, evidence of violence against Jews. They had also been horrified in Berlin, where they witnessed hundreds of Hitler Youth marching through the streets. She quotes a discussion Dad had over lunch with "Mr. Ribbentrop," as he was known then.

"Mr. Ribbentrop, I know you are a supporter of Hitler, but if that man ever gets into power, I'm very concerned about what will happen to the Jews," Mother quotes Dad as saying.

"Don't worry, Mr. Bronfman, if Hitler rises to power, it will be Jewish money that puts him there. He won't do anything to hurt the Jews," the Nazi said. He was, by the way, the first to be hanged after the Nuremberg trials.

Eighty-four years after my parents had lunch with a Nazi, seventy-one years after the Holocaust, sixty-eight years after the establishment of the State of Israel, after so much terror and killing, the world can't seem to cleanse itself of anti-Semitism. But the success of Birthright Israel gives me great hope. I have also seen firsthand how Palestinians and Israeli Jews can actually like each other. Abu Ala, the chief Palestinian negotiator, has been to my home. He told me that he'd spent so much time with Israel's chief negotiator, Uri Savir—more than he spent with his wife—that they really liked each other. I've also had representatives of the 106 retired Israeli generals, former Mossad chiefs, and former commanders of the National Police Force to my home. These people, who know better than anyone the experiences of war and conflict, are signatories to a petition that promotes a two-state solution and an end to the occupation. In spite of the tension, there is always hope when such a group comes forward to protest the status quo. In my worldview, hope trumps despair every time, particularly when it comes to Israel, the insurance policy and homeland for the Jewish people. Thinking back on Ribbentrop's words, I couldn't be more certain of that.

As for my fear of confronting Edgar, it's hard to understand how I could be that way when at the same time I could travel to Ramallah, the heart of Palestinian territory, to dedicate a centre that we funded for the physically disabled, or live in Jerusalem while hearing the sounds of the Intifada from Bethlehem, or travel to Gaza under the protection of black-clad PLO gunmen, or meet the group's leadership. Or so convinced that we should not cancel Birthright trips when things got rough in Israel.

How do I reconcile the emotional fear of a brother with little to no fear for physical safety? I don't have physical fear, but I've had emotional fear. The tangled relationship between the human mind and the human heart are much like Churchill's description of Russia, "a riddle wrapped in a mystery inside an enigma." I have been a success on many fronts—philanthropy, the Expos, my dealings with DuPont, Israel, my children, and my stepchildren. As I know from my baseball days, no one bats a thousand. But as I look back, I'd say that I have a damn good batting average.

I've come to realize that my life is the story of a person who blossomed late. There are fast starters, slow finishers, there are steady folks, and then there are slow starters and fast finishers. There are also those who are brilliant in school yet have difficulty earning a living, and those who don't graduate yet do very well. I was a slow starter, had difficulty in school, and always had a sense of being number two. But since then, my life has been back end–loaded with accomplishments. Although I had successes at Seagram Canada when I was in my early twenties and thirties, I didn't start to gain positive traction until I invested in the Expos at the age of thirty-eight, and it took a few years for that enterprise to find its feet. Just as I prefer the buy-and-hold approach when it comes to investments—like Dad—my personal strength and record has built over time, a bit like laying down a good whisky and letting it age properly. I needed to age properly too.

I didn't begin to find my true calling—philanthropy— until my mid-fifties. Since then, I've come to realize that my victories have been the result of a series of wonderful partnerships. Maybe it was my insecurity when I was younger, but I've always sought out people with skills I don't have. I first started to notice the power of partnerships when I played in golf or tennis tournaments. With a good partner, I could relax and we could help each other. I've also always been able to trust a good partner. And what a group I've been blessed with, starting with Leo Kolber, the friend of a lifetime; the late Mel Griffin and Jack Duffy, who were my dear colleagues at Seagram; and the late John McHale at the Expos. During our tenure at DuPont, I worked with three of its CEOs—two of them intimately, Ed Jefferson and Ed Woolard, both fine executives and even finer people. Then, there are my foundation partners and friends, Jeff Solomon, Janet Aviad, Tom

Axworthy, and Ann Dadson—all so smart, so wise, so superb. What a team. And Birthright Israel would not exist without the initial partnerships I had with my dear friend Michael Steinhardt and our incomparable first CEO Shimshon Shoshani. In all of these cases, each brought strengths I don't have, but each needed what I *do* have.

Sadly, even though I bloomed late, my brother, Edgar, and sister Phyllis didn't seem to notice. Although Phyllis and I now have a friendly relationship and Edgar and I repaired ours, his recognition of my accomplishments and business instincts came too late. That was a partnership that should have been, but never was.

"Edgar took it as a given that he was the boss over everything," Leo says. He was unable to have a partner. Maybe that's why we couldn't confront him together with full force when it came to his son and DuPont. Yet I kept hoping for that partnership, or thinking it somehow existed, while there was never any hope of one.

Dad had sized us all up. Edgar would run the business and Minda and Phyllis would marry rich men. As for me, he figured I would help burnish the family name. I'm not a boaster, but when it came to me, he wasn't wrong. In certain respects, we share traits. He was never flamboyant, nor am I. He never lived an extroverted lifestyle, nor have I. He was never good at small talk, nor am I. He had great passion for what he did, and I have as well. I have never had his vision, but the kid who started out as a sickly, scrawny basket case has evolved into a contented, accomplished man with more friends than he can count. I have a wonderful life.

Acknowledgements

My grateful thanks to Howard Green, who collaborated with me on this project. It was a joy to work with him. He's a serious man who did yeoman work in ferreting out from others, and from endless interviews with me, the person I was and the man I've become. I also wish to express gratitude to those with whom I've been associated these many years. Each of them has played an important role in my life. I'd like to thank all my colleagues, those who are in the book and those who are not—at Seagram, DuPont, the Expos, Major League Baseball, CEMP and later Claridge Investments, philanthropy in Canada, the U.S., and Israel, in the public realm as well as the foundation world, and ACBP.

For his recollections, thank you to my son, Stephen Bronfman, and to both him and my daughter-in-law, Claudine, for welcoming Howard to tour their home, as it's the house where I grew up. Equal thanks to my daughter, Ellen, and son-in-law, Andrew Hauptman, for their generous contributions and supporting documents.

My deepest thanks as well to a long list of those who helped by sharing memories, recollections, or in numerous other ways: Phyllis Lambert, Barbara Bronfman, Tom Axworthy, Erwin Bottinger, George Bushnell, Ann Dadson, Maria and Jim Fanning (who passed away in the spring of 2015 at the age of eighty-seven, a few months after being interviewed for this book), David Fisher, Larry Fisher, Sharna Goldseker, Michael Hallows, John Hoover, Jill Collier Indyk, Leo Kolber, Amanda Levine, Arnie Ludwick, Sam Minzberg, Ed McDonnell, Sarah Anne Wilkinson, Barbara Plotnick, Franklin Silverstone, Liz Sokolsky, Michael Steinhardt, Michael Vineberg, Danielle Oristian York, and Bill Zabel.

In Israel, heartfelt thanks to Shimon Peres, Ehud Olmert, Aliza Olmert, Shimshon Shoshani, Gidi Mark, Nissim Matalon, Hirsh Goodman, James Snyder, Tzaly Reshef, Jonathan Kolber, Rivka Saker, Uzi Zucker, Keren Luzon, Sam Goldman, Karen Tal, Amitai Ziv, Tali Gottlieb, Sigal Yaniv, Meira Yagid, Yona Bartal, and Or Kornhauser.

While several people have read this manuscript and helped root out inaccuracies, any errors are mine and mine alone.

—Charles Bronfman

First and foremost, to Charles Bronfman for inviting me to be his collaborator and for his respect, generosity, friendship, sense of fun, and for entrusting me with his life's story. Thanks to Rita Mayo for her kinship as well—not only is she a spirited tennis player, but she also makes a great coffee cake. Like Charles, I am indebted to all of those listed above, including those who spent time speaking with me during the gathering of material for this book. I am deeply grateful to Jeffrey Solomon for his quiet advice over a glass of scotch or while he puffed a cigar on starry nights; to Janet Aviad for thoughtfully and graciously guiding me through Israel; to Charles's long-time executive assistant, Angela Forster, for her good humour and brio in dealing with my countless requests; to Anthony Wilson-Smith; and to Michael Levine and Carolyn Forde at Westwood Creative Artists. In Israel, in addition to those listed by Charles: Oren Cohen Magen, Amos Mendel, Sagit Klayman, Uri Raviv, Yousef Hiekhal, Yaakov Shabat, Daliah Guri, Levana Dvash, and Ilana Fleischman.

Charles's manuscript would not be a book without the wonderful team at HarperCollins in Toronto—Jim Gifford, Iris Tupholme, Leo MacDonald, Michael Guy-Haddock, Noelle Zitzer, Maria Golikova, Lloyd Davis, Rob Firing, Alison Woodbury, Norma Cody, Melissa Nowakowski, Shannon Parsons, Alan Jones, Amy Frueh, and Lesley Fraser. Finally, thank you to my mother, Roselle Green, for a lifetime of unlimited love and wise counsel, and to my spouse, Lynne Heller, for her boundless support, enthusiasm, and love.

— Howard Green

A Note on Sources

While my (Charles's) recollections provided the building blocks to construct this book, mortar came via other people's work on the various subjects touched upon in this memoir, specifically my mother's two privately published memoirs as well as Michael Marrus's first-rate definitive history, *Samuel Bronfman: The Life and Times of Seagram's Mr. Sam.* Jonah Keri's *Up, Up, & Away* was an invaluable source about the history of the Montreal Expos. My friend Leo Kolber's *Leo: A Life,* written in collaboration with L. Ian MacDonald, provided a great deal of useful background, detail, and corroboration. My brother Edgar's book, *Good Spirits: The Making of a Businessman,* let Howard hear his "voice" in the absence of hearing it physically, as did another book he wrote, *The Making of a Jew.* Obviously, both furnished Edgar's point of view on a number of matters. The documentary *Whisky Man* by David Paperny provided rich quotes from family members, including me, Edgar, Phyllis, my cousin Edward, and Edgar Jr. Ari Shavit's *My Promised Land* assisted in tackling what must be one of the thorniest questions on earth, the question of Israel.

Ten Days of Birthright Israel: A Journey in Young Adult Identity by Leonard Saxe and Barry Chazan was equally important to understanding the genesis of that initiative. My books on philanthropy and nonprofits, *The Art of Giving* and *The Art of Doing Good*, written with Jeffrey Solomon, again helped Howard get into the headspace of a philanthropist. Helping to distill the history of DuPont was Adrian Kinnane's *DuPont: From the Banks of the Brandywine to Miracles of Science*, as well as Gerard Colby's *Du Pont Dynasty*. Rod McQueen, who has a long history of business writing in Canada, provided a trove of information, background, and colour in *The Icarus Factor: The Rise and Fall of Edgar Bronfman Jr.* To glean an understanding of Jean-Marie Messier of Vivendi, *The Man Who Tried to Buy the World: Jean-Marie Messier and Vivendi Universal*, by Jo Johnson and Martine Orange, proved very useful.

There were also unpublished works. Carl Brauer's independent assessment of the Heritage Project, which included a history of Heritage Minutes, was quite helpful, as were other original documents, such as letters and memos, provided by Tom Axworthy. Patrick Watson's account of the birth of the Heritage Minutes from his autobiography also added depth and colour—as did Marsha Boulton's *Just a Minute*. My manuscript owes a debt to all these publications, documents, books, and films and their authors and producers. They are just some of the sources tapped to help fill in the blanks. Please see the full bibliography for a complete list.

Bibliography

Books

Bar-Zohar, Michael. *Shimon Peres: The Biography.* New York: Random House, 2007.

Bliss, Michael. *Northern Enterprise: Five Centuries of Canadian Business.* Toronto: McClelland & Stewart, 1987.

Boulton, Marsha. *Just a Minute: Glimpses of Our Great Canadian Heritage.* Toronto: Little, Brown, 1994.

———. *Just Another Minute: More Glimpses of our Great Canadian Heritage.* Toronto: Little, Brown, 1997.

Bronfman, Charles R. *Israel Reports.* Self-published. May–August 2002, May–August 2003, May–August 2005, May–August 2006, June–August 2007.

Bronfman, Charles R., and Jeffrey Solomon. *The Art of Doing Good.* San Francisco: Jossey-Bass, 2012.

———. *The Art of Giving.* San Francisco: Jossey-Bass, 2010.

Bronfman, Edgar M. *Good Spirits: The Making of a Businessman.* New York: Putnam, 1998.

———. *The Making of a Jew.* New York: Putnam, 1996.

Bronfman, Edgar M. *Why Be Jewish? A Testament.* Toronto: Signal, 2016.

Bronfman, Edgar M., and Zasloff, Beth. *Hope, Not Fear: A Path to Jewish Renaissance.* New York: St. Martin's Press, 2008.

Bronfman, Saidye Rosner. *My Sam: A Memoir by His Wife Saidye Rosner Bronfman.* Privately published, 1982.

———. *Recollections of My Life.* Privately published, 1986.

Bronfman, Samuel. . . . *From Little Acorns . . . The Story of Distillers Corporation-Seagrams Limited.* First appeared as a supplement to the 1969–70 Annual Report of Distillers Corporation-Seagrams Ltd., October 1970.

The Canadian Journey: Rivers of Memory, River of Dreams. The Seagram Company Limited. 1980.

Colby, Gerard. *Du Pont Dynasty: Behind the Nylon Curtain.* Don Mills, ON: Lyle Stuart, 1984.

Didion, Joan. *The Year of Magical Thinking.* New York: Knopf, 2005.

Faith, Nicholas. *The Bronfmans: The Rise and Fall of the House of Seagram.* New York: Thomas Dunne, 2006.

Flanders, Kappy, and Andy Bronfman. *Sis & Pa: Our Family Album.* Privately published, 2003.

Gilbert, Martin. *Conversations with Charles Bronfman.* Unpublished, 2003.

Goodman, Fred. *Fortune's Fool: Edgar Bronfman Jr., Warner Music, and an Industry in Crisis.* New York: Simon & Schuster, 2010.

Green, Howard. *Banking on America: How TD Bank Rose to the Top and Took on the U.S.A.* Toronto: HarperCollins, 2013.

Hotchner, A.E. *Doris Day: Her Own Story.* New York: Bantam, 1975.

Johnson, Jo, and Martine Orange. *The Man Who Tried to Buy the World: Jean-Marie Messier and Vivendi Universal.* London: Penguin, 2003.

Keri, Jonah. *Up, Up, & Away: The Kid, The Hawk, Rock, Vladi, Pedro, Le Grand Orange, Youppi!, The Crazy Business of Baseball, & the Ill-fated but Unforgettable Montreal Expos.* Toronto: Random House, 2014.

Kinnane, Adrian. *DuPont: From the Banks of the Brandywine to Miracles of Science.* Wilmington, DE: E.I. du Pont de Nemours and Co., 2002.

Kolber, Leo, with L. Ian MacDonald. *Leo: A Life.* Montreal: McGill-Queen's University Press, 2003.

Lambert, Phyllis. *Building Seagram.* New Haven: Yale University Press, 2013.

Marrus, Michael R. *Samuel Bronfman: The Life and Times of Seagram's Mr. Sam.* Hanover, NH: Brandeis University Press, 1991.

McQueen, Rod. *The Icarus Factor: The Rise and Fall of Edgar Bronfman Jr.* Toronto: Doubleday, 2004.

Norman, Philip. *John Lennon: The Life.* Toronto: Anchor, 2009.

Newman, Peter C. *Titans: How the New Canadian Establishment Seized Power.* Toronto: Viking, 1998.

———. *Bronfman Dynasty: The Rothschilds of the New World.* Toronto: McClelland & Stewart, 1978.

Oz, Amos. *How to Cure a Fanatic—Israel and Palestine: Between Right and Right.* London: Vintage, 2004, 2014.

Saxe, Leonard, and Barry Chazan. *Ten Days of Birthright Israel: A Journey in Young Adult Identity.* Hanover, NH: Brandeis University Press, 2008.

Shavit, Ari. *My Promised Land: The Triumph and Tragedy of Israel.* New York: Spiegel & Grau, 2013.

Snyder, James S. *Renewed: The Israel Museum, Jerusalem, Campus Renewal Project.* Jerusalem: The Israel Museum, 2011.

Watson, Patrick. *This Hour Has Seven Decades.* Toronto: McArthur & Co., 2014.

Wills, Maury, and Mike Celizic. *On the Run: The Never Dull and Often Shocking Life of Maury Wills.* New York: Carroll & Graf, 1991.

Wright, Lawrence. *Thirteen Days in September: The Dramatic Story of the Struggle for Peace.* New York: Vintage, 2014.

Articles

Axworthy, Tom. "Creativity and Convergence in the CRB Foundation: Andrea and Charles Bronfman's Philanthropic Method," in *Reflections: Thirty Years of Focused Philanthropy.* Andrea and Charles Bronfman Philanthropies, 2015.

———. "Transforming Society: The Role of Philanthropy." *The CRB Foundation: The First Decade.* Montreal: The CRB Foundation, 1996.

———, interview with CharityVillage.com, 2004.

Aharoni, Ido. "Why Birthright Is the Real Game Changer for Israel." *The Jewish Week,* April 24, 2015.

Associated Press. "Jackson Escapes Pot Prosecution." *Daytona Beach Morning Journal,* November 25, 1976.

Bell, Michael. "Jerusalem: Is There a Solution, or Just Blood?" *The Globe and Mail,* November 19, 2014.

Berenson, Alex. "The Sun Is Setting on Seagram Empire." *The New York Times,* June 20, 2000.

Bianco, Anthony. "Deal Time at Seagram." *Businessweek,* June 26, 2000.

Bruck, Connie. "Bronfman's Big Deals." *The New Yorker,* May 11, 1998.

———. "Friends of Israel: Is AIPAC Losing Influence?" *The New Yorker,* September 1, 2014.

Carreyrou, John, and Martin Peers. "How Messier Kept Cash Crisis at Vivendi Hidden for Months." *The Wall Street Journal,* October 31, 2002.

Caton, Mary. "Hiram Walker's Clifford Hatch Jr. Dies at 72." *Windsor Star,* September 24, 2014.

Dash, Eric. "Richard Metrick, Veteran Bear Banker, Dies at 69." *The New York Times,* August 5, 2010.

Ebeling, Ashlea. "Cross-Pollinator Angelica Berrie Tells How to Give Away a Fortune." *Forbes,* February 11, 2015.

The Economist. "Messier's Mess." June 6, 2002.

———. "Mr Bronfman in Tinseltown." November 19, 1998.

Fabrikant, Geraldine. "As a Sale Looms, Questions on Leadership and Strategy at the Seagram Company." *The New York Times,* June 15, 2000.

———. "At Seagram, Waiting for the Glitz to Pay Off." *The New York Times*, September 18, 1997.

———. "Divorce, in Style." *The New York Times*, May 13, 2011.

———. "French Media Conglomerate Is Reported Negotiating to Buy Seagram." *New York Times*, June 14, 2000.

———. "Ovitz Won't Head MCA as Big Hollywood Deal Collapses." *The New York Times*, June 6, 1995.

———. "Seagram Puts the Finishing Touches on Its $5.7 Billion Acquisition of MCA." *The New York Times*, April 10, 1995.

———. "Seagram's Chief Says He Has No Candidates to Lead MCA." *The New York Times*, June 7, 1995.

Fabrikant, Geraldine and Bernard Weinraub. "Having Gotten the Part, Bronfman Plays the Mogul." *The New York Times*, February 4, 1996.

———. "One Deal Off. One Deal On. Well, That's Entertainment." *The New York Times*, June 19, 1995.

Fortune. "Seagram in the Chips." September 1948.

Gilpin, Kenneth N. and Schmitt, Eric. "Edgar Bronfman Jr. in Line at Seagram." *The New York Times*, February 27, 1986.

Gopnik, Adam. "Expos Nation: The Extraordinary Past—and Possible Future—of Major League Baseball in Montreal." *The Walrus*, October 2014.

Harper's Magazine. "Forum: Israel and Palestine." September 2014.

Harris, Kathryn, and Joe McGowan. "Edgar in Hollywood." *Fortune*, April 15, 1996.

Holson, Laura M. and Geraldine Fabrikant. "A Wealthy Family Humbled by Its Own Moves." *The New York Times*, July 3, 2002.

Johnson, Jo. "Return of the Prodigal Son." *Financial Times*, February 7, 2009.

Kandell, Jonathan. "Edgar M. Bronfman, Who Built a Bigger, More Elegant Seagram, Dies at 84." *The New York Times*, December 22, 2013.

Karpel, Dalia. "Principal Player." *Haaretz*, September 2, 2011.

King, Norm. "Dan McGinn." *Society for American Baseball Research Baseball Biography Project*. http://sabr.org/bioproj/person/101cb07f.

Leinster, Colin. "The Second Son Is Heir at Seagram." *Fortune*, March 17, 1986 (Research Associate Nancy J. Perry).

Leonard, Devin. "The Bronfman Saga: From Rags to Riches to . . ." *Fortune*, November 25, 2002.

McQuiston, John T. "Howard Head, 76; Designed Metal Skis and Tennis Racket." *The New York Times*, March 5, 1991.

Milner, Brian. "Beware Would-be Media Moguls Bearing Visions." *The Globe and Mail*, December 5, 2000.

———. "Bronfman Hands Tied as Messier's Vivendi Unravels." *The Globe and Mail*, May 17, 2002.

———. "Bronfman Hunt for Vivendi Assets Is 'All About Image.'" *The Globe and Mail,* May 26, 2003.

———. "Bronfmans to Take a Pass on Buying Vivendi Pieces." *The Globe and Mail,* July 19, 2002.

———. "Convergence Has Become a Four-Letter Word." *The Globe and Mail,* July 29, 2002.

———. "Bronfman Fade-out Predictable." *The Globe and Mail,* December 7, 2001.

———. "Seagram Dynasty Down the Hatch." *The Globe and Mail,* June 20, 2000.

———. "Seagram Deal in Final Phase." *The Globe and Mail,* June 19, 2000.

———. "So Charles Bronfman Was Right After All." *The Globe and Mail,* July 6, 2002.

———. "The Unmaking of a Dynasty." *Cigar Aficionado,* March-April 2003.

———. "Vivendi Play Undoes a Dumb Deal." *The Globe and Mail,* December 18, 2001.

———. "Vivendi Saga Promises New Twists." *The Globe and Mail,* October 21, 2002.

———. "Vivendi Universal Great for Investors if They Sell Stock Fast." *The Globe and Mail,* October 17, 2000.

Norris, Floyd. "Bronfman Follies: From Oil to Movies." *The New York Times,* April 9, 1995.

———. "The DuPont Deal Was Done with Taxes Much in Mind." *The New York Times,* April 8, 1995.

Olijnyk, Zena. "Charles Bronfman (Live and Learn)." *Canadian Business,* May 26, 2003.

Palmer, Joanne. "Angelica Berrie's Amazing Journey." *The Times of Israel,* November 29, 2013.

Philadelphia Inquirer Wire Services. "Seagram Co., DuPont Agree on Stock Sale: The Chemical Firm Will Pay $8.8 Billion for 156 Million Shares That Seagram Has. The Beverage Firm Is Likely to Use the Money to Buy MCA Inc." April 7, 1995.

Pogrebin, Robin. "David Geffen Captures Naming Rights to Avery Fisher Hall with Donation." *The New York Times,* March 4, 2015.

———. "Lincoln Center to Rename Avery Fisher Hall." *The New York Times,* November 13, 2014.

Remnick, David. "The One-State Reality: Israel's Conservative President Speaks Up for Civility, and Pays a Price." *The New Yorker,* November 17, 2014.

Rudoren, Jodi. "Young Jews' Exodus to Berlin Splits Opinion in Israel." *New York Times International Weekly,* October 25–26, 2014.

Sorkin, Andrew Ross. "The Refrain That Follows Bronfman." *The New York Times,* March 4, 2008.

Slater, Joanna. "Born into Riches, Edgar Bronfman Grew into Philanthropy." *The Globe and Mail*, December 27, 2013.

———. "Charles Bronfman Opens Up About Seagram's Demise: 'It Is a Disaster.'" *The Globe and Mail*, April 5, 2013.

United Press International. "Albert Speer Dies at 76; Close Associate of Hitler." *The New York Times*, September 2, 1981.

Vogel, Carol. "Seagram's Owners Are Preparing Its Art Collection for Auction." *The New York Times*, December 12, 2002.

Weinraub, Bernard, and Geraldine Fabrikant. "Plot Twist Upon Plot Twist in Bronfman's MCA Thriller; Hollywood Turnaround Story Lapses into Turmoil." *The New York Times*, April 20, 1998.

Zummach, Nicole. "Funder Focus: Thomas Axworthy and the Historica Foundation." charityvillage.com, January 5, 2004.

Speeches

Axworthy Tom. *Memory Matters! Notes for an Address to the Winnipeg Canadian Club*. December 10, 1997.

Bronfman, Charles. *Hebrew University of Jerusalem Convocation Address by Charles R. Bronfman, O.C.* June 4, 1990.

Films and Videos

Andrea Morrison Bronfman: The Charles Years.

Bronfman, Edgar Jr., interview by Charlie Rose, *Charlie Rose*, PBS, March 14, 2001.

Bronfman, Charles, interview by Howard Green, *Headline with Howard Green*, Business News Network, October 19, 2012.

Bronfman, Charles, interview by Howard Green, *Headline with Howard Green*, Business News Network, April 10, 2013.

Lambert, Phyllis, interview, *Venture*, CBC, May 25, 2003.

Goodman, Karen, and Simon, Kirk. *Strangers No More*. New York: Simon & Goodman Picture Company, 2010.

Paperny, David. *Whisky Man: Inside the Dynasty of Samuel Bronfman*. Paperny Films, 1996.

Other

Brauer, Carl M., *The Heritage Project: An Early History*, October 3, 1995.

Business Wire. "Edgar Bronfman, Jr.'s Remarks to News Media Following Seagram's Shareholder Meeting and Vote to Approve Merger With

Vivendi and CANAL+." Press release, December 5, 2000.

Canadian Centre for Architecture. "About CCA." http://www.cca.qc.ca/en/about.

Discovering Israel at War: The Impact of Taglit-Birthright Israel in Summer 2014. Waltham, MA: Brandeis University, Maurice and Marilyn Cohen Center for Modern Jewish Studies, 2015.

"Official New York Mets Website." New York Mets. http://newyork.mets.mlb.com.

Personal papers of Ellen and Andrew Hauptman.

Personal papers of Thomas Axworthy.

Saxe, Leonard, Benjamin Phillips, Theodore Sasson, Shahar Hecht, Michelle Shain, Graham Wright, and Charles Kadushin. *Generation Birthright Israel: The Impact of an Israel Experience on Jewish Identity and Choices.* Waltham, MA: Brandeis University, Maurice and Marilyn Cohen Center for Modern Jewish Studies, 2009.

Saxe, Leonard, Michelle Shain, Graham Wright, Shahar Hecht, Shira Fishman, and Theodore Sasson. *Jewish Futures Project: The Impact of Taglit-Birthright Israel: 2012 Update.* Waltham, MA: Brandeis University, Maurice and Marilyn Cohen Center for Modern Jewish Studies, 2012.

Saxe, Leonard, Michelle Shain, Leonard Saxe, Shahar Hecht, Graham Wright, and Micha Rieser. *Jewish Futures Project: The Impact of Taglit-Birthright Israel: Marriage and Family.* Waltham, MA: Brandeis, University, Maurice and Marilyn Cohen Center for Modern Jewish Studies, 2014.

Saxe, Leonard, Theodore Sasson, Shahar Hecht, Benjamin Phillips, Michelle Shaine, Graham Wright, and Charles Kadushin. *Jewish Futures Project: The Impact of Taglit-Birthright Israel: 2010 Update.* Waltham, MA: Brandeis University, Maurice and Marilyn Cohen Center for Modern Jewish Studies, 2011.

Seagram Company Limited. Form 8-K. Filed June 19, 2000.

Shain, Michelle, Leonard Saxe, Shahar Hecht, Graham Wright, and Theodore Sasson.

Shain, Michelle, Shahar Hecht, and Leonard Saxe. *U.S. Jewish Young Adults React to the Gaza Conflict: A Survey of Birthright Israel Applicants.* Waltham, MA: Brandeis University, Maurice and Marilyn Cohen Centre for Modern Jewish Studies, 2014.

The Canadian Encyclopedia. Historica Canada. http://thecanadianencyclopedia.com/en/

Vivendi Universal. "Vivendi Universal Acquires 16.9 Million Vivendi Universal Shares Sold by Bronfman Family." Press Release, May 29, 2001.

Vivendi, The Seagram Company Limited, and CANAL+ S.A. Joint proxy statement for shareholder vote on merger of Vivendi, The Seagram Company Ltd. and CANAL+ S.A., November 2, 2000.

Appendix

Winners of the Charles Bronfman Prize

2004 Jay Feinberg, founder and executive director, Gift of Life Bone Marrow Foundation

2005 Alon Tal, founder, Adam Teva V'Din and Arava Institute

2007 Dr. Amitai Ziv, founder and director, MSR-The Israel Center for Medical Simulation

2008 Rachel Andres, founder, Jewish World Watch Solar Cooker Project

2009 Mike Feinberg and Dave Levin, co-founders, Knowledge Is Power Program

2010 Jared Genser, founder and president, Freedom Now

2011 Sasha Chanoff, founder and executive director, RefugePoint

2011 Karen Tal, former principal, The Bialik-Rogozin School; co-founder, Education Insights

2012 Eric Greitens, founder, The Mission Continues

2013 Eric Rosenthal, founder and executive director, Disability Rights International

2014 Sam Goldman, founder and chief customer officer, d.light

2015 Rebecca Heller, director and co-founder, International Refugee Assistance Project (formerly Iraqi Refugee Assistance Project)

2016 Etgar Keret, storyteller

For more information, see www.thecharlesbronfmanprize.com.

Index

INDEX

INDEX